Nightmares

Religion, Theology, and the Holocaust
Alan L. Berger, *Series Editor*

Other titles in Religion, Theology, and the Holocaust

Bondage to the Dead: Poland and the Memory of the Holocaust. Michael C. Steinlauf

The End of Days: A Memoir of the Holocaust. Helen Sendyk

Exodus Affair: Holocaust Survivors and the Struggle for Palestine, 1947
    Aviva Halamish; Ora Cummings, trans.

Himmler's Jewish Tailor: The Story of Holocaust Survivor Jacob Frank. Jacob Frank, with Mark Lewis

The Last Lullaby: Poetry from the Holocaust. Aaron Kramer, trans. & ed.

The Man Who Stopped the Trains to Auschwitz: George Mantello, El Salvador, and Switzerland's Finest Hour
    David Kranzler

The Meeting: An Auschwitz Survivor Confronts an SS Physician. Bernhard Frankfurter, ed.;
    Susan E. Cernyak-Spatz, trans.

My War: A Memoir of a Young Jewish Poet. Edward Stankiewicz

New Dawn: The Triumph of Life after the Holocaust. Helen Sendyk

Second Generation Voices: Reflections by Children of Holocaust Survivors and Perpetrators
    Alan L. Berger and Naomi Berger, eds.

Sun Turned to Darkness: Memory and Recovery in the Holocaust Memoir. David Patterson

Survival: The Story of a Sixteen-year-old Jewish Boy. Israel J. Rosengarten

Three Homelands: Memories of a Jewish Life in Poland, Israel, and America.
    Norman Salsitz with Stanley Kaish

War in the Shadow of Auschwitz: Memoirs of a Polish Resistance Fighter and Survivor of the Death Camps
    John Wiernicki

Who Will Say Kaddish? A Search for Jewish Identity in Contemporary Poland
    Larry Mayer, Text; Gary Gelb, Photographs

Will to Freedom: A Perilous Journey through Fascism and Communism. Egon Balas

NIGHTMARES

Memoirs of the Years of Horror
under Nazi Rule in Europe
1939–1945

•   •   •

Konrad Charmatz

•   •   •

Translated from the Yiddish
by Miriam Dashkin Beckerman

Edited by Matthew Kudelka

SYRACUSE UNIVERSITY PRESS

Copyright © 2003 by Esther Birenzweig and Miriam Dashkin Beckerman
All Rights Reserved

First Edition 2003
03 04 05 06 07 08   6 5 4 3 2 1

Yiddish edition copyright © 1975 by Der Nayer Moment Publishers
First Edition 1975, São Paulo, Brazil.

The paper used in this publication meets the minimum requirements of
American National Standard for Information Sciences—Permanence of
Paper for Printed Library Materials, ANSI Z39.48–1984.∞™

Library of Congress Cataloging-in-Publication Data

Charmatz, Konrad, 1910–
[òKoshmarn. English]
Nightmares : memoirs of the years of horror under Nazi rule in Europe, 1939–1945 / Konrad
Charmatz ; translated from the Yiddish by Miriam Dashkin Beckerman ; edited by Matthew Kudelka.
p. cm.—(Religion, theology, and the Holocaust)
ISBN 0–8156–0706–7 (pbk. : alk. paper)
1. Charmatz, Konrad, 1910– 2. Jews—Poland—Biography. 3. Holocaust, Jewish (1939–1945)—
Poland—Personal narratives. 4. Poland—Biography.
I. Title. II. Series.
DS135.P63C46313 2003
940.53'18'092—dc21
2003007565

Manufactured in the United States of America

This book is dedicated to the memory of my mother,
Esther Rachel, of blessed memory,
who was tortured to death in Treblinka,
and of my brother, Akiva, his wife, Frieda,
and their children, Ruth and Maier,
who perished through Nazi hands in 1943.

May the Almighty avenge their blood.

Konrad (Elkana) Charmatz was a noted journalist in São Paulo, Brazil, where he lived for more than twenty years. Born in Ostrowiec, Poland, in 1910, he was imprisoned in Birkenau-Auschwitz and Dachau during the Nazi occupation. Charmatz arrived in Brazil in 1946, where he became the editor of the "Yiddishe Presse" and pioneered a Jewish television program and ran a Jewish radio show from 1954 to 1967. In 1964 he became the owner of the main Jewish newspaper in Brazil, *Der Nayer Moment*. Charmatz was an active figure in the Jewish community in Brazil, which won him several awards from both the Brazilian and Israeli governments.

Nightmares was originally published in Yiddish and Portuguese and went on to win the World Farband of Jewish Partisans and Concentration Camps Survivors prize in Israel in 1985.

Charmatz died in 1986, and, according to his wish, he is buried in the Mount of Olives, in Israel. He is survived by a wife and two daughters, all of whom currently live in Toronto, Canada.

Miriam Dashkin Beckerman is a renowned Yiddish translator and a member of ALTA (American Literary Translators Association). She has translated numerous stories from the Yiddish by writers such as Yehuda Elberg and Dovid Katz among them. Her translation of the Yiddish book by Rivka Lozansky-Bogomolnaya was published in 2000 as *Wartime Experiences in Lithuania* by Vallentine Mitchell, UK. Beckerman was awarded a prize in 1998 by the Dora Teitelboim Foundation for her accomplishments in translation.

Contents

PART TWO

Acknowledgments

The family of Konrad Charmatz would like to acknowledge those who helped in so many ways to see this book through: Miriam D. Beckerman, Jordan Jacobs, and Matthew Kudelka.

In particular, we wish to thank Alexander Grossman, who spared no effort to further this project as a means of honoring the author.

Introduction

Twenty-nine years have passed since the destruction of Europe, the bloodiest period in all history, during which one-third of the Jewish people were murdered, six million souls, over one million of them children. Six million worlds were destroyed during the Second World War when Hitler—may his name be blotted out—set out to destroy, God forbid, all the Jews to the last remnant of the people of Israel. Just as happened with all the enemies of the Jews, he came to a despicable end. But before he died he succeeded in destroying the most beautiful Jewish community in Europe and in blotting out forever thousands of old Jewish settlements that had played an important role in Jewish life.

We, the ones who escaped the gas chambers and the crematoria, the ones who were not murdered or incinerated, the remaining few from that huge community, once we were freed and met the Jews in free countries, felt a certain disappointment and bitterness. While in the concentration camps we had fantasized that Jews in the free lands, our sisters and brothers, were allowing themselves no rest but rather were storming the world organizing street demonstrations and protest meetings; that they were sending their children to fight the Nazis as volunteers; that they weren't celebrating any bar mitzvahs or festivities. We fantasized all this, and our fantasies gave us courage and the strength to endure our agonies. But once we were freed and saw the reality, we saw how naïve we had been—that politicians had promised something would be done, but nothing was ever done. Jews had not been forceful enough in the political arena. Instead they had carried on with their festivities, celebrated anniversaries, and even arranged dances. Quietly, from time to time, some would sigh to themselves. Those who were more sentimental would let a tear drop, and with that the matter ended. Except in

Israel, where Jews organized rescue operations and formed the Jewish brigade, hardly anything was done in the diaspora to save the unfortunate ones in the concentration camps.

♦   ♦   ♦

I did no writing in the concentration camps because I did not have the means, but I did keep a diary in the ghetto, which I carried with me all the way to Auschwitz. There they took away from us all our baggage and all our documents and threw them in a large heap. We never got our things back. But in my mind, scenes were etched, pictures, episodes, events, meetings, and experiences, and these left a deep mark on my heart and in my soul.

When I became a free man again I felt compelled to write a book to immortalize those who had died. So I started to make notes, to gather material, to write. But soon I saw how so many Jews resented hearing about the Holocaust, how it disturbed their peace of mind and made them lose their appetites, and I lost my desire to write and publish my memoirs. To release my memories into such a cold and indifferent world would have been an offense to my feelings. It would also have profaned the sufferings of six million martyrs.

But later still, I told myself that I must not keep historical material to myself. My memoirs would be a monument to my friends who had perished. I also felt that my children and grandchildren had to know what I had endured, what the tattooed number on my left arm signified. When my children were young and asked me about that tattoo, I used to tell them it was a telephone number that I must never forget. But now they are grown and must be told the truth. Perhaps they will learn something from this. In writing this book I am bowing to the wishes of my many friends and dear ones. Now I will tell the world what I remember. It is late, and the memories are old, but it is never too late to tell the truth.

PART ONE

• • •

1

Not God, Not Man, but the Devil Himself

Many people still didn't believe that war was imminent. Many comforted themselves with the thought that at the very last moment catastrophe would be avoided—that all of this was merely a political struggle that would somehow be settled before war descended on the world. The tension was palpable and so was the danger. Hitler was making fiery hate speeches and threatening total war if his demands were not met. The ravings of hundreds of thousands of his followers could be heard ceaselessly: *Sieg Heil!* The commander of Poland's army, Rydz-Smigly, proclaimed, "I will not relinquish even a button from my uniform," and declared his readiness for the struggle to defend his homeland.

By the last days of August 1939, most people felt that war was inevitable. Every day the newspapers declared with alarming front-page headlines that the storm was coming. On the radio we listened to Hitler thunder that he would annihilate anyone who opposed him. Diplomatic interventions by Chamberlain of Britain and Deladier of France helped not at all. The lion had broken his chain and could no longer be held back.

The Polish army mobilized all its troops and reservists. Young people with knapsacks were everywhere, gathering at assembly points. Each night blackouts were rehearsed, enveloping the city in darkness. Air force commandos came around, checking that everyone was following the blackout instructions. Searchlights lit up the skies, probing for enemy planes. The younger of us were amused by this spectacle.

The August nights were mild. The air was scented with ripening fruit and grain. Young men and women wandered the streets laughing, carefree, amusing themselves in the darkness. They looked up and listened to roar of

3

steel birds patrolling the sky. It all seemed like a joke. Poland was preparing to defend itself, though no one believed it would be necessary.

Jews generally have a good sense of danger, and certainly sensed trouble then. Wealthy Jews immediately acquired passports. Others were sending money out of the country in case they had to flee. The poor tried to console themselves that all was mere saber rattling, idle threats to frighten the masses, that at the last moment a miracle would happen. "Strategists" among us calculated that Hitler wasn't ready to wage war; that the entire world would oppose him; that his tanks and cannons were made of plastic; that it was all swindle and bluff. In the cafés, loud discussions took place amidst joking and laughter.

◆　◆　◆

In the last years before the war, I was living and working in Sosnowiec, an industrial city in Poland, only seven kilometers from Katowice, the capital of Oberschlesien. That was very close to the German border, where people expected the first battle to be fought. Anyone in that district who could fled from the border. Even those who didn't believe war was coming wanted to be far from the border until the threat had passed.

I myself had the same idea, for two reasons. The first I have just noted. The second was that at this critical time, I wanted to be near my mother, who was living by herself in Ostrowiec. True, she was living with her family—her mother, a brother, nieces, and other relatives—but none of her children were with her. Since I had no wife, I considered it my duty to be at her side at such a critical time. So I went to the train station, purchased a ticket, and on Wednesday, August 30, 1939, left for Ostrowiec. I learned later that my train was the last civilian train to leave Sosnowiec.

At the station the tension was thick. Nervous soldiers were around, and reservists, recruits, and nurses hurrying to their garrisons. The train sped quickly past several stations, as if it had no time to stop. Everywhere the same scenes: confused people, fear in their eyes, running back and forth, shoving one another. In Skarzysko, where I had to transfer, I barely squeezed onto the regular coach train, which was crammed with army personnel who smelled of sweat and strong spirits. I heard many drunken voices singing military songs, many of them full of longing. The locomotive whistled, the wheels turned, and the engine steamed, and the wind carried these sounds across the land, through thick forests and across endless plains, past sunk-in-sleep villages.

Late at night I arrived at Ostrowiec station. I could barely squeeze my way out with my valise. In the darkness the coachman, Yosel Kobaleh, recognized me. He grabbed my valise, pushed me into a packed wagon and brought me to the sleeping city. My mother, trembling with fear, hearing my voice, opened the door and rejoiced at the sight of me, as though God himself had sent an angel to her. She would at least have one child beside her in the dreadful days to come. When I was a child, I would cuddle up to her like this, seeking her protection when there was thunder and lightning outside.

2

My First Contact with the Shtetl

The following day, the villagers saw me on the street and looked at me won-deringly. I had used to come to the shtetl sometimes for the high holidays, but they couldn't understand what I was doing there on an ordinary Thurs-day. What had happened? They started to question me: "Is it true that there is already fear at the border?" Since I had just come from there, they assumed I must know.

First I visited the grave of my father, bless his memory. This was beside the home of the Ostrowiec rebbe, Reb Maier Yechiel Halevi, bless his mem-ory. While I was praying at the grave site, a cool wind blew and the branches of the trees swayed as if praying together with me. I left the cemetery com-forted, and feeling that I had fulfilled a holy obligation on which my destiny depended.

Outside, Jews came to greet me, to say *shalom aleichem,* as if they needed proof that I was truly back among them. The news of my arrival had spread quickly and was being discussed in every home. My appearance had instilled fear and anxiety in everyone's heart.

It wasn't long before people's fears were realized: the very next day—Friday, September 1, 1939—at dawn, the German Luftwaffe bombed the outskirts of Ostrowiec. The shtetl was in a part of Poland called "The Secu-rity Triangle." The Polish government had planned that if the Germans at-tacked Poland's western border and the capital, Warsaw, it would transfer itself to this zone, between Congressional Poland and Galicia. But in the first hours of the war the Luftwaffe was already bombing our district. This sowed great panic in the shtetl and throughout the land. It was utterly unexpected; people were already dying. In the chaos, ambulances sped back and forth.

This was the Germans' warning to the Polish government: You have no place to run because we will always precede you.

There was no longer any strategy; there wasn't even time for the army to organize itself. Immediately, in the first hours, everything had fallen apart. The Germans were attacking the border and the hinterlands at the same time, and preventing the Polish armed forces from establishing defenses.

We sat by the radio listening to the reports of war correspondents. We also listened to the German *Rundfunk,* which triumphantly, to the accompaniment of military marches, announced the rapid advance of German land forces. Polish airspace was now entirely dominated by the Luftwaffe. Reports soon arrived that German troops were in Krakow, in Kielce, in Radom, that they were already marching toward Warsaw. On Sunday reports began arriving that the Germans were only ten kilometers from Ostrowiec. At the same time we began hearing gruesome reports that Jews were being murdered by German troops.

Panic fell over Ostrowiec. People scuttled through the streets like poisoned mice, not knowing where to run or where to hide. Our neighbors, Jews and Christians, had left the city during the night. My mother, pale and frightened, came running to me with the news, wringing her hands and asking in a shaking voice: "Maybe you also should escape from the city? My heart is fearful. I will remain because I don't have the strength to run and wander. I'm too old for that. But as for you . . . What do you say?"

So it was that we decided that at dawn the next day I would leave for Solec in the direction of the Vistula River, where it was thought that the Polish army might make a stand against the Germans.

3

People on the Run

Before dawn my mother saw me out of the house. With tears in her eyes and a prayer softly spoken, she accompanied me as far as the outskirts of the city. In her glistening eyes I saw the whole impending tragedy.

People were fleeing Ostrowiec in all directions, on wagons, on bicycles, on foot. The former prefect of the city fled with me—a neighbor of ours, Kazik Bushko. We ran as if someone was already chasing us. It was impossible to hire a wagon at any price, so we fled on foot. Once the sun rose and the air grew hot, running became harder. Sweat started to pour from me and my shirt started clinging to my skin. I went into a village hut and left my jacket there, as well as some other things that I was no longer able to carry. I asked the peasant woman to keep my things for me until I was able to return.

My legs grew more and more tired and sweat kept pouring from me. Refugees were already running back from the river, and telling us it was hell there. All of us who were fleeing—civilians and military—were an easy target for the Luftwaffe planes, which were dropping bombs and firing machine guns at us. Hundreds had already been killed. The German planes descended over and over to observe us. Each time they spotted military uniforms among us, they sprayed us with bullets. We were already encountering dead bodies in pools of fresh blood. There was no need for them to run any farther.

We decided to stay off the main road and away from military targets, and to flee in small groups. After the terrible news from the river, we decided not to run in that direction but rather to look for refuge nearby. I remembered there was a village nearby called Baltev, some distance from the main road and too small for the German planes to bother with, and we decided to go there. It was already dusk when we reached it. The sun had just set, leaving

8

behind a fiery red sky, which quickly vanished with nightfall. When we arrived at the Jewish estate that was our destination, the house was already full of refugees.

We collapsed like the dead, utterly exhausted, and fell asleep on the straw that had been spread on the floor. Here we did not hear the shooting or feel the panic of the other refugees. We did encounter a few deserters from the Polish army, who were quickly provided with civilian clothes. In the distance we heard tanks rumbling, machine guns firing, and bombs exploding. It was our salvation that there was no railway to the village—the only access was by road. It meant we were cut off from the world.

We lived at Baltev as if we were shipwrecked. We ate, drank, swam, and went for walks. Terrifying news reached us from the city. On entering Ostrowiec the Germans had killed everyone in sight. Later they had dragged out the town's most prominent citizens and shot them in the middle of the street. They did this to frighten the civilians and to warn them against sabotage. On hearing this news, we decided to stay put. Besides, there was no place to run, since the Germans had already advanced. But how long could we stay in the village like this? Rosh Hashana was approaching. We longed for our friends and relations. Every day we received news from peasants about what was happening in the city and on the roads leading to it. Comforting news began to reach us: people were no longer being murdered, and life was returning to normal.

On Tuesday, September 12, the day before Rosh Hashana, I decided to return to the city. I changed into peasant clothes, and with a group of peasants on a cart I set out for the market in Ostrowiec. When I reached the main railway station, I encountered German soldiers for the first time. They searched our wagon to make sure we weren't hiding weapons. They shouted, cursed, and in German asked us if we had hidden anything. The peasants motioned with their hands that they didn't understand, and I imitated them. That is how I returned safely to the city.

4

The First Rosh Hashana under German Occupation

The Rosh Hashana of 1939 I shall never forget. The synagogues were closed
so we gathered in private homes for the Days of Awe. All our neighbors organized a *minyan* (quorum for prayer) in my mother's house. The curtains
were drawn and the doors and gates locked, and just as in the time of the
Marranos we conducted the Yom Kippur prayers. All of us, women and
men, worshipped quietly and tearfully. Later we stood in the corner and
talked about the gruesome events, especially about the first murders, when
our city's most prominent citizens had been dragged from their homes and
shot on the street. Our lives were now worthless, so it seemed to us, and the
enemy could do what they would to us. Some tried to point out that Poles
were also being murdered, that in every war there are victims. Others noted
that some Jews were already doing business with the Germans and that the
devil is not as black as he is portrayed. But we were deluding ourselves. We
were in the lion's jaws, and we all knew it and also knew we would need
great mercy not to be devoured.

In the middle of worship someone came running in with a warning:
"They are on the march! Germans!" We quickly removed our prayer shawls
and hid in any holes we could find. It turned out to be a false alarm: they had
merely been passing by. All of us were pale, with fear in our eyes, as if we had
been sentenced to death. When the cantor struck too high a note, we all became alarmed and called out, *"Sha . . . Sha . . . "* (Quiet! Quiet!). From the
street newcomers kept arriving. They told us how Jews were being dragged
out to do slave labor. When the Germans "discovered" a minyan, they took
away all the men to clean the streets with their prayer shawls and polish the
military vehicles. My mother stood in the corner with her *Korben Minchah*
(the women's prayer book) and sobbed bitterly. She would raise her eyes to

me and begin to cry, trembling all over. She looked at me as if I had been sentenced to death and as if she wished her tears could save me from it.

Yom Kippur was even more tragic. I am certain that on that Yom Kippur all Jews fasted, even children and the sick. Our worship was like *vidui* (the final confession before death). The Angel of Death was hovering over us, sword in hand. Jews beat their chests with their fists when asking forgiveness for their sins, as if trying to redeem themselves for sins they had not even committed. They distributed charity with an open hand and were warm and friendly toward the poor, who walked the streets like chosen ones. They themselves were in danger, but found solace in the fact that the wealthy and the prominent were in the same position as themselves and that all lives now had equal value. Everyone was suffering bitterly. Many people, no longer able to hold back their tears, began thrashing about as if in convulsions, as if the tears all of us had shed had overflowed the troughs. The Torah scrolls were looked upon prayerfully and wrapped with care in sheets and prayer shawls. After prayers all of us slipped back to our homes with fear in our hearts, awaiting whatever fate had in store for us.

5

Getting Used to the Troubles

The shtetl began to adjust to the new regime and its new decrees.

It quickly became clear that this was not a short-term situation. The Germans were crushing all opposition. All of Poland had been occupied. The Poles made no attempt at opposition: at the least sign of it, the invaders punished not just the guilty but the entire city, dragging away the most prominent citizens, who were never seen again.

Though the punishment for it was severe, commerce began again, albeit covertly. Goods began disappearing from the stores. With the help of the Poles, the Germans were stealing everything. German war equipment and other contraband began to appear on the black market.

Every day the Germans made new demands on us and posted new decrees. For the first time, I was seized for forced labor after a young Pole pointed me out: "Jude!" (Jew). I was taken away to clean military transport trucks.

I grew tired of having nothing better to do. Also, I wanted to return to Sosnowiec to see what had happened to my business. But it was difficult to part from my aged mother under such circumstances. I couldn't bring myself to leave her alone at such a dangerously unsettled time. Just the thought of my leaving sent a shudder through her. What frightened her was not her own fate but the thought of me setting out on dangerous roads. After two months of going around nervous and distraught, she agreed that I should return and see what had happened to my property. But she insisted that I return as soon as I knew.

The trains weren't yet operating normally, so many tracks having been bombed. I squeezed onto a freight train, which rolled through the countryside for two days and two nights. I saw many destroyed cities and villages, collapsed bridges and twisted railway tracks. People were dashing around like birds that had lost their nests. On November 1, 1939, we passed through Jederzejów station. It was All Saints' Day, when people go to the graves of their fathers and pray for the souls of the dead. At the station I saw graves, recently dug, of Poles who had died fighting the Germans. Candles were burning beside them, and women in black were kneeling and praying. Children clung to their mothers with tears and fear in their eyes.

Everywhere were masses of refugees—lost souls with frightened and desperate eyes. They were fleeing in panic, with packs and satchels. Each time the train stopped at a station, hordes of them came running. They threw in their packs and then themselves, over the shouts and curses of others. The shouting had no effect. The refugees would shout back, "What do you think? That you're traveling first class or in sleeper coaches? If you're looking for comfort stay home."

With much difficulty, I arrived at Sosnowiec on November 2. I started to look for my house, my friends, and my acquaintances.

6

Sosnowiec

I barely recognized the city. Many shops had been closed, others had been pillaged, and many people had fled. This was an important industrial center, and right on the border, and on the day of the invasion the German *Sturmkommandos* (assault commandos) had reached it within minutes.

I was told immediately that many of my best friends had been shot on the very first day. Moishe Merin, a short, thin man with mousy eyes who was known as an idler, as a professional gambler, and who was always looking for a loan, which he would never repay, had been chosen by the Germans to be the "Jewish elder." He himself had applied for this position during the first two days, when all of the city's thousands of Jews had been locked up in the cellars of the city hall on Pierackiego Street.

The cellar had been so crowded that people almost suffocated. And there was no water. People were ready to destroy the building's plumbing, even though they would drown by doing so, simply to wet their tongues with a little water. In the night the *Obersturmbannführer* came and demanded that the rebbe of the city be brought forward. If he was not he would immediately shoot ten Jews. The rebbe was not among those locked up, so to save ten Jews from death, sixty-five-year-old Avraham Shtiglitz declared that he was the rebbe. The Germans grabbed him, tore out half his beard, beat and kicked him, and threw him back into the cellar, all bloodied, with the demand that he and all the Jews should say their last confession. The Jews, in one voice, called out, *"Shma Israel!"* in the belief that their end had come. The German beasts were delighted that they had scared the Jews to death. Later an order was given that they should sing.

The following day the Jews were led out of the cellars, arranged in rows, and given the command, "Run!" Confusion reigned. To the accompaniment of shouts, insults, beatings, and gunfire, they were driven into the factory of the Shine brothers. Soon after that, all Jews who were barbers were told to step forward. These men were ordered to fetch their work tools within ten minutes, otherwise they would be shot. After they returned, more dead than alive, with sweat pouring from them, they were commanded to cut off everyone's hair and beards.

When the German beasts tired of this spectacle, they ordered all the leaders of the Jewish community to step forward. No one did. Moishe Merin saw this, and saw a chance to become a somebody. The Germans stared at this pathetic little bundle of bones: Was this the leader of the Jewish community of Sosnowiec? But since no one else had declared himself, they honored him with a beating and then took him away. Merin was no fool. He also had nothing to lose. So he went along with them for whatever it would be worth to him.

The Jews were kept for three days and three nights in the factory cellar. Later the Germans started letting people out. First, those with a trade. The others were taken to the jail on Towarowa Street. A number of Jews were later bought out with bribes. The remainder were shot a few days later.

On September 9 the synagogue on Dekerta Street was set on fire. The Jews in the neighboring houses were not allowed out, nor was it permitted to rescue the Torah scrolls. Everyone who approached the synagogue was shot. The following day the Jews were made to clean up the damage and sweep the street. Germans like order.

7

Terror and Evil Decrees

A wave of terror began: shootings and mass executions. At the slightest pretense—for mere suspicion of sabotage or rebellion—entire streets of people were led out and shot. One decree followed another, one command followed another, so that people lived in constant fear, with no time to think, to organize, or to look for solutions. They were too busy trying to stay alive.

First the Germans separated the Jews from the rest of the population. Jewish businesses and factories had to have Germans as commissioners. These commissioners then confiscated those businesses and became the new owners. Jews' homes were also taken over this way.

Entire streets were emptied of Jews, who had to leave everything behind except hand luggage. They were forced into crowded tenements, two or three families to one flat. On the right arm they had to wear a white band with a blue Star of David. Later this was changed to a yellow patch with the word *"Jude."* Jews would later be forbidden to travel by train or bus or to leave the ghetto.

At first, on the train between Sosnowiec, Bedzin, and Dabrowa, one car was provided for Jews. The Germans constantly raided this car, and for the most trivial reasons would take passengers away, never to be seen again. So Jews avoided the train.

On searching a Jew the Germans might find money, or food, or documents. This much was enough to bring down punishment, so Jews avoided the ghetto's streets. All Jews were suspect and in danger of arrest for the slightest reason.

The Germans forced their way into Jewish dwellings, stealing everything they could and making arrests as they did so. Jews were not allowed to purchase from non-Jews or in non-Jewish stores. They could receive rations only from their own community sources. Every Jew was allowed 200 grams of bread per day, 100 grams of margarine, 100 grams of sugar, and 100 grams of marmalade per week. It was not enough to keep anyone alive, so everyone sought to buy something on the side.

Jews weren't allowed to go to any theater or cinema. Jewish children were not allowed to attend government schools, and the Jewish schools were always closed. In the evenings Jews were not permitted to show themselves in the street, so after six o'clock everyone was confined indoors. All radios were confiscated. German broadcasts were forbidden, and so of course were foreign broadcasts. If a radio was found in any house, everyone in that house was arrested. So there was nothing to do at night but stay indoors or visit neighbors.

8

The Tricks of the Nazis

The Nazi machine worked with absolute precision and according to a strict plan. The Nazis deliberately confused and disoriented the people so that no one could tell what their intentions were, so that rage or desperation would not congeal into a general revolt. They wanted Jews to think they could still save themselves. To this end, they always issued decrees for only one part of the population. The purpose of this was to create privileged Jews and to plant the hope among them that they weren't the real targets, that if some Jews were sacrificed, the others—the more useful elements—would have a better chance of survival.

The Nazis could not have succeeded without the cooperation of some Jews, and some Jews did indeed allow themselves to get drawn into the net. The Nazis established the Judenrat and a Jewish militia, both of which would help them carry out their plans for the liquidation.

First, they demanded that contingents of young people be turned over to them for the slave labor camps. The point of this was to encourage the young to think that if they went quietly, their parents would be able to live in the city until the war ended. Later the Nazis ordered the older people to give themselves up, and to bring with them the children and the sick. To the Nazis these people were an unproductive element whom they did not have the resources to keep alive in such a difficult war. Still later, the Nazis liquidated everyone else. Throughout all this, they were aided by the Judenrat and the Jewish militia.

Moishe Merin, Sosnowiec's Jewish elder, argued that if the Judenrat didn't do it the Nazis would do it themselves, and much more harshly. When the Germans come to us with their demands, he contended, we still have some control, to drag out the decree, to argue a little, to rescue a few. In the meantime we leave the best and most useful element for as long as possible, and maybe save some of them from annihilation.

Jews who accepted this argument were only fooling themselves. Those who belonged to the Judenrat were out to save themselves and their families, at very least to ensure they were the last ones liquidated. Perhaps a miracle would happen meanwhile and they would survive. But the Nazis were much smarter and more sophisticated than these Jews were. They thought to themselves: Why should we ourselves do this dirty work when there are Jews who will do it for us? In fact, these cooperative Jews can help us spread false illusions. Let the Jews destroy themselves. Once the Judenrat has completed its task, we will snuff out its members, too. In the meantime they are supplying us with everything we ask: people, gold, silver, furs. For helping us, they will be the last to die, so it's worth their while.

9

The Judenrat

As already stated, the leader of the Judenrat in Zaglebie was Moishe (Manyek) Merin, who quickly learned how to deal with the Nazi functionaries and the SS. He met all their demands; in return, they supported him and gave him all kinds of privileges. Besides carrying out all their orders, Merin showered them with gifts and bribes. This did not stop the brutalities, nor did it end the shower of decrees, but at least these would be carried out with the knowledge and help of the Judenrat. Merin was also able to protect his relatives and friends and to gain certain small privileges for them.

As an example of his personal influence, Merin pointed to the workshops at Sosnowiec and Bedzin, which he had had a hand in establishing and where a few thousand Jews were employed. The Jews at these shops received *Arbeitskarten* (work cards) from the Germans as employees of the *Arbeitseinsatz* (labor units). This employment helped them avoid being sent to forced labor camps. The German owners grew rich from these workshops. First of all, they had access to all kinds of experienced craftsmen at cheap-as-dirt prices. Second, they received large bribes and expensive gifts from workers who had no skills but who were looking to save themselves from transportation. People paid large sums to Gestapo officers and workshop owners for the protection these workshops provided. The German administrators also benefitted, because they were not sent to the front, engaged as they were in essential war work such as supplying the Wehrmacht with uniforms, clothing, boots, shoes, and other necessities.

His success at establishing these workshops gave Merin the chutzpah to try to become the leader of all the Judenräte in the German Reich and its conquered territories. The Gestapo allowed him to travel to Berlin, Prague, Warsaw, Lodz, Krakow, and other cities, and at each of these cities he urged the Jewish communities to unite under a central committee. And, of course, at each city he nominated himself as candidate for president of that committee, on the basis of his good intentions and his experience, giving as an example the Judenrat of Zaglebie under his leadership. In each city he pointed out the flaws of the local leaders and promised to do better. But the local leaders were skeptical. Merin's appearance told against him: he was a small man with beady eyes and an oily smile. To them he was the perfect image of a cheap careerist, a product of Jewish suffering and Jewish destruction.

Dr. Feivl Viderman, a Jewish intellectual and community leader from Bedzin, in his book *Di Blonde Bestia* described a meeting in the Judenrat under the chairmanship of Moishe Merin at which the latter reported on his visits to a number of Jewish centers and their liquidation. Said Merin:

You have heard that I and Frau Charney [his secretary and personal assistant] have visited the largest Jewish centers so that we know exactly what is happening there. We have even been to Berlin and Prague and what we saw there can only be described as desperation. There is lacking a strong hand that can be effective in a difficult situation. The leaders of the German and Czech Jews lost their heads. The Jews there do not have any influence regarding the deportations. When I was there I reminded the leaders of their negative stand to my suggestion of a half-year ago that we should establish one central body for all the Jewish communities in Germany and the annexed territories but they did not want to hear of it, all because of their dislike of Polish Jews. Today they are against the establishment of a union of all communal bodies, fearing that the influence will fall into my hands, the hands of Moishe Merin, a Polish Jew who does not have a good command of the German language, not trusting me to deal in their name with the Germans . . . Because of their faults, the German and Czech Jews are suffering so badly today. Today we need energetic, courageous new leaders because the former diplomacy has gone bankrupt and that explains my great success . . . That's how it is on the Western front, but it's no better in the East. There, too, helplessness and desperation prevails. I foresee that in the near future all Jewish communities will be wiped out, and no sign of them will remain. That, *meine Herren,* is the result of false politics which the heads of the communities are practicing: Rumkofsky in Lodz and Czerniakow in Warsaw with whom I can't come to terms. At a meeting with them, during my talk which lasted three hours, I could not convince them of the falsity of their approach and the correctness of my politics. They did not want, or simply were not capable of understanding me. Because of this the sad consequences won't be long in coming.

This makes clear the general situation and the part that Merin played in the destruction of the European Jewry. He wanted to be "king of the Jews," as the Germans ironically called him. He wanted to go down in Jewish history as the chief liquidator of European Jewry. He behaved like a dictator. The Judenrat he led had other members, but he barely listened to their opinions. He himself made all the decisions, and the Judenrat simply carried them out.

In the hands of Moishe Merin rested the fate of the one hundred thousand Jews of Zaglebie. He sent to death whomever he wanted, and whomever he wanted he temporarily let live. His German patrons granted him this power in return for his help in liquidating the Jews of Zaglebie. Everyone feared him and tried to get on his good side. At one of the mass meetings on the "Rialto," when he appealed to the people to come forward for the next selection, a rebbe called out—either from courage or stupidity—that we were lucky the Almighty had sent us such a leader, because "since Moishe Rabeinu until Moishe Merin, there has not been one like Moishe."

For the Judenrat Merin chose people who were ready to do whatever he directed. He preferred intelligent people with a good reputation in the community. He also enlisted a number of informers who knew the city well—that is, who knew which people had hidden away money and other valuables. Other informers had connections with various streets and provided him with intelligence about underground movements and various other events. A young man from Bedzin, a handsome and popular fellow, had found a good position with Merin: "officer of the women." For the "king of the Jews" he recruited the most beautiful women. What woman didn't need a small favor? One needed a place to live, another a place to work, another food, a fourth wanted her dearest ones to be spared from transportation. All were at Merin's mercy and did whatever gained his favor. If a husband was in the way, he could be quickly dispatched with the next group to forced labor.

10

The Problem of Shelter in the Ghetto

Shelter was a severe problem. As the ghetto's area was further and further reduced, Jews were thrown out of their living quarters and packed into tenements, two, three, or more families to each flat. Sanitary conditions were terrible. The wealthier families were the most affected because they had been used to so much better. In charge of shelter was a traditional Jew named Hersh David Kaiser. When he was out on the street, scores of people would run after him, pleading for a roof over their heads or for an opportunity to move elsewhere because they could not tolerate their neighbors. It was Kaiser who could appeal to Merin's people on their behalf. Under such a system, anyone without money or valuables for bribes was in dire straits.

When I was forced to give up my place on Mascickiego Street right opposite the Ogrodek, the city park, where the air was nice and fresh, I felt bitter. True, I was a bachelor and didn't own much and had only been renting space from the Grytzers. After much intervention I found a room to share with another bachelor, a young man named Schlesinger, whose family had been liquidated a few weeks earlier. The five-room apartment was on Targowa Street near the Judenrat and had once belonged to his family. After they had been sent away, the son was permitted only a single room; the others were assigned to prominent people. In one room lived the Jewish police *kommandant,* Kleiner. In another lived a tall, red-haired girl, an appointee of the Judenrat, along with her family. In the remaining room I lived with the bachelor.

I pitied Schlesinger. He was seventeen perhaps and completely alone in the world. Sadness was etched on his face. He felt abandoned and endangered, and feared that he would also be sent off. He worked night shift in a shop and slept during the day. Each day he became thinner and paler. I tried to befriend him and cheer him up, but he no longer trusted anyone.

Once he came to me and asked for advice. Influential acquaintances, friends of his family, had arranged a place for him with the Jewish militia, and he asked me whether he should accept it. This placed me in a very tight bind. Personally, I felt that a Jew should not accept any position with either the Germans or their Jewish servants. Yet I could not bring myself to advise him to refuse, since refusing might amount to a death sentence for him. So I told him it was a personal matter, a matter of conscience, and that only he could decide.

This wasn't good enough for him. He put me on the spot and asked me, "If you had the chance, would you accept the offer?" Now I was really on the spot, because I had already had that opportunity and had emphatically refused it. It came about this way:

I was working as a stockkeeper in the plate glass workshop that I had once owned. The shop was also on Targowa Street, at number 11. It was a large shop that shipped glass by the wagonload all the way to Russia. As a "trustee," I managed this shop. First it was for a German from the neighboring shtetl Swiétochlowice, a man named Poshled. He had been a customer of ours before the war and had become a friend. Later, when he took over my shop, he treated me with politeness and respect. It was he who arranged for me to be the stockkeeper and who provided me with a work card. Later he was replaced by another German, this one from Riga, a man named Platzer. This one looked at me askance and wanted to get rid of me. When he learned that I had once owned the shop, he became frightened—if the Germans were defeated quickly, I might well take it back from him, and he had already put money into it. At first he didn't dare do me wrong, but later he decided it was better to get rid of me. Naturally, I tried to please him, to be quick and conscientious. I also did the work of three hired hands because I knew the business well. But he made it clear he resented me.

I discussed the situation with my relatives and friends and asked them for advice. I had a cousin in Sosnowiec whose mother, a sister of my mother, lived with her husband in Olkusz, a shtetl eighty kilometers from Sosnowiec. Their eldest son had married a girl whose sister was the wife of the Jewish police commissioner. One day my uncle came to me and suggested I join the Jewish militia. He would use his influence on his relative, the police commissioner, to arrange for me a position on the force. On hearing this suggestion, I froze. I, a militiaman! I would have to seize Jews and escort them to transports. I would be helping the Germans and their Jewish servants. No way would I do that! My uncle and aunt and their friends argued with me for hours. A militiaman's cap would protect me from the transports, they said. Militiamen would be the last to be deported. I would have food to eat and would not starve. "Your present commissioner will make sure you're liquidated," they continued, "because you don't let him rest in peace. Why wait till it's too late? Get yourself a safe position."

My aunt began to cry. How could she allow me, her own blood, a child of her eldest sister, to be deported to Auschwitz? But I stood firm. I wasn't going to herd Jews together and walk them to the transports simply to save myself. I did not want to become a cruel Jew. Still they tried to change my mind, arguing next that a militiaman didn't have to be cruel. I could be a *good* militiaman, one who saved people and helped them at times of need. They worked on me for an entire week, but I wouldn't change my mind.

So when Schlesinger asked me what I would do, I didn't tell him I had faced the same question, and I avoided giving him a clear answer. In the end, he did accept the position. One day he appeared in a blue-and-white militia cap with a stiff brim. The hat did not suit his face. His smile was refined, subtle, hardly the smile of a law enforcer and arresting agent. To this day I don't know what happened to him. Some time later I was sent away with a transport, and he remained in Sosnowiec.

11

A Jewish Café in the Ghetto

Strange as it sounds, there was a Jewish café in the Sosnowiec ghetto, on Mandzever Street. It belonged to two partners, Yechiel Landau and the wife of the *kommandant* of the Jewish police, Kleiner, who were good friends of Merin. People outside were starving for a crust of bread, yet in the café one could get coffee, tea, and freshly baked bread. This was the meeting place for the ghetto's informers, for its smugglers, for the high functionaries of the Judenrat, for anyone with influence. All kinds of shady deals took place there. Valuables were bought and sold, foreign currencies were exchanged, work cards were traded. The German police rarely appeared there, nor did SS troops. It was a thieves' den, and anyone who habituated it had to be up to no good. Simply to be sitting there during work hours eating unrationed food was *treif* (nonkosher). Obviously the Judenrat was protecting this café, and this had to be with the Gestapo's permission. The system required a meeting place where illegal transactions could be carried out.

At the café one could hear gossip about all the latest events and decrees. Every night something out of the ordinary happened in the ghetto. Sometimes entire blocks of people were taken away, to be transported the following day. People were arrested because they were found with food for which they had no ration cards. One time the SS broke into a house and took away some young people who belonged to the underground. Another time an entire family poisoned themselves.

The following day at the Jewish café there would be talk about all these things. Here one could also hear news from the fronts, from people with contacts among the Germans. One could also hear what deportations would be taking place soon. Merin himself used to frequent this café, especially when a government official was visiting or a guest from another community.

He wanted to show these people how well the Jews were living under his command.

By doing everything they demanded, Merin had forged links with the Gestapo, with the leaders of the slave labor camps, and with SS men like Knoll, Linker, Muchinsky, and Ludwig. From time to time he saved a few Jews by delaying their deportation. For allowing this the SS received large bribes in the form of money and valuables. The Germans were thinking: This business pays since the Jews are ours anyhow. Nobody will grab them away from us. Let Merin buy time for a few more Jews for fantastic prices. We'll get them later.

These token rescues raised Merin's prestige among the Jews, many of whom believed he was accomplishing a great deal. This enabled him to continue to serve the Germans as a loyal servant. Merin knew that the small advantages he got from the Germans were at the price of helping them. The day that he could no longer help them, that he could no longer hand over the required number of victims, he would himself be liquidated.

The Germans had made a good deal with Merin. Why should they have to do all the work when there were Jews willing to do it for them? Let the Jews liquidate themselves. If Merin thinks he is outsmarting us, he is making a grave error: he won't escape our hands.

12

Liquidations

With German precision, the Nazis steadily liquidated Europe's Jews, one community after another. The method was always the same: confine them in ghettos, prevent them from earning a living in any way, extract from them all their money and valuables, and step by step reduce their population by working them to death in slave labor camps or by killing them outright in gas chambers and crematoria.

Sosnowiec was one of the oldest Jewish communities in Poland. There were thirty thousand Jews in the city before the war, over one-fifth of the population. After the war began, as the smaller Jewish communities in Zaglebie were liquidated, the city's Jewish population grew to forty-five thousand.

The liquidations actually started in 1939. In October of that year, three hundred young men were transported from Sosnowiec to slave labor camps. The Germans' intention was to eliminate the young Jews, who were most likely to lead a revolt. This would make it easier to finish off the elders. The Judenrat organized the transports. We were told that Germany, being at war, needed workers for its factories to replace those who had been called into the Wehrmacht. Merin told us that if we sent the young to the work camps, the old would be permitted to remain in the city. We learned later that the transportees, together with contingents from Katowice and Konigshütte, had been shipped to the Soviet border at Nisko, and forced to cross over under the threat of being shot.

At the same time, Jews were being transported to Sosnowiec from Czechoslovakia and put to work in the factories of the Shine brothers on Maja Street 1. The Jews of Sosnowiec helped them as much as they could, though this wasn't much. Every morning we watched them march to work

28

under the watchful gaze of the SS in their black uniforms. These Czech Jews had been told they would be deported. Instead, in July 1940, with exit visas in their pockets, they were sent to slave labor camps.

Meanwhile, the Germans were steadily liquidating smaller communities: Katowice, Konigshütte, Oswiecim, and others. Often the Jews of these towns were murdered on the spot. They were forced to dig pits, then they were murdered en masse and their bodies thrown in. Some were sent to slave labor camps, and some were brought to Sosnowiec and Bedzin. The Germans did not want the Jews thinking they were to be annihilated. They did not want to extinguish all hope: better to plant the idea that once the useless elements were done away with, the rest would be able to save themselves. Until they arrived at the liquidation camps in Auschwitz and elsewhere, people still stubbornly believed that *"Arbeit Macht Frei."*

Jewish factories and shops were confiscated and turned over to Aryan commissioners, most of them *Volksdeutsche,* the so-called *Treuhändler* (trustworthy ones). Jewish houses also were taken over by the German administration, and so were all valuables: gold, silver, and jewelry. Jews found in possession of these things after being told to surrender them were shot on the spot. With the help of the Judenrat and the Jewish militia, the Nazis stole from us everything we possessed. Had the Germans themselves done the thieving, they would not have gotten even half, because Jews would have burnt, buried, or destroyed what they owned to avoid handing it over to the bloody enemy. Merin persuaded the Jews that if they handed over their possessions voluntarily they would not be harmed but would be allowed to live in peace. So Jews sought to buy their freedom. What did possessions matter when their very lives were in danger? They paid a great price for their peace, which they never got. This was the aim of the Germans—to get the Jews to willingly forfeit everything of value. Merin had an easy time helping the Germans with this. And in return for his help, they let him survive and prosper in the role of "king of the Jews."

13

Labor Camps

The Gestapo instructed the Judenrat to set up a labor camp and supply it daily with slave laborers. This was done. These people cleaned the streets and the trains and loaded and unloaded trucks and train cars. The Judenrat persuaded the Germans not to grab people in the streets but instead to let them provide the necessary workers. As a result, the wealthy avoided being taken while the poor were sent to work. The poor actually went willingly to work, because at least they got a piece of bread and some soup. A worker was paid fifteen marks for two weeks' work. On the black market a loaf of bread cost twenty-five marks, a kilo of meat seventy. This was a great source of income for the Judenrat. To avoid winter work and work on the trains, Jews were willing to pay any price. With the bribe money the Judenrat collected, it bought the laborers meager rations. After the Gestapo were paid off, there still remained something for those in charge to pocket.

The Judenrat had as many as fifteen hundred people on its payroll. This included a great many guards, as well as spies whose job it was to ensure that no underground revolt broke out. There were also women on the payroll who were simply concubines of Judenrat officials.

The Judenrat headquarters was Targowa Street 12, in one of the houses of the Radomsk rebbe, the militia headquarters directly opposite. The Judenrat was constantly perfecting its apparatus, always giving the Germans exact information about the Jewish population. In return for this, it received a food ration from the German authorities. Jews who weren't registered were not entitled to food rations. The Jewish militia was well organized and was fully backed by the KRIPO (Kriminal Polizei Amt) and the Gestapo as long as it carried out their orders conscientiously, so the Judenrat could do with the Jews whatever it wanted. And since the Judenrat was a personal extension of Merin, everyone's lives depended on the caprices of one individual, who was himself a bit of a psychopath. His secretary and assistant was his wife, Fanny Charney, who spoke and wrote German fluently—a simple, decent woman who faithfully carried out his orders without really understanding them.

In 1941 a new round of anti-Semitic decrees began. The *Arbeitseinsatz* (forced labor unit) was established for the purpose of reducing the Jewish population through selections and transportations. The *Arbeitseinsatz* was supervised by General Heinrich Shmelt. His representative, the chief inspector, Henchel, installed a *Dienststelle* (placement office) in Sosnowiec where healthy young people were selected for forced labor camps. As helpers, Henchel gathered together a band of murderers and sadists: Heinrich Lindner, Bruno Ludwig Kuchinsky, Messner, and Knoll. It was these men who gathered and prepared contingents of Jews for transport. The Judenrat immediately placed itself at the service of this group, promising to supply the demanded quantities of slave laborers. There were actually Jewish boys and girls working in the *Dienststelle* office; the Judenrat had supplied them! When the *Dienststelle* gave an order to the Judenrat to supply a few thousand slave laborers, it immediately prepared a list of names and ordered those listed to join the slave labor force. Those who did not present themselves, the Jewish militia sought out and forcefully brought to the transport. No resistance was allowed to take root, no underground organizations were ever allowed to stir people to revolt. The Judenrat left little for the Germans to do. But when the contingents didn't appear on time, the Germans would invade the streets to grab whomever they could.

The Hebrew high school at Skladowa Street 5 was used as the Dulag (transport assembly point). Here, people registered themselves before being sent off. For a huge bribe, some were able to rescue themselves. Such bribes probably ended up in the pockets of the SS and the Gestapo. It did not matter to them: the people were theirs anyhow. If they let one out, they grabbed three in his place.

Here at the high school were also kept all those suspected of underground activities. From here they were sent away with the next transport. Opposite the Dulag was a small building called the *Tvilag* (a waiting place). Here the *Ersatz* (replacements) were kept. If anyone failed to show up for work or at the *Arbeitseinsatz* and could not be located, members of his family—parents, wife, brothers, children—were taken here, and kept as long as the missing one did not appear.

As soon as the first transports began leaving for Germany, filled with Jewish slave laborers, the Judenrat, with Moishe Merin at the head, set out to persuade people that the young should volunteer for work, with promises that they would return in six weeks. This was a German trick: people never returned from the camps. After the young were sent away, their families were liquidated—sent off with the next transport. Later we learned that these people worked under the harshest imaginable conditions, twelve to fourteen hours a day with hardly any food. The sick and those who were simply exhausted were sent to the *Himmelkommando,* in Auschwitz.

In 1942 the situation in the ghetto grew even more desperate. There were no longer any young, healthy men for the Germans to transport. At that point the Germans began shipping everyone to the concentration camps—young and old, women and children. From those camps, the young and able were sent to slave labor camps. The older ones, and women and children, were led to the gas chambers and crematoria. Jews were dragged out of the workshops where they had been employed as craftsmen. Strict inspections were conducted in Jewish homes, and if anything illegal was found, such as illegal rations, the people were removed to no one knows where. What Jew could exist on two hundred grams of bread and one hundred grams of margarine per week? Every Jew did as much as possible to avoid dying of hunger. People sold everything they had avoid starvation. As a result of all these measures, the captures increased.

In March 1942, exactly at Purim, Jews were forced to witness the hanging of Marek Lieberman and Mangel in a garden on Mandzever 32. They had been accused of falsifying documents. On the same spot a few days later, another four Jews were hanged for illegal trading: Nachum Lon and his son, Yehudah Vorman and Feffer. The Judenrat itself had prepared the gallows. In Jewish homes candles were lit at night in sorrowful memory of the dead.

14

The First Transfer

In April 1942 the Judenrat announced that Jews were to pack suitcases, blankets, underwear, sleeping cots. Part of the population was to be transferred. Even the destination was announced—Theresienstadt. At the same time the Judenrat had prepared a list of those who were employed and those who were not. It was made to look as if every unmarried working man would be able to protect his parents. This was a new trick that the Gestapo was playing to confuse the Jews. The women and children of the men who had been sent to forced labor were treated as unproductive. Indeed, a transport of the "unproductive" ones was dispatched immediately to Auschwitz.

By now the Jews were beginning to see through all the Nazis' tricks, to understand that gradually, according to a plan, the entire population of the ghetto was to be liquidated. The young people's underground organizations—Poalei Zion, Hashomer Hatzair, Dror, Hanoar Hatzioni, and Bund—had distributed leaflets in all Jewish homes calling for an uprising. When the Judenrat ordered five thousand Jews to assemble on May 10 at ten in the morning at Demblinski Street 10, at the old Jewish school, with ten kilos of baggage, ready for transfer, only a handful of people showed up. It was now obvious that the Judenrat was misleading people and was merely a tool of the Gestapo.

At this point Moishe Merin saw that he was losing his influence in the ghetto, that his actions were stirring up a revolt, and that his life was in danger both from the Jewish underground and from the Gestapo, which would blame him for the failure of its plans. Once he could no longer fill the transports, and could not keep the Jews quiet, what did they need him for? He would be liquidated instantly. We knew something was about to happen, but no one knew what. Yet it didn't take us long to learn.

On the evening of May 10, it happened. As soon as night descended and homes were locked, the entire ghetto was surrounded by military police with machine guns, searchlights, and police dogs. Jews were chased out of their homes into the open. At that time I was living with a Jewish family at Targowa 2. Beside me lived an elderly couple, the Nechemias, their daughter, son-in-law Kopelovitsch, and granddaughter—a three-year-old with blond hair. We were sitting around the table talking, discussing the day's events. Suddenly we heard pounding on the door and harsh shouts: *"Alle Juden heraus! . . . Schnell! Schnell! . . . Ihr Schweinehunde!"* (All Jews out! . . . Hurry! hurry! . . . You swine!). Like wild beasts they stormed the house with machine guns, bayonets flashing, striking us with whips and guns: *"Heraus! Sofort heraus!"* (Out, get out now!).

All of us ran out, almost naked. I could not even grab my documents, which were in my room in my jacket. The young woman grabbed her naked child from the bed, and we quickly slipped downstairs. The yard, a pie-shaped area, was already full of Jews—old men and women, young women and their children, all shaking with fear. The yard was lit up by searchlights; movie cameras had been set up. I was standing in the front row with my neighbors. The little blond girl was terribly afraid—trembling like an autumn leaf. Standing in the row with us was the rebbe of Sosnowiec, Yeshiah Engelhart, with his long black beard and radiant face. Surrounding us were SS and Gestapo troops and criminal police, who carried their machine guns in outstretched arms while messengers raced back and forth. From overhearing them we knew that someone had been found hiding indoors. Such people were shot immediately.

The people in the yard were scared out of their wits, doubling over with fear and panic. Many men and women wore only their nightclothes. The searchlights on the roofs and building ledges flooded the entire area with light: there would be no hiding. It was a dreary night, gray and cold. The sky was overcast, as if trying to shut us off from the world. Before long, lightning began to strike and thunder to clap, and immediately after this the rain began to pour down. I looked into the rebbe's face, which was still as a bronze mask. Rain was streaming down his face and beard.

I stood near my neighbor, the young woman, who held her daughter in her arms. The child was shivering. Instinctively she felt the danger and began to cry. She choked back her tears but her heart was fluttering with fear.

A few meters away I saw a guard I knew, an older German in a Wehrmacht uniform, who used to come among the Jews, encouraging them and sometimes even supplying them with food. I knew him as a decent and liberal man who did not ascribe to Nazi ideology and did not support the Nuremberg laws. Often I had talked to him quite openly about all kinds of issues. He regretted and criticized the Nazis' cruelty and their treatment of Jews. Now he was serving with a helmet on his head and a machine gun in his hands. Feeling terribly sorry for the child, I tried to intervene with this guard. Slowly, I approached him and asked him to let me go upstairs to the house to find a blanket for the child, who was shivering from the cold and soaking wet from the rain. Or perhaps he could go upstairs for me and bring a blanket down.

It was as if I had dropped a bomb on him. He was not at all the same good-natured man. His eyes flamed like a wild beast's. He raised his fist and screamed madly: *"Mach das du weg kommst, sonst ershiess ich dich wie einen Hund!"* (Get away from here or I'll shoot you like a dog!).

That is how the "good Germans" acted when they were serving the state.

◆　◆　◆

We were held in the yard until at least midnight under heavy guard, then escorted to the lobby of the Rialto, the cinema on Warszawska Street. In front of me the rebbe walked bent over, his eyes downcast as if trying to sink into their sockets. From his beard flowed rain mixed with tears. His lips were moving, but the words I could not hear.

This same night the Gestapo, aided by the Jewish militia and the Judenrat, led by Merin himself, invaded the heavily populated buildings at Mandzever 32, Dekerta 14, and Targowa 2 and 11, from which they took away all the Jewish residents, men, women, and children. These people were assembled at the Rialto and at the *Volkskirche* (people's church) on Jasna Street. At five in the morning the leader of the *Dienststelle* appeared, an SS man named Kuchinsky, with his gang of murderers, who began examining everyone's papers. Unfortunately, my *Kennkarte* (identity card) and working papers were in my coat, which I hadn't been able to grab when I was rushing from the house, so I was in serious danger. But a miracle happened: a neighbor and friend with a good *Sonderkarte* (special pass) was among the first to be released, and I asked him to save me—to go to my house and bring me my documents. And that he did. He brought me my papers, and I was able to show them at the very last moment.

I learned later that that night's detainees hadn't been enough to fill the transport, so people were grabbed from the street. While I was at work around eleven the next morning, I saw the Jewish militia, accompanied by the Gestapo and police dogs, running through the street. They surrounded the same houses again and dragged out all the people they found, even those who were employed and those who belonged to the Judenrat. All were packed into wagons and taken to the transport. Approximately 1500 people were sent to Auschwitz that day with the transport. In that same transport, Rebbe Engelhart and his family, bless their memory, were also sent off.

Merin, not wanting to lose his influence, or his head, thought up yet another lie, this time saying that the transportees had been taken to work camps. A rumor was even spread that the transport had returned. People ran to the train station in the hope of seeing their relatives and friends again. They quickly returned, disappointed and embittered. Clearly, the people had not been taken to work, since the old, the sick, and the children had been taken. A train worker told us later that the transport had been bound for Auschwitz. Most of the people had been led straight to the gas chambers.

A bleak mood descended on the ghetto. In this action there was not one family that hadn't lost someone near and dear. A terrible hopelessness enveloped those left behind; they sensed that their end was near: the fate of the Jews had been sealed. One after the next, we would all end the same way.

The Germans kept trying to fool us with all kinds of tricks and lies. Through their loyal servants in the Judenrat, they announced that unproductive Jews would have to be evacuated. The rest—the productive ones—would be permitted to remain and work undisturbed for the Wehrmacht.

Merin again promised that what had happened would not be repeated. He insisted that he and his team had had no choice but to help with the raids: only in this way had it been possible to save the rest; had they not cooperated, everyone's fate would have been sealed.

But this quickly proved to be another lie: in the first days of June, the shtetl of Olkusz, eighty kilometers from Sosnowiec, was liquidated with the help of the Judenrat and the Jewish militia. Almost everyone was sent to Auschwitz. Only a few—the relatives and friends of the Judenrat—were saved and brought to Sosnowiec. This bone the Nazi murderers allowed their loyal servants. In the latter half of June, the second transport from Sosnowiec was carried out.

15

The Second Transfer

In the second half of June 1942, the second large transfer of the Jews from Sosnowiec took place.

At night the Gestapo, with the help of the militia, encircled Panska and Ostroguska Streets and dragged out nearly all the inhabitants. In this district there lived mainly poor, hard-working folk who had struggled all their lives. It seemed that the Judenrat, with the "king of the Jews" at its head, had decided it was time to throw the poorest Jews to the insatiable Nazi beast. Whenever the Germans demanded laborers immediately, the Judenrat had always tapped the people of this district. The rich bought their way out of work with money or valuables. These poor working-class souls had no means to do that; besides, they were used to hard work, and even thanked God for the bit of warm soup they were given. So while the wealthy Jews sat in the cafés discussing politics, the poor went to work in their place. But the German devil now needed more victims, so the Judenrat went looking for them among the poorest and most defenseless. Men, women, and children were dragged out and led directly to the wagons.

That same night, the Jewish hospital was encircled and all the sick were taken away. The sick who could still walk tried to flee over the fences. They were caught like mice by the SS and their Jewish helpers. To anyone who still wondered where these transports were going, it was obvious now. The sick were thrown onto the platform like sacks, the next atop the last. Those who could not move were tossed onto the train cars like garbage. To our great disgrace, even this work was done by Merin's militia. At a distance stood the Gestapo officer Freitag, who enjoyed watching Jews carry out his commands. He urged them to work harder: *"Macht, Jungens, macht es schneller! Bewegt euch!"* (Hurry it up, guys, hurry! Get moving!).

38

Around eighty children from the orphanage were also loaded on the transport, some only babies, others as old as five. Some of them cried. Others tried to tear themselves away, and raised their eyes in fear as if asking, "What do they want from me here?" In all, two thousand people were loaded onto the train that day and sent to Auschwitz to the gas chambers.

The remaining Jews now knew their fate was sealed: there were no more reserves, no more substitutes, so their turn was next. The desperate fear of death was in everyone's eyes. Up to that point the Nazi beast had been fed with the poor and the helpless. But now there were no more poor people, no more sick or mentally ill or orphans or unemployed. From this moment on the healthy and the rich had nothing but themselves to offer up to the German devil.

In Landau's café the "prominent" Jews were still sipping their coffee and eating their pastries. But even they, the officials, the "family of the king," were distraught. No more illusions: they knew they were candidates for the next transport. The sick from the hospital and the children from the orphanage cast such a dark shadow that it was hard to catch breath. No more hope: the ship was sinking, and no salvation was possible. Despair pressed on everyone's heart.

More and more people were committing suicide, the one sure escape from the Nazis' claws. Any young people who possibly could escaped from the ghetto into the forests, where they joined the partisans. They were placing themselves in great danger, but they wanted to at least die fighting.

The Judenrat officials and the privileged Jews began behaving as if the end was in sight. They sold everything they had, bought themselves liquor and lost their inhibitions. Morality vanished. They gathered in private homes and staged orgies. The women shed all their shame and began cavorting like prostitutes, surrendering to every man before every other man's eyes. Death was near, if not today then tomorrow, so why not take all they could while they could? All that was holy was turned on its head. Ethics was vanquished by jungle law. Whoever was stronger and had more to offer, that one gained everything. Life had become random, so the few days or months that remained had to be used to their limit. People sought to drown all their feelings in the hope of killing their despair. Judgment Day was almost here—days or perhaps hours away—and there was only death to await. Only days before, they had enjoyed their families and friends, but Auschwitz had swallowed them up. It was as if no one wanted to hope any more, no one wanted illusions. All belief in the world was gone and would never return.

Ever since the Nazis seized Poland, some Jews had risked listening to the radio. Anyone caught with one was shot on the spot, along with his relatives, who were guilty of not denouncing him. Even his neighbors were sent to the death camps. There were other Jews who fantasized news and brought it as the latest information from the BBC or the Voice of America. People told one another fantastic stories about Allied victories, fiery speeches, German battlefield disasters, and so on. These fabrications served two purposes: they gave importance to those who created them, and they gave courage—and perhaps the will to survive—to those who believed them. Often the lies were about speeches by great statesmen offering Europe's peoples hope that freedom would soon come again. The news was called *Yivo* (Yidn Viln Azoi).

In the ghetto there circulated a joke. The Lodz ghetto had been liquidated. There were no Jews left in that great Jewish city. The last two Jews had been caught and were being led to their execution. After the judgment was read and the nooses were put around their necks, one Jew turned to the other and whispered in his ear: "Did you hear, Berl, yesterday Churchill made a speech and said any minute now we'll be free."

By this time, anyone who came to the Jewish café and tried to tell the latest news from secret sources, was told to hush—nobody wanted to listen. They were chased away with bitterness, these weavers of falsehood.

16

The Third Mass Transfer

The 12th of August of 1942 will go down in history as the most diabolic of all the days in the destruction of the Jews of Zaglebie. Moishe Merin, the "king of the Jews," had by then lost the trust of the Jews who remained in the ghetto. To them he was their liquidator, a servant of the Gestapo. It was common knowledge where the transports were going and what was happening when they arrived. Everyone knew about the gas chambers and the crematoria. After the sick, the old, and the children were sent away, no one had any illusions.

Merin had decided to hand over all Jews to the Nazi devil for the sake of saving his own life and the lives of his relatives, and everyone knew it, so no one believed him any more. The underground resistance had done all it could to tell the Jews where the transports were going and what happened to Jews at the end of the line. As a result, nobody was going to appear for transports voluntarily. On the contrary, more and more people were joining the underground, running off to the forests.

So when the Gestapo demanded another contingent for transport, to assemble on August 12, Merin grew frightened that he wouldn't be able to provide it. If he couldn't, the Germans would have to gather the contingent themselves. His failure would signal to the Germans that he had lost all influence over his Jews, and that the time had come to liquidate him.

So he decided that the Judenrat would organize clarification meetings. Speakers at these meetings appealed for volunteers to come forward to the prescribed gathering place on August 12, saying that this merely would be a re-registration of the working Jews, whose documents would be restamped.

Merin himself led the meeting at the Rialto cinema on Warszawska Street. There he explained that the Jews should come willingly to the city stadium. There, all of them would get legal documents entitling them to live and work in the ghetto. He promised that nothing would happen to anyone and insisted that having received their new documents they would no longer be persecuted. At the same time, he spoke of his accomplishments, about his efforts in "high places" to save the remaining Jews of Zaglebie who were useful elements for the Wehrmacht. As an example, he pointed to the "shops" that had been set up in the ghetto as a result of his efforts so that Jews wouldn't be shipped to places unknown, but could remain in their community doing productive work.

He ended with the words, "Come, all of you, men, women, and children, in your festive clothes, as to a joyous occasion, because at the gathering place you will get your legitimization and be protected from the raids and transports." One of the rebbes who was present spoke in support of this, declaring that Merin was "our savior, our leader."

Merin appealed to the German commissioners in the shops to let their workers have August 12 off so that they could be present at the stadium for re-registration. He also had posters put up in the streets urging Jews to appear at the stadium on the appointed day. To confuse the situation even further, in July the Gestapo had conducted re-registrations in three nearby Jewish communities—Czeladz, Mondrzew, and Strzemieszyce—during which they had indeed stamped documents and then sent the people home. To the Jews of Sosnowiec, this was a good omen.

On August 12 the Gestapo gathered around sixty thousand Jews in the stadium, including the Jews of Bedzin and Dabrowa. The underground's warnings had done little to dissuade the Jews from gathering there. They went en masse with their wives and children to the assembly points. That day they were permitted to walk through the streets, even to leave the ghetto. Even before dawn, they were hurrying to the stadium of the Unia to grab a good spot, as if they were attending a football match. Even the sick were brought so that they could also be legally registered.

In Sosnowiec alone around twenty-six thousand Jews assembled voluntarily. Only a very few stayed away. People came in their holiday clothes, as if to a festival. The older women dyed their hair in order to appear young and capable of work. The men also tried to look younger and stronger than they were. Once all the Jews had assembled, the Germans—the Gestapo, the SS, and the security police, all armed with light and heavy machine guns—cordoned off the area and forbade anyone to leave. Under a burning sun, every-one was ordered to remain seated. Anyone who stood was shot immediately.

Only in the afternoon did SS officers appear, along with leaders of the *Arbeitseinsatz*, accompanied by leaders of the Judenrat. Tables were set up and document inspection began. The commission that examined the documents divided the Jews into four categories.

Group 1 comprised those who were doing vital war work and who had no children or old people to support. These were released as soon as their documents were stamped. Group 2 comprised those who were young but who either had no specific jobs or were engaged in private businesses. These were assigned to slave labor and immediately sent to the Dulag. Group 3 comprised those who had jobs but had jobless people in their family, or older parents and children. With these, the Germans had to exercise judgment. If the worker had essential skills, the other, "unnecessary" people were taken from him since they were a burden; he himself was released. If he did not have essential skills, he was sent with his family to the transport. Group 4 comprised all the unproductive elements: old people, children, the unemployed, and those employed in nonessential businesses. This group was assigned for transportation to Auschwitz for liquidation.

The leaders of the Judenrat saved their relatives and friends. After that, they saved the wealthy ones, the ones who could still offer bribes. The Gestapo and officials of the *Arbeitsensatz,* drunk, made a game out of the faith of the people, as though they were garbage.

It was a sultry day, the sun harsh, the suspense unrelenting. People were frantic, their faces burning with sweat, tears, and panic. Some lost their nerve and all control of themselves. When the ones assigned to Groups 3 and 4 tried to flee, the Gestapo began shooting, and many fell dead. In the evening rain began pouring down. The children cried as they clung to their parents, but their parents couldn't help them, and this broke their hearts. Old people were collapsing into the rain puddles. In this way the people remained all night, awaiting death as a savior.

On Thursday, August 13, as the gray morning broke over the stadium, two masses of people lay on the field like two piles of soaked garbage: the twelve thousand to fifteen thousand men, women, and children of the doomed Groups 3 and 4. For some in Group 3 survival was still possible if they had the bribe money, and all night long those people traded in souls with the Gestapo and the Judenrat. All of Group 4, however, were fated for death, and waited for the transports to take them to Auschwitz. After a day of hot sun and a night of cold rain, everyone was half-dead anyhow. Many were too weak to stand, and many others lay dead on the ground. In their terrible suffering, the living envied the dead.

While it was dark those yet standing were escorted from the stadium by the SS, the Gestapo, and the *Shupo* (security police). In the faces of the victims, smeared with mud and dehumanized by despair, one could see the shadow of death. They dragged themselves along as if nothing mattered to them any more, as if they longed for death to release them. In their thousands they were packed into Kolataja Street numbers 4 and 6, which had been emptied to take them. There they were locked in and placed under heavy guard.

In those houses terrible things happened. Some tried to escape through the attics and over the roofs. A handful escaped by tunneling to neighboring buildings, Targowa 8 and Kondzever 16, or by dressing as sanitation workers or militiamen, having paid huge sums for the clothing. Some even escaped by feigning death and being taken away on tumbrels. Knowing their fates were sealed, some jumped from the upper floors to hurry their suffering to its end. Many others went mad and tore the clothes from their bodies. All of this lasted until August 18, when approximately eight thousand Jews were loaded onto train cars and carried to the Auschwitz gas chambers.

17

The Mournful Mood in the Ghetto

In every house in the ghetto, in every family, the people mourned for family or friends. The empty houses cast deep shadows of dread. The breath of those who had just been torn away could still be felt. Within the old walls could still be heard their sobs and wails. In the empty houses it was as though the cupboards, the beds, the empty vessels were mourning the terrible destruction, and longing for a human word, a breath, a sound, or the cry of a child.

The SS did not let any houses remain empty for long. They packed those Jews who remained tighter than before, just as if they were piling refuse after a sweeping. They shrank the ghetto even further, pulling the noose as tight as they could. In this they were following a precise plan to the letter. After the previous action these brutes assured the Jews, through their servants in the Judenrat, that things would calm down and that the remaining Jews would be allowed to stay and do productive work for the German war machine.

The Germans put the remaining Jews to work manufacturing clothing, boots, furs, and underwear for the German army. They even increased Jews' rations, to suggest that normal life was returning. But this was only to put the Jews off their guard and soften their hatred of the Germans, who wanted the Jews to think they were now safe and shouldn't rebel or try to escape.

For a while there were no more transports, although from time to time people would be grabbed off the street and sent to Auschwitz. Every week there was a train car to Auschwitz, and for the sake of efficiency the Germans always made sure it was full. For the slightest excuse people would be taken away to the death camps, never to be seen again. The Nazis called these Jews "serious lawbreakers," even when they had done nothing wrong.

45

The Judenrat was made to sign a proclamation stating that these were criminals who were damaging the community.

At this point the Germans started sweeping up young people for shipment to forced labor camps. First they took those who worked for commercial firms. Then they scaled down the factories and took away the unskilled workers. After that they liquidated all workshops except those essential to the war effort. All the young people caught in these sweeps were sent to the *Arbeitseinsatz*. And throughout all this, new decrees were made, and actions were taken on their basis, to reduce the population of the ghetto.

In January 1943 the Nazis decreed that all remaining Jews in the ghetto of Sosnowiec must leave the city for a smaller ghetto in the suburb of Szradula, where the poorest Jews lived, and which bordered another shrinking ghetto in Bedzin. There they were crammed into a few small houses and assured that they would be permitted to remain in them. The Nazis' real purpose was to concentrate the Jews in an ever smaller area, the better to watch them and the easier to liquidate them.

At first the Germans left a few Jews behind in the Sosnowiec ghetto, in a few isolated streets: Wiejska Street, Ciasna Street, and smaller streets than these. But soon enough these streets were also cleansed of Jews, till only Szradula remained. The Jewish homes were handed over to Poles.

Just before the transfer to Szradula, all the Jews had to appear before a doctor. At this time all of them got new regulation cards. Each of these blue cards had the letter T for *taglich* (daily) or O for *ohne taglich* (not daily). Those who got the blue card with the letter O were destined for Szradula. All the others were sent back to the handful of streets in Sosnowiec. The Jews who were ordered to remain in Sosnowiec understood very well that they were the next candidates for Auschwitz. The wealthier ones, those who still had bribe money or valuables, tried to buy their way into the Szradula "paradise." Many put an end to their doglike existence by killing themselves.

The underground warned the Jews that their end was approaching, that the ring was tightening, that they were all going to be liquidated in just the same way the smaller communities in the district had been rendered *Judenrein* (free of Jews)—that now it was the turn of the last two concentrations of the Jews of Zaglebie, namely, Sosnowiec and Bedzin. Yet people did not want to hear such talk. The Nazis were still feeding them illusions, and perhaps they lacked the strength to flee into the forests. They still struggled to believe that the Germans wouldn't kill *them*. The Judenrat, for its own survival, did everything it could to reassure the remaining Jews that in this small ghetto of Szradula, they would be able to live out the war.

18

The Turn Comes to Liquidate the Workshops

In November 1942 the Germans suddenly encircled the Helden workshops on Mandzever 20, Sadova Street, and Pilsudskiego 70, sweeping up the workers and sending them directly to forced labor camps. This was the first sign that the shops were also to be liquidated and that those employed in them were no longer protected.

Moishe Merin had always been proud of the shops and had taken credit for them. Exerting his pull, he had convinced the "ones in high places" of the need to establish these places, where skilled Jews could labor for the German war machine. German entrepreneurs had jumped at the idea, for various reasons.

First of all, they got access to good, cheap workers to produce vital war products such as steel, uniforms, furs, and underwear. Second, the German central authorities considered these entrepreneurs and their shop foremen to be essential to the war effort, and thus exempt from active duty. Third, there was plenty of money to be made from the Jews themselves, who were willing to sell their most precious possessions—furs, underwear, jewelry, gold—for mere pennies. With the vast sums they extorted from the Jews, these entrepreneurs were able to enlarge and expand their workshops so as to gouge still more Jews. In addition to this, Jews bribed them outright just to get into the shops. The Judenrat itself negotiated these bribes. Merin made it out that the shops were the best shelters for Jews, because once employed in them, they would be able to remain until the end of the war. The Jews, therefore, were ready to pay any price to get in. The entrepreneurs, for their part, bribed anyone necessary for the right to establish shops and to employ Jews to work in them.

But this system was now collapsing. In November 1942, liquidation of the shops began. The "iron bridge" started to collapse. In March 1943, SS and Gestapo storm troops surrounded the workshops of Helden, Garetzki, Shvedler, and Express, taking away all the workers of the first and second shifts and shipping them to Germany. Only a few highly skilled workers were left—enough to fill existing orders. In March 1943 most of the workers—I among them—were transported to slave labor camps.

The last safety plank had collapsed. There was nowhere else to hide, no one left to offer protection. No Jew was needed now. Hitler had kept his word: his fiendish project to destroy all the Jews was being carried out according to plan. The angels of destruction, Peikert, Dreier, and Cott, were in charge of liquidating the shops.

It seems that the Germans had decided to liquidate the Jewish ghettoes quickly. The war news from the front was getting worse for them every day. There were no more victories for them to celebrate, no more advances. In Stalingrad they had suffered their first major defeat. In Africa, the Allies had launched a major offensive and driven back the German "heroes," who suffered heavy losses. The Russians were beginning to attack now. The winter of 1942–43 was a catastrophe for the German soldiers in the east, where they found the harsh cold unbearable.

The German forces were losing their belief in victory, losing their morale, losing their courage. They began to let out their anger and bitterness on the defenseless Jews. Furthermore, the SS brutes, by cracking down hard on the Jews behind the front lines, were able to avoid being sent to the front. How could they be pulled away from such "brave" and important work when they were succeeding so well at it? Earlier in the war, when the Germans were advancing rapidly, plenty of SS troops had gone to the front willingly, for the sake of being part of a great victory. Now they did all they could to avoid it because active service now meant death in combat, or death from the cold, or capture by the Russians. Finally, they were destroying helpless Jews to ensure there would be no witnesses to their crimes.

19

The Last Action

The end was approaching for the Zaglebie Jewry, the end of one thousand years of history. The Zaglebie Jews had written one of the most glorious chapters of the diaspora. Here in this profoundly spiritual community had been learned Jews, great religious scholars, Jewish artists of worldwide reputation, Jewish industrialists, Jewish intellectuals and scientists. All of this was and is no more. With his Nazis bandits, Hitler—may his name be erased—destroyed one of the most beautiful and vibrant Jewish communities in Poland.

On March 10 the only Jews left in the Sosnowiec ghetto were a few with the necessary connections—with relatives or close friends in the Judenrat—and a handful of their concubines. On that day the final transfer took place. No one was permitted to leave the ghetto except to work in the shops. The Judenrat and the Jewish militia were also installed in Szradula. The crowding was horrible. Ten to twenty people were packed into each apartment. People took turns sleeping. When some workers rose to go to work, others took their beds. The sanitation was dreadful. People lay in the streets and yards like dead bodies. Merin's last act was to collect all the remaining gold and silver from those who still had any. He appealed to the Jews to forfeit this willingly to avoid yet another deportation. He himself placed on the table his gold cigarette holder and his gold watch and ring. Jews brought their jewelry, silver, candelabras, and *hanukiot* (Hanukah menorahs); these were packed in cases and sent to the Gestapo. The Jews handed everything over, thinking that they were saving their skins by doing so. Merin probably now saw that he had run out of German protectors and that the water had risen to his neck.

20

The Liquidation of the Judenrat

Some Jews who still had hidden valuables, foreign bank accounts, and connections in "higher places" tried to get foreign identity papers. For huge sums it was possible to arrange these documents from Switzerland or from Latin American countries such as Paraguay and Bolivia. In June 1943 a number of Jews, including a group of young people from Hanoar Hatzioni, were informed that they had been recognized as foreigners and were to report to the police station, from which they would be sent to an *Ulag* (an internment camp for foreign nationals). There, transport out of the country would be arranged for them. These "fortunate ones" rejoiced, said their good-byes to relatives and friends, and went to the police station with their bags packed. Everyone envied them.

The same day, the police telephoned the Judenrat and instructed them to mount a guard for the foreigners being transferred to the internment camp. There was nothing suspicious about this—it was routine for the Jewish "authorities" to be at hand when a transport took place. Moishe Merin himself appeared to say farewell to the foreigners; his secretary, Fanny Charny, was also there, and so were Chayim Merin (Moishe's brother), Berenstein, and Levenstein. But as it later turned out, this was another Nazi trick. None of these people ever returned. A Polish worker at Auschwitz later said he saw a car arrive there from Sosnowiec with twenty people in it, presumably the leaders of the Judenrat, together with the "foreigners."

Merin and his servants had done all that had been demanded of them. But once they had nothing more to offer, they were useless to the Germans, and potentially disruptive, so they were liquidated. The Jews remaining in Szradula would be easy for the Germans to grab up and destroy without help.

The following day, when the Gestapo chief of train transports, Dreier, came into the ghetto, he pretended not to know what had happened and asked for Merin. Then he immediately appointed a replacement.

Once Merin and his gang had been liquidated, the Jews realized their last hour had come. The Germans had surrounded the ghetto with barbed wire. In the workshops the Jewish workers were being replaced by Poles. Everyone sensed that the last act was drawing to a close. Indeed, in June 1943 the SS proceeded to empty out the Szradula and Bedzin ghettos. This time the SS themselves dragged the Jews out of their houses. The Gestapo chief, Dreier, himself led this action and gathered the transport. That day four thousand Jews were sent to Auschwitz.

After this, a black mood fell over Szradula. Suicides increased. The Jews felt cornered and beyond salvation. Even if a Jew could cross the barbed wire, the police were certain to catch him and turn him over to the Gestapo.

Yet even now, the Nazis tried to convince the Jews that they would be able to work in the shops and see the end of the war. There was even talk that they would move some of the workshops to Szradula. In this way they tried to spark false hope among the despondent Jews.

21

The Completion of the Liquidation

On August 1, 1943, the last phase of the liquidation of the Zaglebie Jews took place. In the middle of the night the ghettoes of Sosnowiec and Bedzin were encircled. SS and Gestapo storm troops entered, and they and Ukrainian bands of murderers started shooting left and right. Many Jews had hidden in underground shelters, which they had prepared beforehand in premonition of this hour. The Gestapo called forward the new "kings" of the Jews and warned them that any Jews found hiding in bunkers would be shot on the spot. The rest would be transferred, with their belongings, to Birkenau, where they would be able to work unhindered.

At daybreak, SS *Kommandos* and military units forcibly entered the houses and dragged out every last Jew. This liquidation lasted an entire week. Every hole was searched and many bunkers were dynamited. Jews were pulled out of their hiding places and shot on the spot. The streets were full of dead bodies. The Germans shot children who were trying to save themselves. They tossed the wounded and sick into the freight cars as if they were garbage. They carried on until they had cleared out and liquidated every last Jew. The final one thousand were taken to the gas chambers in Auschwitz. This is how the Sosnowiec Jewry, a community that once had numbered thirty thousand—eighty thousand when Bedzin, Dabrowa, and the surrounding district were included—came to its end, murdered by Nazi bandits.

In the Szradula ghetto there remained, after this last deportation, a few hundred Jews, who were left to live and work until January 13, 1944, when they also were cruelly liquidated. With that the Zaglebie Jewry had vanished, destroyed by the Nazi murderers and their Polish and Ukrainian helpers.

53

PART TWO

• • •

My Personal Fate

Now for my own struggle to avoid death. Scores of times, some mysterious hand saved me from the claws of death. When people ask, "How did you save yourself?" I do not know what to answer. I was not stronger or smarter than many of my friends who did not survive. It was pure coincidence, a predestination, my personal fate. I was among the few who were meant to be saved. In my descriptions you will see how destiny sometimes arrives at the most unnatural outcomes. Perhaps it was my destiny to serve as a witness, to write about the Holocaust as a memorial to the fallen. That is why I consider it my duty to describe the inhumanity I saw, to recall names and tell about that tragic period. Let this book be material for future historians of the Nazi era, which soaked Europe's soil with the blood of six million Jews.

22

I Fall into the Grasp of the Gestapo

When I came back to Sosnowiec, in the first days of November 1939, I began to liquidate my business. I saw that it would not be possible to continue the undertaking, a plate glass wholesaling firm. It was obvious the Germans would soon grab it. In my absence, many Jewish businesses had been sacked, but since I was not trading in food or clothing, thefts from my shop hadn't been too significant. My storage rooms were full of glass stock, so I quickly sold whatever I could.

I had already been instructed to prepare accounts listing everything I had in stock and to present it to the authorities. I also had to sign papers stating that I had "voluntarily" donated everything I owned to the state. The situation grew worse with each passing day. In these circumstances I decided to leave Sosnowiec and join my family. Whatever would happen to them would happen also to me. Above all, let us be together.

It was a long journey to Ostrowiec, so I decided to make Krakow my destination. There I had a married brother and many relatives. Krakow was on the other side of the border and belonged to the *Generalgouvernement;* even so, it was only two hours from Sosnowiec.

I started to prepare for the journey. I sold everything I possibly could and with the money bought gold and jewelry, which would be easy to carry and to convert into cash. Jews were forbidden to obtain traveling passes, but with enough money one could buy one. Yosel Landau, a friend and neighbor, introduced me to an intimate friend, a former partner, a *Volksdeutsche* from Katowice, a certain Polaschek, who declared himself ready to escort me safely across the border for a fat fee. We agreed that on February 8, 1940, at dawn, he would come by my house. From there we would leave for the train station, which was close to my house. All of this was done. On February 8, at seven in the morning, the man appeared as arranged. I gave him a large part of my valuables and removed my armband with the Star of David, and we left for the station.

It was a lovely, sunny winter day. Close to the station I saw two men in civilian clothes walking back and forth. Instinctively, I was frightened because I had never seen either of them before. I thought, *"Oifn Ganef Brent Dos Hitl"* (a thief always feels suspect). Besides, what connection could there be between me and these two people?

We purchased tickets and boarded the train, which left the station immediately. I sat on one side and my companion on the other, to make it look as if we did not know each other. Right away, the two strange men entered our train car, appearing to be looking for seats. They went into another car and came right back out as if they had not found seats there, and sat down in a corner near us. I was anxious and inexplicably afraid. I felt feverish and short of breath. There was danger in the air, and I didn't know what to do.

In the shtetl of Szczakowa we had to change trains for the one to Krakow. As we stepped onto the platform, I did not look at my companion at all, but instead tried to disappear into the crowd. Suddenly a strong hand grabbed me. I turned and saw the steely face of one of the two strangers. He commanded me in German, "Come along with me!" It was as if I beheld the Angel of Death. I grew weak and dizzy and nearly collapsed. Immediately the two spies hoisted me by the arms and led me into the office of the train director. They also brought in my companion. Immediately, they asked if I was a Jew.

A Gestapo officer arrived soon after. They took me back to Sosnowiec to the headquarters of the Gestapo on Pierwszego Maya Street. My companion was freed immediately. I later learned that he himself had notified the Gestapo that he was bringing to the *Generalgouvernement* a suspicious Jew carrying a lot of valuables. The second suspicious character was his own son, who was serving in the Gestapo as *Volksdeutsche*. He was trying to show his loyalty to the Fatherland in the hope of being rewarded with a Jewish business.

I was strip-searched. I had hidden valuables in my clothes and even in my body orifices. While I was undressing I slipped a three-karat diamond ring into the finger of my glove. Soon they brought things from my house:

documents, papers, letters, and writings, all tied up with the straps of my phylacteries.

The first interrogation started.

While looking through my personal belongings, one of the SS, a redhead, who was sitting and writing, called out to me: *"Jude, weisst du was man mit misseh mishina meint?* (Jew, do you know the meaning of the expression 'hard luck'?) That's what you're going to get today."

They started to torture me, tearing at my flesh. They were determined to know who I was in contact with and what sorts of underground missions I had performed, whether I had any contact with the underground and who I knew in that movement. They were experts at torture and at extracting confessions. It was not only the inquisitor who beat me, but also two specialists, who tortured me in shifts.

They also read my writing and poetry, searching for evidence that I was working against the Nazis. They scalded me with hot irons. They pulled out my fingernails, and then they administered electric shocks. By various similar methods they tried to force me to talk, but I did not talk: I was silent as the wall. My head swelled, my eyes became full of blood. Bruised and battered as I was, I could still hear them speaking among themselves: *"Der Schweinhund will nicht reden. Mir werden ihn aber reden machen"* (The swine doesn't want to talk, but we'll make him talk).

Outside, when they learned that I had been arrested and was being questioned by the Gestapo, many people hid, cleared out, in fear that I might betray them, that some secrets would be extracted from me. I was very familiar with the entire underground and youth movement and knew many secrets. It was also known that the Gestapo had specialists for extracting information.

My interrogators tried every means to convince me that as soon as I disclosed the names of members of the underground—even only a few—I would immediately be freed and even be protected against retaliation. At one point they threatened to shoot me. They took me naked into the yard, in the snow, and told me to face the wall to be shot. I ran as though the devil was chasing me.

I pleaded with my torturers, "Shoot me, because I can't endure any more." But they teased me: "You will die when we're ready." They were like wild beasts. When they heard me say, "I don't know, I can't," they tore at my flesh. Blood was running down me in sheets but I did not succumb and did not surrender. I thought to myself, *I am going to die; there is no way I will escape these murderers. If I betray others they will only extend my agony with even more tortures. It will only make things worse.* I made a firm decision not to talk. When my head was swollen, my eyes filled with blood, I heard, more by instinct than through my ears, as though through a fog, one say to the others, "He will have to talk. We'll make him talk. He knows a lot."

In this way they tortured me a whole day on February 8, 1940, until nightfall, without ceasing. Also, for an hour they put me in a narrow, dark chamber where it was impossible to sit or stretch out and I had to stand with sharp stones digging into my flesh. In the evening I was thrown into a jail cell, a pack of broken and bleeding bones. This was a cell where bandits, criminals, and rapists of the worst kind were kept. When they saw my condition, they knew how cruelly I had been handled. Taking pity, they washed the blood from me and pressed cold compresses to my wounds.

The next morning I was again led out for questioning. Once more they started to torture me, with new methods, trying to extract information. I prayed for death to quickly end my suffering.

23

Those in the Prison

When one finds oneself in prison, behind bars, one encounters a new and totally different world. Until then, I had never encountered criminals. I had read and heard a lot about prison life, but only when I actually found myself behind bars did I realize the horror of that world, reduced to a few cubits of damp and foul air. Above the cell was a small strip of sky; seldom did a ray of sun enter.

I was sharing a cell with political prisoners and career criminals. The latter were the élite and always had the upper hand. They set the tone in the cell: it was they who classified the other prisoners and who assigned the chores. The "headmen" of the cell were the violent criminals, the armed robbers and the murderers of police. Below them were the break-and-enter men, who might strike their victims but who never killed them. These latter had little influence and looked up to their more powerful cellmates like students to their professors. Yet they had more status than the petty thieves, the pickpockets, and those who were charged only with assault. One of the thieves in our cell had been arrested for stealing chickens. Though he had a threatening manner, he quickly fell silent when someone called him mockingly, "chicken thief." His crime had shamed the trade, so he had to keep his mouth shut and just listen to the others. The political prisoners also had their categories. Those accused of high treason, of spying, had the most prestige because they were in danger of the death sentence. Sometimes one of them was removed from the cell at night, never to be heard from again.

Some of the political prisoners had been arrested because they had demonstrated against the Germans. Some were Polish patriots and political opponents of Nazi Germany. These men were regarded with contempt, especially if they had been prominent in society on the outside: politicians,

61

diplomats, industrialists, and so on. To the other criminals these men were the old ruling class, the servants of law and order, the ones who had mistreated them and then given them stiff sentences.

From time to time we heard the prison doors open with a screech, and all eyes turned to the door because we knew that more prisoners were being brought in. As soon as the heavy door slammed shut, the headmen of the cell began questioning the new arrivals: Who are you? What are you here for? Often the victims were so broken from their interrogation and so confused by their strange situation that they began crying, or mumbling incomprehensible words. If the new "guest" did not find favor with the cell's headmen, he was assigned a spot right beside the slop pail, which he had to scrub and keep clean.

The most powerful man in the cell, the "president," was a Pole of around thirty-five with a scar that stretched across his entire left cheek and half his skull. He had already spent more than half his life behind bars. He had escaped prison a few times, had hidden in caves and fought gun battles with the police. He was in jail now for armed robbery. He had been robbing a bank when the police surprised him. There had been a gun battle during which he shot one dead and wounded three others. Now he was awaiting trial. He too wasn't much concerned about his fate because in prison his status was lofty and he had certain privileges. His "second" was a young blond gentile around twenty-seven with a mustache. He was also accused of armed robbery—a "hot job." He had been robbing a jewelry shop with three other colleagues. They had shot a security guard; soon after, they had had a shootout with the police during which two police were killed by machine gun fire and a third was wounded.

He was a good-humored and sympathetic gentile with laughing eyes, always in a good mood. His beloved was behind bars in the women's section for participating in a different crime. Often he would mount the shoulders of a friend to peek through a hole in the front of the cell. Through it he could glimpse the outer yard, and see if his beloved was there cleaning the furniture and carpets of the prison warden. When the others teased him that the warden was replacing him as his wife's lover, he answered that their wives weren't sitting at home either. "If I knew that my wife was sleeping with the warden, I'd strangle them both," he said.

When the other prisoners saw my battered condition, they took pity on me. When they learned that I hadn't broken under questioning, they treated me with great respect. I was assigned a place not among the prominent, but rather among the minor prisoners, not too near the slop pail. I was terribly confused and in great pain. From the corridor outside we could hear a transistor radio. News from the Western front was being broadcast, announcing that the Germans had crossed the French border, had broken through the Maginot Line and were conquering one city after another. This depressed me even more. It seemed to me that the whole world was going under. The Germans' success in battle shocked me terribly. I was full of pain. My greatest wish then was to fall asleep and never wake up. My mind was as sharp as a knife. I kept thinking about what would happen in the morning, when the murderers would once again take me for questioning.

When I opened my eyes next, the lights were on and there was shouting in the corridor. I heard hinges screeching and the loud curses of the guards. The air in the cell stank terribly. There were between sixty and seventy of us in a sixty-meter cell, which also contained an overflowing slop pail. The first thing the cell's headmen did when they opened their eyes was tell what they had dreamed and call for someone to interpret their dream. The old "cats" knew well how to do this. Then the "dupes" were ordered to clean the cell quickly and empty the slop pail. Anyone who was too proud to follow orders was severely beaten.

After "coffee" we were escorted to the prison yard for our morning walk. We marched in a row and afterward had to run and sing. My bones ached and my head and eyes were swollen, yet I breathed easier out there. It was a cold, snowy morning. When we were ordered to sing, I reminded myself of the *Avinu Malkainu* (a Hebrew prayer). I sang it with all my heart, as if wanting to cry my heart out to the Creator. I also reminded myself of my Hebrew name, Elkana, which has this Hebrew horoscope: "Fortunate is the one who notices the poor, because in a time of misfortune, God will notice him." So I prayed quietly to myself: "God, observe this poor beaten man and protect me from evil." For a moment I forgot myself and started to sing aloud: *Avinu Malkainu.* The guard halted me and asked: "What's that you're singing?" I quickly came to my senses and answered, "I'm singing to the Almighty that he should protect us from evil." The guard gave me a shove with his keys and replied, "Fool, your God is dead. Get going!"

Soon we were back in the cells. The criminals had already made contact with other cells while outdoors. The blond gentile had seen his beloved from a distance, and sent her a note. Quickly the guards started to call people out for questioning. My turn soon came. I was shown new documents that had been found in my house and office. They started to beat and torture me again. Suddenly I heard, in the next room, Yosel Landau, my neighbor, who had put me in touch with the *Volksdeutsche* Pole, the one who had betrayed me to the Gestapo. I knew they would lie to him that I had talked, to draw from him information that would put me in more trouble, so I began declaring that I had told them nothing, declaring it in a voice loud enough for Landau to hear. The Gestapo immediately saw what I was doing, and gagged me and pulled me into another room. But it was too late: Landau had heard me.

The Gestapo tortured me for days on end without a break. They kept bringing in fresh torturers and interrogators, and tried both soft means and harsh, but they could not break me down. They would have happily killed me, but they hadn't given up hope of forcing me to talk.

Once a prisoner came into our cell who seemed to want to become friends only with me. The criminals realized immediately that he was a jailhouse plant, and signaled me to be careful what I said to him. A few days later he was pulled from the cell.

One day almost the entire city council of Dabrowa Gornicza was brought into our cell. These men were suspected of conspiring against the Germans. Our cell's headmen received them with spiteful glee. The oldest councilor, the former prefect, was immediately ordered to clean the slop pail. The criminals hated former officials like these, the lofty ones, the judges and police commissioners. These men were treated especially badly by the criminals, who had revenge to extract. If they fought back—tried to reason and protest—they were beaten even worse, to the accompaniment of vile insults.

Sometimes during the night, the cell door opened and the Gestapo and criminal police entered and called a few names. These men were executed the very same night. One night a strange man appeared in our cell, a hatchet-faced little man with piercing eyes. He looked like a Jew, but he would never admit to being one. The "interrogators" in our cell could not understand why he had been arrested. He never dropped a single hint: their questions bounced off him. Yet we could tell he was important and had something to hide. He became friendly with me and I eventually gained his trust. He admitted to me he was a spy, one who gathered economic information for the enemies of the Germans. A few times he was called for questioning. Then one night the guards pulled him out of the cell and led him away. As he was leaving he grimaced at me, knowing this was good-bye.

Another time, two German storm troopers were brought to our cell. They had been part of the Germans' motorcycle brigade during the first days of the invasion. They had been caught having sexual relations with Jewish women and were about to go on trial for shaming their race.

24

A Cell of Jews Only

On the eve of Passover of 1940, all the Jewish prisoners were gathered into one cell, away from the other prisoners. Nobody knew why. Immediately two groups formed: the pessimists and the optimists. The former believed we were about to be executed. The latter were more hopeful: the Judenrat must have arranged for us to be supplied with matzos and other Passover foods, and that was why we had been separated. Many of us didn't sleep that night in the Jews' cell. We all knew we might be taken away in the night. But that didn't happen, nor was any food brought to us. The Judenrat had more important concerns than to provide Jewish prisoners with Passover foods. Apparently the Germans simply wanted to gather us up for any eventuality, because Jews had a special status.

One person who was not afraid and did not lose any sleep was a known Sosnowiec underworld character named Wolf. He was a tall, handsome blond fellow with blue eyes who had already been in prison on criminal charges. When he was free he was a professional card player. There were a few like him in Sosnowiec, who dressed elegantly and mixed in high society, who earned their living at the gambling tables, extracting money from "suckers." Suckers are everywhere, he told us. We became friendly with him, and he passed on to us some of the secrets of winning. Professional gamblers used marked decks, the marks barely detectable, that always let them know which cards their opponents had, when to buy a card and when not to buy. Even fresh packs that had just been unwrapped had their marks. He also told us how he used to seduce other men's wives, later to blackmail them.

Every day new "guests" were brought into our cell. One for black market trading, another for hiding forbidden possessions in his house, a third for not declaring all he owned, and so on. The men caught us up with the news from outside, such as of new decrees and recent transports. By this time the headman of our cell was Wolf, who for his seconds had two professional criminals—forgers and the like—who had already done prison time.

We were all glad to be in an all-Jewish cell. We felt uncomfortable among non-Jews. There were criminal elements among the gentiles, violent men and homosexuals. The latter often hunted for victims. Many of the career criminals also had venereal diseases. One night one of the criminal prisoners tried to rape a boy. His target screamed. The guard entered with two policemen, and they took the perpetrator to a punishment cell. The boy who had been attacked was also removed; otherwise the colleagues of the first would have killed him. Later it turned out that the perpetrator was in the tertiary stages of syphilis.

Among our own kind, we felt friendlier and more secure. Sometimes on the Sabbath we quietly hummed a Sabbath hymn and told one another stories. Among us was a Sosnowiec Jew named Pinchovsky, a feather dealer, who knew Hassidic melodies. Another of us, a man with a deformed face, could tell Hassidic tales. Once a young boy named Lieberman was brought to us. He was from a prominent Sosnowiec family. He had been caught falsifying documents. He had a beautiful voice, so we would listen to his sentimental melodies. He was later hanged in a garden on Mandzever Street.

From time to time we would get up and start to walk. We would imagine what streets we were walking through and what our destination was. This helped us endure prison life. Sometimes our relatives from the outside would send us food parcels, and we would divide these among ourselves. Twice I also received food parcels. To this day I do not know who sent them to me, because I did not have any relatives.

For those of us who smoked, the greatest of joys was getting a package of tobacco. To strike a light, they would extract some cotton batting from their clothes and rub a stone on a piece of glass until sparks flew and the cotton caught fire. Cotton batting gave me no end of trouble. I have already related how, during interrogation, I had slipped a diamond ring into a finger of my glove. Later I worried that the glove might be taken from me and the ring with it. So I quietly sneaked it out of the glove and buried it in the cotton lining of my winter jacket. When the smokers started to pull cotton batting out of my clothing, I became afraid they would also pull out the ring.

25

My Mother Appears to Plead My Case

The window of our cell had a tin lining that shut out the outside world. In this lining someone had made a hole through which it was possible to see a part of the street. More than once I looked through this hole to watch free people going about. Once when I was doing that, I got the shock of my life: my mother and her sister were looking up toward me. How had *she* gotten here? I couldn't imagine how. An old, sick mother had come from so far away to see her son. I rejoiced at the sight of her, yet I was also fearful. I looked at her gentle face, her tear-filled eyes, and wondered: Who had brought her here?

She had learned I had been arrested and could find no peace. Sick as she was, she locked her house and set out on the road. Jews were not allowed to travel by train so she traveled in wagons or on foot, crossing borders illegally until she came to Sosnowiec. Along the way she stopped at Olkusz, where her sister lived. From there both of them came to Sosnowiec to save me, her youngest son. That's what a mother is capable of. She stayed in Sosnowiec as long as she had to, doing whatever she could, knocking on doors, parting with her last few pennies until she had freed her son from prison, where he had been held for four months under Gestapo interrogation.

On the eve of Shavuot (Pentecost), June 6, 1940, I was released. My mother was waiting for me at the gate. She fell into my arms and covered my face with tears and kisses. We proceeded directly to Olkusz, directly to my aunt's house, where we celebrated the festival. My mother radiated joy at her success in freeing me from prison. All I could give her was the diamond ring, which I dug from the lining of my winter garment, with much love and gratitude.

My mother remained with me for some time but later returned to Ostrowiec. I promised her that as soon as I could liquidate my business I would join her there, but unfortunately, this became impossible when travel grew increasingly dangerous. So it was that I never again saw her.

It was told to me later that she was deported to Sandomierz and from there to Treblinka, where she died a martyr's death after terrible suffering. May the Almighty avenge her blood.

26

The Noose Around My Neck Gets Tighter and Tighter

Life in the ghetto became increasingly difficult. I had been given a position in my old business, because the German who had taken it over needed my expertise. But I was certain he would send me away as soon as he didn't need me any more: he wouldn't want the former owner around. Naturally, I hung on as long as I could, but I knew that eventually I would be dispensable.

Also, I found it impossible to clear myself with the Gestapo. Six months after my release from prison, they were still calling me to court for the crime of attempting illegally, with a false pass, without a Jewish armband, and with a bag full of jewelry and gold, to cross the border into the *Generalgouvernement*. I was enormously lucky that most of the gold and jewelry had ended up in the pockets of the Gestapo themselves; it made my defense somewhat easier that they had stolen much of the evidence against me.

It cost me a lot of money to have my punishment reduced. That is how I was sentenced to four months' imprisonment, less time in interrogation. Since the interrogation had lasted four months, I was set free. However, according to the precise German records, I still had three-and-a-half hours left of that sentence to serve, so I had to enter prison to stay for another three-and-a-half hours.

One day later on, when I arrived at work, I was told that the Gestapo was searching for me. This was not the Gestapo from Sosnowiec, but rather the Gestapo from the *Generalgouvernement*. Since I was not there at the time, they left a note stating that they would return and that I should be ready. When I read this I trembled. What more did they want from me? Hadn't they tortured me enough? Where should I hide?

I decided on the spot to flee. I understood that if I remained in Sosnowiec they would eventually find me, and if not they, then the Jewish mili-

70

tia. So I decided to go into hiding until I could find out why I was wanted. Until then, I had better clear out. I decided to go to my aunt's home in Olkusz, eighty kilometers from Sosnowiec. I was not allowed to travel by train or minibus so I set out on foot, hoping that along the way some better mode of travel would appear.

It was winter, very cold, with snow falling and visibility poor. So as not to be noticed by police patrols, I covered my Jewish star and followed a wagon carrying bricks, pretending I belonged to it.

I arrived at Olkusz at night, more dead than alive. When my aunt answered my knock, she had the shock of her life: I looked frozen to death. I told her the whole story and asked her permission to stay in her house until I could learn why the Gestapo was looking for me and could come up with a plan to fix the situation. She pitied me, but I could see reluctance to help me in her eyes, and even more in the eyes of my uncle. If the Gestapo found me in their house, they would face accusations of hiding a criminal, and this would put their own lives in danger. We could all be sent to Auschwitz as a result. My uncle told me then that a German "loyal" had been placed in charge of his lumber supply business and was billeted in their house. They also told me he was a treacherous Nazi and that if he learned of my presence he was likely to turn me over to the Gestapo.

I explained to them that it was only a matter of a few days—only until I could learn what the Gestapo wanted. Not having any other choice, because they could not throw me into the street, they decided to tell the German that I was a relative from a small shtetl who had come to consult a doctor in Olkusz. I ate a meal with them, took a bath and went to bed. The following morning, when the German came down, they told him the story. He also saw that a doctor had been called for me and that medicines had been placed around me.

This German was a short, blond man with a shock of hair over his eyes, and he knew how to talk nonstop. He introduced himself to me as one of the "leaders" and heroes of Germany, as a man responsible for the entire economy of the German Reich. He was conceited and impudent, a braggart and a fast talker. He was constantly planning what he would do after the victory. He was certain that a province would be placed under his jurisdiction, because he was one of the Führer's closest confidants. He was constantly bringing home loot he had stolen from Jewish homes. Once he came home with a German paper with news from the front. In it he read that the Russians had launched a counteroffensive, so he got up on a chair like Napoleon, shook his shock of hair, and cried out:

"Ya, now I'm going to the front. I'll show you how one fights."

I forced myself not to smile.

I could not remain longer in Olkusz; my presence was raising suspicions. I did not receive any good news from Sosnowiec because no one could learn what I was accused of. I only got promises from friends of my aunt that they would look after me. My aunt and uncle would never have chased me out of their house, but I could detect in their faces that they were frightened and wanted me gone. So I decided to return and report to the Gestapo. Whatever would happen, would happen. A free ride on a coach wagon was arranged for me, and I returned to Sosnowiec.

First I sought out a "fixer" I knew who had connections with the Gestapo. I gave him a sum of money and he promised to look out for me. When I reported to the Gestapo they immediately took me in to the officer of the SS who was the local contact for the *Generalgouvernement*. After questioning me, they placed me in a solitary cell for a few hours. Then they led me out and placed me on a wagon, and an SS officer drove off with me. I didn't know where he was taking me. It was only when we came to the border with the *Generalgouvernement* and he reported to the border guard, pointing to me as his "catch," that I realized we were heading toward Krakow.

On reaching Krakow, I was immediately imprisoned on Senatorska Street near Grodzka Street. The following day I was called for interrogation. It was only now that I learned the charges. When I had been arrested the first time, they had found among my documents various notes relating to goods that I had purchased in Ostrowiec and that I afterward had transferred illegally to Sosnowiec. I had made these transactions while last visiting my mother. At that time, when I traveled back to Sosnowiec, we had had to stop at Skarzysko.

When I got off at that station to make my connection, I saw that the police and the Gestapo were encircling the building and sorting the travelers, separating out the Jews and packing them into freight cars. I felt the danger and saw hell gaping. I was carrying large sums in money and valuables. At the checkpoint I watched several men represent themselves as *Volksdeutsche*.

These were immediately allowed to pass, so it occurred to me quickly that I had to risk doing the same. I spoke German, so I gathered courage, walked boldly up to the guards and told them I was a *Volksdeutsche* who had been visiting my family in the *Generalgouvernement* and was now returning home to Oberschlesien.

The officer looked at me, examined me and asked, "Where do you live?"

"In Katowice," I answered boldly.

He returned my false document to me and waved me through the barrier.

After they found the notes in my house, they had started to investigate the matter in Ostrowiec. That is what this new round of questions was about. I was lucky this wasn't a political case but only a tax matter. I was tortured and questioned for a day and a half. Then I was released and ordered to leave the city within twenty-four hours. To this day I don't know why they let me go. I'm certain someone intervened for me. Perhaps Elijah the Prophet . . .

27

"If a Misfortune Is Destined, It Will Come Right into the House"

My old business, where I was now working as a stockkeeper, was continuing to grow. When the Germans invaded Russia, they severely damaged many cities and towns, which now had to be rebuilt. Since the Russian glass factories were also badly damaged, glass had to be sent to Russia from the Reich. Many wagons of glass were dispatched from my old business in Sosnowiec to the Ukraine as far as Charkow. I had to prepare and document all these transports.

Since glass was a vital war business, my "position" was secure, and this saved me from being transported for all of 1942. The business was prospering, but it needed bank loans to expand. One day an inspector from the Dresden Bank, a man in his fifties, appeared at the shop to inspect the business. He took an interest in my plight, and his sympathy seemed genuine. I came to trust him instinctively. He spoke to me frankly and condemned the Nuremberg decrees. At one point we were alone in the storage room, where I was sure no one could overhear us, and I risked asking him:

"I see that you are a refined and intelligent man of liberal views, and I know you are honest in your sympathy for me. So I want to ask you: How is it that you are wearing the insignia of a PG (party comrade)? Do you agree with the party's ideology?"

He smiled at me and answered: "I was never a Party man, I never let myself be drawn into the Nazi Party. I even opposed the movement because I am against extremism and terror. But one day, Hitler came to our city, and a colleague of mine dragged me along to hear him speak. His speech was so convincing, so patriotic and so logical. Not only that, but his public speaking skills enchanted me, so much that I decided to register in his party. True, he's a demagogue, a showman and an extremist, but the Germans see him as a savior, because he set out to raise them from their despair and make them a great and proud nation. That is why all the downtrodden people, the ones without hope, joined his faction and why it grew so rapidly."

◆　◆　◆

For as long as *Volksdeutsche* were running my old business, it was still conceivable that I could keep my position. But then a new commissioner arrived, a German from Riga named Platzer, and my chances plummeted. In 1942 he decided to buy the business from the government. As soon as he did, he set out to get rid of me. He wanted nothing to do with the business's former owner, so he prepared a team to replace me. I saw and felt the ground sinking beneath my feet. I walked the streets worried and tearful.

One day, on leaving my yard, I encountered a woman acquaintance, a former neighbor, for whom I had always carried warm feelings. She used to torment me softly with her beauty and grace. She was a brunette with pale eyes and complexion and a pleasing figure.

Before the war, many men had pursued her. But she hadn't given herself to any of them. Among her admirers was a wealthy young man, the son of a dry goods wholesaler, who was crazy about her. Yet he was among the weakest of the candidates, being overweight and dull-witted and far from handsome. But then came the war. The girl's father became impoverished, and the wholesaler's son became a big shot. So he sent matchmakers and good friends to the girl's father. He pursued her relentlessly, offering wealth and protection, until finally the girl agreed to marry him. Everyone considered this a "pot of gold" match—that is, a marriage arranged for money.

But it didn't take long before the gold ran out. The wealthy wholesaler became a fat target for influential men chasing bribes, and it wasn't long before he fell into poverty. He was sent to a concentration camp as soon as he ran out of bribe money. The young wife was left alone, at the mercy of any thug who had influence with the Judenrat. Moishe Merin wanted her for a mistress, but nothing he could say or do was going to persuade her to submit to this. She loathed him and did not want to become one more concubine of the "king of the Jews." Besides which, she was almost certain he had arranged for her husband's deportation, simply to render her vulnerable to his advances.

When I saw her coming through the gate she stopped. Her eyes lit up and she extended her pale hand to me. It was a Sunday, and she invited me to go for a walk. So we went into the gardens behind the Ogrodek in Ostrogorka, which had been planted by Jews. The Judenrat had arranged for the poor Jews to be granted this plot of ground—it had belonged to Jews before the war—where they could plant vegetables for themselves. They had set to work, plowing and planting until the whole area sprouted. This, of course, was another German ruse to spark the people's hope that they would be allowed to survive. On Sundays Jews used to spend the whole day in this garden to breathe some fresh air.

We strolled there for a few hours. I had not known anything about how her husband had been deported, or about Merin's designs on her. She opened her heart to me, telling me how lonely she was and how isolated from those around her, how Merin's thugs were trying to force her into sin. When people started staring at us, she suggested we go to her home. I walked her there. She insisted I have supper with her, but since the night was almost on us, we had to hurry so that I would have time to reach home before curfew.

After this we began to meet often. She was very grateful for someone to talk to and with whom to enjoy herself. I visited her house, and sometimes she would visit mine.

Merin learned quickly that she and I had become friends and that we often met. Soon enough, one of Merin's business associates looked me up. He was a handsome young man with a high rank in the Judenrat. He was also the Don Juan of the "White House," as the Judenrat headquarters was called.

He began to question me about my relationship with this young woman. Then he asked if I would like to come with her to Merin's headquarters to join the "king of the Jews" and his henchmen for an evening of fun. It soon became obvious to me that he wanted me to persuade her to join this gang's orgies. He also made it clear that it would be dangerous, perhaps fatal, for her and her friends to reject Merin's generosity.

I replied that I did not own her or anyone else. She was not my wife, nor was she my lover; she was only a close friend who sought my friendship and company and to whom I gladly offered both. If she wanted to enjoy herself in other company, I had no objections, but I would not force anything on her, nor would I trick her into attending Merin's parties, because that was not my way.

While talking to my friend later, I mentioned to her that one of Moishe's men had approached me, and what he wanted. Later, other members of Merin's gang approached me to point out that I ought to be a little friendlier to Merin. It did not pay to be otherwise.

I told her that if she decided to meet with that crowd, she should not let me hold her back, because nothing tied us except friendship. My words upset her; she began crying and pounding her hands on the table.

"I don't want to! I won't! Even if I knew it meant dying of hunger. I detest that whole gang. And *you*"—she looked at me with so much tenderness—"if you're frightened of Moishe, I can release you from our friendship and we can stop seeing each other."

It was as if she was questioning my courage. I embraced her and said:

"Perhaps you misunderstand me. I'm not going to chase you away from me, because I know how important I am to you in these difficult, bitter times. I promise not to end our friendship even if I know that it will endanger my very existence. I only wanted you to know this is a dangerous game. Your husband has already become a victim, and your freedom is already in danger, and perhaps so is your life. If you decide you must bend to Moishe's demands, but I stand in your way, I'm willing to pull back and leave you free to deal with him in your own way. I'm willing to jeopardize my own freedom, but not yours."

Again she started to cry, and cuddled up to me, as if wanting to become one with me.

A few days later, when my friend was in my house, we were so busy talking that we forgot to look at the clock. Because of the curfew it was too late for me to walk her home, so we continued to sit there and talk. We had completely forgotten that one of my doors led directly into the living quarters of the Jewish police *kommandant*. There they probably heard the voice of my friend. Before long we heard a commotion in the next room, and among all the voices we recognized Moishe Merin's. He of course, had the right to break curfew, since it was his men who enforced it. I knew right away this was not a chance visit and that I would pay heavily for my carelessness.

28

I Get a Notice to Report to the Dulag

That visit quickly had repercussions. A few days later I received a notice from the *Arbeitseinsatz* to report immediately to the Dulag. My turn had come to be sent to a concentration camp. I knew this was Merin's revenge on my friend for having rejected him.

My first reaction was to not give myself up. I hid in the warehouse of the glass shop, to which I still had the keys. I slept there on a pile of straw. The Jewish militia looked all over for me, even in my friend's home. I let my relatives know I had received a notice to report and told them where I was hiding. I asked them to help me if they possibly could.

Two days later my uncle came to tell me that all his interventions had failed: I was to report immediately, otherwise my name would be passed to the Gestapo, who would search till they found me.

I felt caged, with no way out. And I understood something else: Having reported voluntarily I might be sent to a work camp, from which I might still be able to save myself. On the other hand, if I was captured by the Gestapo they would either shoot me on the spot or, the best case, send me to Auschwitz where my chances of survival were nil. So I decided to report to the Dulag.

On March 1, 1943, I reported to the Dulag at Skladowa 5, where I joined a mob of people waiting for their transport. The official registered me, and I was locked into the building. Below, on the street, in front of the assembly point, a large crowd had gathered—elders, women, and children, all trying to glimpse their relatives for what they knew was almost certainly the last time. I looked out, hoping perhaps to see some of my relatives. I was astonished when I suddenly spotted, in this huge crowd, my friend. She was pale and her eyes were full of tears. When she looked up and saw me, she took out a handkerchief and began to wave, throwing kisses my way. Though she was the cause of my being deported, I was not angry with her. Not at all. I merely pitied her, knowing that the noose around her neck was tightening. She would not be able to fight much longer, and would have to give in to the monsters who had encircled her. I knew that I was now a victim of this same "gang," but I had nothing with which to fight them, so there was no hope for me. It was time for me to come to terms with my destiny. Let the waves carry me where they would.

Two days later, the transport was assembled. We were lined up in a long corridor. Our names were called one by one until the necessary number for the transport was ready. With all the troubles, when we saw that our end was drawing near, that we were being transported to a place of no return, when everyone had to reply, "Here!" when their name was called, one of us in the crowd decided to joke and answered, *"Iber der hur"* (a pun on "here" and "whore"). Everyone started to laugh. The SS did not understand what the laughter was about. It puzzled them that in such bleak circumstances there should still be a desire to laugh.

29

We Arrive at the Slave Labor Camp

We were taken to Niedershlesien in locked freight cars. At the shtetl of Otmet we were placed in barracks. The following day we were let out in groups to work. Most of us were put to work paving a road from Berlin to Moscow. I was assigned to a group that was sent to a large shoe factory, where mainly women worked, the men having been sent to the front. We did not stay there long. Soon after, we were transported to a nearby shtetl, Gogolin, where we were regrouped and segregated. Many of us were sent to Ober-Lodzisk in Oberschlesien.

This was a forced labor camp for industrial construction. Here steel plants were being built. A number of German construction companies carried out their production here. The largest were "Borsick" and "National." Before dawn we were led out to work, after dark we were led back home, utterly exhausted. Our diet consisted of watery soup, 200 grams of bread, sometimes a bit of margarine, and sometimes a piece of horse sausage.

The work was back-breaking. We carried iron beams, blocks, boards, and sacks of cement. The worst task of all was climbing 60 meters into the air and hanging on somehow while fitting the beams—very dangerous work requiring training and experience that I did not have. The first time I made the climb, my head started to spin until I nearly fell. I clung to the beams so as not to fall, and it was a miracle I got down safely. Some of my friends could not manage this. They became dizzy and fell, and died on the spot. The second time I did not want to go up. I pleaded with the man in charge: "I can't go up—I get dizzy and can't do my job." He pounced on me like a tiger, and beat me so mercilessly that I had no choice but to go up a second time and sweat it out.

Sundays we did not work, but if trainloads of material arrived on that day we had to unload them. A block of us would be escorted out to unload wagons of coal, iron, or other building materials. Mainly, though, we rested on Sundays. We would gather, chat, remind ourselves of home, and reflect on our fate. Around this time I became acquainted with a French artist. If memory serves, his name was Mincov. He sketched a portrait of me with a piece of coal. Here I also met a Parisian doctor, Avraham Suchodolsky, with whom I became close friends. He worked in the camp as a doctor, so he often arranged rest days for me.

One day I got an abscess on my right foot, right on the sole, so that I couldn't walk. In the camp it was forbidden to be sick. There were no medicines, nor was any time permitted for healing. As soon as a worker was no longer able to work, there was no playing around—he was sent directly to the gas chambers. Dr. Suchodolsky cut out the abscess with an ordinary knife, drained the pus and healed my wound.

He was fed slightly better than the regular slave laborers. He sometimes got a roasted potato and a piece of meat or a piece of liver sausage. From this he always hid a portion for me. We lived like brothers. He told me about his student years in Paris, which I found fascinating. He revealed an entirely new world to me. He also told me about his fiancée, to whom he had been engaged only a short time. In turn, I told him about my life, episodes of my wild youth. We became very close.

Dr. Suchodolsky had an assistant, an older man in his fifties. His name was Hollander, and he was from Chrzanów. If I remember correctly, he was a diamond broker just before the war, in Belgium. He was a very fine Jew from a Hassidic family. Dr. Suchodolsky wanted to give me his position, but I refused because it would have meant that Hollander would have to do hard labor. When his assistant found out about this, he shook my hand in gratitude.

On a Sunday in the spring of 1943, on a bright, sunny day, I felt like dressing a little better than usual. At that time we all still had our belongings packed in suitcases. I took out a clean shirt, gray trousers, a jacket, and a red tie. While we were strolling in the yard, the camp supervisor came out, a nobody, a little guy, a cripple with red hair and a large nose. He brought a few soldiers along with him to gather thirty men to plough and plant the garden. He watched us work the whole time. I cannot say that I worked with much enthusiasm. It bothered me that this Sunday, our day of rest from hard labor, was being broken.

My pace did not please the supervisor, or perhaps he didn't like my elegant appearance, so he began picking on me, telling me I wasn't working hard enough. He began jabbing me with his fist, but he couldn't make me move faster. My jacket and red tie had got under his skin, so he was trying to humiliate me, calling me a mere slave who ought to look the part. He was making my life miserable. When I straightened up, he saw how short he was compared to me, and this made him even angrier.

At this point I asked him angrily: "What do you want from me? I'm working hard." I told myself I could take him in a fight, but I also knew I would be shot if I struck back. My words enraged him even more, and he shouted:"You dare get fresh? You're asking for trouble. I'll teach you how to work!" He tried to throttle me, but not being able to reach my throat, he grabbed my tie and tried to pull me down to his level. He actually tore my tie, but he couldn't pull me down. As punishment for this he ordered me to sweep the entire yard and half the street, with only a broom. Three soldiers watched me to make sure I carried out my punishment. I never wore my festive clothes again.

◆ ◆ ◆

The construction work became more unbearable by the day. Working on the same project were British and French prisoners of war, who received much better treatment than we Jews: better rations and warmer barracks. They also received food packages from the Red Cross. We, on the other hand, were treated like slaves, starved and beaten until our bones broke. The Germans regarded us as worms to be stepped on. One day—this was after April 19—we noticed to our surprise that the Germans were looking at us differently than before, with more respect. We couldn't understand why, because we were cut off from the world outside. When we looked out through the gates and saw people moving about freely, we envied them. How fortunate they were!

A few days later, at work, I encountered a Polish worker. He whispered in my ear: "Your brothers are fighting like lions in the Warsaw ghetto. They're making the Germans pay, I tell you!" That evening I gathered my friends and told them the news. That night we slept in peace, because Jewish honor had been saved.

We began to get used to life in slavery. On Sundays and in the evenings,

I would write poetry and write in my journal. Later on I was assigned to lighter work, constructing barracks outside the factory. On that detail it was possible to "organize" a few potatoes, a piece of bread, and a few cigarettes, which I would sell for a piece of bread or some soup. I thought to myself that perhaps I and my friends might survive the war, if things kept up like this. This regime wasn't too severe.

Then the situation grew worse again when one from our camp ran away. His wife appeared one day outside the barrier, signaled to him, and got him out. The authorities started to plague us, reducing our rations and holding us for hours at roll call. Security was strengthened. They started working us harder and punishing us for the slightest reason.

Summer came. For us it was as if we had chains around our arms and legs. Before dawn we were harried out to work; after dark we were returned to the camp, exhausted, with swollen feet and empty stomachs. It was hard to fall asleep on an empty stomach. When we closed our eyes, it was from fatigue.

We had no calendar, but we kept track of the date. In 1943, in the slave camp at Ober-Lodzisk, during lunch break, after a bit of watery soup, one of us announced, "Today is Shavuot." Each of us breathed a sigh as we reminded ourselves of past holidays, when our families were near and our homes were fragrant with baked goods and vegetables. All of us reflected quietly until we heard the harsh, croaking voice of the foreman: "*Auf!*" (Get up!). We rose from our memories and dragged ourselves bitterly and painfully back to work.

Around the time of Sukkot, the news reached us that the ghetto of Sosnowiec had been emptied and all its inhabitants, including Moishe Merin and his gang, had been liquidated. Many were glad that the liquidators themselves had been liquidated—that they, the "decorated" ones, had met the same end as the others. Still, it was painful, because it reminded us that the Nazis were determined to carry out Hitler's plan of liquidating every last Jew. We understood that our turn, too, would come. As soon as the Nazis had extracted every last ounce of blood for their war machine, they would liquidate us with the rest.

30

The Day Arrives

On a cold November morning after a heavy snowfall, after we were awakened, we felt a change occurring. We were not led out to work but instead were told to wait in the barracks. We felt that something terrible was about to happen, but none of us knew what. As dawn broke we were ordered to pack our belongings and gather outside. Immediately we saw a group of well-armed SS men and at their head their commander, Lindner.

We were lined up and roll was called. Then we were kept in line until the transport trucks arrived. We were packed into these and driven off. Soon enough we recognized the district—Chrzanów and Szczakova—and knew we were going to Auschwitz. A few hours later the trucks came to a gate, above which we read the sign *Arbeit Macht Frei* (Work Liberates), and we understood that our last day had come.

We were shoved into a large paddock area, where we were made to throw our belongings into a pile. We clung to one another like sheep before the slaughter. Around us we saw people with striped clothing. There were also a few civilians who spoke Yiddish, but it was a disgrace, this Yiddish they spoke. One did not hear Yiddish like this among the worst underworld characters.

"Hand over your money and gold," they told us, "because you're going to the ovens anyway." Soon after that the head *Kapo*, the notorious "Pinkus," delivered a speech to us, each word striking us like a hammer blow. Pinkus was a Polish Jew who had lived in France. When he spotted Dr. Suchodolsky beside me, he recognized him from the transfer camp for French Jews in Drancy, and greeted him with a *"Mi Sheberach."* He could not forget that my friend was a camp physician while he was merely a regular prisoner. So he scorned and insulted him, telling him that not only was he going up the chimney, but he was going to torture him slowly first. Dr. Suchodolsky clung to me as if to protect himself from the thrusts of Pinkus's torments. After a time, Pinkus found others to abuse. Meanwhile his "boys from the *Himmelkommando*" searched us roughly—our pockets, clothes, and shoes—and took away everything of value.

Our spirits broke, our limbs buckled. We were commanded to remove our *shmates* (tatters) because we were going to be "deloused." The air stank with quicklime and sulfur. We felt as if we were in hell. We were lined up in front of a barber, who with a dull razor shaved all the hair from our bodies. Then we were herded into a hall, where pipes sprayed us with cold water. From there we were chased out into the snow and told to run. To the accompaniment of curses and blows, we were chased four hundred meters into another hall, where each of us was thrown a bundle of clothes. These were the garments of those who had just been gassed. Each of us got whatever it happened to be. A tall one got short pants and an undersized top, a short one got long pants and an oversized top. When we looked at one another, we had to laugh.

Only the healthy ones survived that day—the ones with the strength to be so angry that they didn't feel the cold. The weak, the old, and the children had already been led off. On arrival we had been lined up five across and inspected by Dr. Mengele and his staff. He kept only those with some strength left to work. The weak ones were eliminated—sent straight to the gas chambers. Mengele decided their fate with a flick of his finger. His smile was thin. From his eyes there sprang a terrifying cold fire. When my turn with him came, standing to my right was a boy of seventeen named Urbach, from Jaworzno, and to my left the Belgian Jew Hollander, who was at least fifty. These two were immediately removed from the line and sent directly to the *Himmelkommando*.

Those of us who were left after all this were led off to have numbers tattooed on our arms. Then we were assigned to blocks at Birkenau, a quarantine camp. I was placed in Block 8, on a top bunk with five other men. The block had the appearance of a horse stable. There were three-level bunks on two sides and in the middle a stove of sorts to heat the barrack. Around the stove the *Stubenälteste* (house elder) ran back and forth. He and his helpers made sure the "animals are properly settled in their stalls."

Those who did not please him or who complained about their crowded bunks, he pulled down and placed on a long bench. There he beat and kicked them to death. Later his victims were tossed out of the barracks like old rags. In the morning a cart collected all the dead and took them to be incinerated.

31

The First Day in Hell

I lay on the bunk as if dead and violated. I felt downtrodden physically and mentally and had one wish: to die! To die as quickly as possible so that my suffering would end because my life no longer had any worth. I could not fall asleep. I had lived through too much that day, and the terrible scenes I had witnessed kept running through my mind.

As I passed under the camp gate and read its sign—*Arbeit Macht Frei*—I knew I was entering the lion's mouth. I saw the electrified barbed wire fences. I saw the watchtowers every ten meters, heavily guarded by SS bandits, who kept their fingers ready on their machine gun triggers. I saw guards with attack dogs on chains. I understood immediately that it was impossible to leave this place alive. What hurt even more was to encounter the Jewish "helpers," who were there as slaves just as we were, but who had come here before us and had offered their services to the Nazi murderers, and helped them torture and humiliate their own brothers and sisters. They themselves had become beasts and let their most base instincts rule them.

I could not forget the crooked, ugly face of Pinkus, the elder of "Zonder Block," who led the gang that received and sorted out the new arrivals. To this task only brutes were assigned, men without feelings. Pinkus (if I am not mistaken, his last name was Chmelnitsky) was the most notorious of all the block elders. He had come to the camp with a French transport and was a true sadist who enjoyed brutalizing his victims and drawing their blood. From suffering under him, we all learned how hopeless our situation was— that sooner or later everyone would be gassed and cremated, that there was no way out.

The Nazis permitted the heartless ones, the ones without scruples, to help torture and liquidate their own brothers. These beasts knew that they themselves were destined to die, and took out their despair and bitterness on the weak and powerless.

The men of Zonder Block were treated better than the rest of us. For now they were left alone. They were fed better, and were permitted to dress elegantly, in the best clothing, which of course originally belonged to the wealthy Jews who had been gassed on arrival. The more brutally they treated the new arrivals, the better the SS treated them.

Pinkus, a short, fat man, dressed like a count in an ironed shirt, spit-polished shoes, and a striped suit that exaggerated his crippled body. His eyes were bloodshot, his voice harsh. He must have come from the underworld because his vocabulary was vulgar enough to make a Cossack blush. His helper, a certain Ziduna, a Jew from Lodz, also excelled in cruelty.

The transports were sorted on arrival. Those who were selected to work in the camp became the responsibility of these Jewish murderers. The others were gassed immediately. They stole everything from the people, carried out the "sanitary" operations such as showering and delousing, and assigned the people to blocks.

The camp commander, an SS storm trooper named Schilinger, stood and watched how hard his Jewish servants were working. Pinkus strutted through the crowds of new arrivals, always looking for another victim to beat with his truncheon, all the while looking up at his patron to see if he was pleased.

"All line up!" Pinkus shouted, making sure Schilinger heard him. "Four in a row! You bags of shit! Faster, faster, you dogs! You were never soldiers . . . Here you'll learn discipline. Soon I'll show you discipline." And passing through the rows of new arrivals, he would kick anyone who wasn't standing straight. He aimed at the belly or below it so that his targets would fall down.

"Stand up, you bag of shit!" he would yell, and if the fallen one didn't rise instantly, his helper dragged him away, never to be seen again.

"Mützen ab!" he now commanded. *"Mützen auf!"* (Down! Up!)

Those who couldn't move quickly enough for him were weeded out right then. When he grew tired of this drill, he started insulting us, and be-littling us, in language so foul that all decent men lowered their eyes. His words hurt even more than his blows because they degraded and humiliated the people and thus broke their spirit. Throughout his display, the SS guards rolled with laughter.

Many of the slaves clenched their fists as if to strike him. When he or his helpers noticed this, they immediately pulled that person out and finished him off. He continued this spectacle with *"Mützen ab! . . . Mützen auf!"* until the Nazis tired of it. Then he commanded:

"Stillstand! Zälen!" (Stand still! Count!). And he made a report to the camp commander, Schilinger. Then he turned to his victims again: *"Der ganze Mist—Um!—Marschieren!"* (You garbage—turn around and march!).

I could not forget the coldly cynical eyes of Mengele, who with a flick of a finger decided people's fates. Actually, he only delayed them, because those he allowed to live were going to die later anyway, after he was finished experimenting with them. Here again, the Nazis were manipulating us, creating the illusion that some would be able to save themselves if they worked hard enough. Absolute despair can generate rebellion; even the slightest hope can quell a revolt.

At most, 20 percent of Jews survived their first day at Auschwitz. After that, people broke down from hard work, hunger, and beatings. Selections were always taking place. People were chased out of their barracks, and stripped and examined to see if they were still fit for work. Those who had boils, scabies, or other obvious conditions were escorted instantly to Block 7 or the gas chambers. Most got sick from pneumonia, diarrhea, and other diseases of malnutrition. Many collapsed on the spot and were tossed into piles for the *Leibenkommando* to cart away later. Many of the people were also used for medical experiments. Doctors visited the camp from all over Germany to use people as guinea pigs for their experiments, to discover ways to heal them or poison them.

32

Block Number 7

Block 7, the most terrifying place in the camp, was right next to our block. It was hell itself, and scarcely anyone who entered it came out alive. Officially it was called the *Lazarett* (military hospital), but actually it was the death block. The people inside it already belonged to the *Himmelkommando*.

Here were those who were waiting for death to come. Some struggled against it, some not. Sores covered their bodies, and high fevers burned in them. Every breath one heard sounded like someone's last. On all sides one heard groaning and pleas for water. The house aides, heartless brutes, tore the shoes off the sick, shouting at them in German, "You son of a bitch, what do you need shoes for? You're going to the *Himmelkommando* anyhow." Even their last pieces of bread were stolen from them.

All of this was told to me by someone who had been saved from Block 7 by a miracle. While he was in Block 7, a friend of his from Paris noticed him, a young man whom Mengele had castrated after conducting experiments on him. In Paris he had been a butcher. He was young and handsome. His task was to bring the sick and the dead to the crematoria, from Block 7 and other blocks.

He recognized my friend and started to cry bitter tears. He told him what Mengele had done to him and how this had destroyed all feelings in him. He showed my friend his strong hands and said: "If I could choke someone with these hands, ignite the whole world, I would gladly do so."

Yet he promised to save his friend. During the next selection, almost all of Block 7 was consigned to the gas chambers. He then threw his friend on top of a pile of corpses and near corpses, and covered him with still more of them. The sick tried to save themselves, but none had the strength to rise, so they lay there while other corpses were piled on top of them. When the freight trains were full for their journey to the crematorium, he returned and pulled his friend out from the pile of dead, thus saving him.

This same man also told me how the sick were taken to the gas chambers. He watched the horrible scene from a hiding place. The trains arrived, with an SS officer at the head, elegantly clad, with white gloves. The block elder and his aides stood and waited for orders. The German asked cynically: "Have the sick received their rations of bread and sausage for the trip? You're being taken to a sanatorium for the sick." Some of the sick wailed: "No, I didn't get . . . I didn't get . . ."

At this the Nazi reprimanded the block elder and his aides: "You bastards, how dare you withhold their bread and sausage? Give it to them right away!"

A hustle erupted in the block, and food was distributed to the sick. The SS officer looked at the victims and said, "Distribute everything, you swine! I'll get even with you later!"

And to the sick, he said: "Now you are satisfied?"

"Yes, yes," everyone answered happily.

And to the block elder and his aides, he ordered: "Place the sick slowly and carefully on the train. No shoving."

This is how the victims were loaded onto the trains. The SS officer then commanded: "Start out, but slowly."

In a few hours the rags of the gassed ones were brought back to be washed in readiness for new victims.

It was rare for anyone to come out alive from Block 7. People were not there to heal but to die painfully. The lice ate them alive. Around the lights one could see them swarming, sucking out the last bit of their victims' blood. The block was always overcrowded. There was nowhere to lie down. On one bunk lay five or six sick people, who became even sicker from each other's diseases. Those suffering from typhus were placed shoulder to shoulder with those suffering from diarrhea and diphtheria. There were no doctors, or if there were, they were not used. Nor were there were any medications, so the sick were abandoned, enduring terrible suffering, until death came to take them.

Often the dead lay for two days on their bunks before being removed, because the block elders wanted to steal their bread and sausage rations. When there was no more room in the block, the sick were dumped in its yard, in the cold, under the sky, hundreds of them, in pain and burning with fever. They begged for a little water to ease their burning lips. Their gazes were heartrending. Many of them began convulsing, others simply lay motionless like the living dead. They did not have the strength to kill themselves by dragging themselves to the electric fence, but they prayed to die. One man tried with gnarled hands to choke himself with a stone, but he had no strength and the stone kept falling out of his trembling hands. Diarrhea poured from many of them, making a foul stench.

There was no water for washing, nor clean clothes or bedding, so the lice, fleas, and bedbugs multiplied till they could be brushed off by the handful. Because the meager diet lacked fats and vitamins, around 80 percent of the camp inmates came down with dysentery. Yet people avoided going to a doctor because it was equivalent to a death sentence. People tried to help themselves by whatever means they could, but every few days there were selections. As soon as a doctor noticed anyone's clothes stained with excrement, he understood that that person had diarrhea and sent him immediately to Block 7 to await the crematorium.

Others had typhus, malaria, swollen bellies. They also suffered acutely from scabies as a result of the filth, crowding, and dreadful sanitary conditions. Jaundice and skin diseases were rife. The sick were robbed of their meager rations of food by the block aides. Since they were destined for death, why waste food on them? Their rations were bartered for cigarettes and whisky. And so it was that the *Kapos* and block elders and their aides were dressed well, with pinstripe suits and shiny boots, while the masses, the captured ones, fell from hunger.

Every person was allowed 350 grams of bread per day. The bread in the camp was awful, a mixture of flour and sawdust, yet on this one was supposed to live for a whole day. The block elders and the *Kapos* divided up the 1,400 grams of bread into six to eight portions instead of four, so each person got roughly 200 grams per day.

Everyone was supposed to get up to a liter of soup per day as well. It was supposed to be potato soup with a meat broth, but the influential ones took the potatoes and the bones for themselves, leaving only the liquid, containing weeds and grasses, for the others. So each day there were more and more sick and starving people.

Not only was there nothing with which to wash, nor water to drink, but there were also no eating tools—no bowls or spoons—so everyone had to share bowls and drink from them directly. As a result, mouth abcesses became endemic. Yet people waited impatiently for a bit of soup to warm their bellies.

Quite often when a house aide was bringing the pot of soup to the blocks, he would be attacked by *Muselmänner* (skin-and-bone people) who had been intoxicated by the smell of the soup. They could not control themselves; they ran to the pots and with their caps helped themselves to some soup in order to silence for a moment their terrible hunger. Often these "soup grabbers" were punished—locked in a barrack and deprived of food and drink. A few days later they would be led to the gas chambers.

As a result of poor nourishment and too few vitamins, many people's bellies swelled, and then so did their arms and legs. Finally they went mad and began racing about wildly until they were caught, bound, and led away to the gas chambers. After they were removed from the gas chambers, they were placed in a lumber warehouse until it was their turn for the crematorium.

The infirmary workers did nothing to help the sick; on the contrary, they helped spread diseases and increase the fatality rate. This was truly a liquidation camp; everything possible was done to liquidate Jews. There were plenty of doctors in the blocks, but there was no interest in using them to heal the sick. Instead people were left to endure terrible suffering till they died. In Block 7 there were usually around 800 sick people, around 150 of which died each day.

The sick did everything they could to avoid entering Block 7, because almost no one left it alive. They continued working in the mud and the dirt as long as they could, however sick with fever they were, because if they reported sick they would instantly be sentenced to die.

33

Life in the Block at Birkenau

The block elder was the absolute ruler of eight hundred to a thousand slaves. He could do with them whatever he wished. Most of the block elders were Germans or Poles who had been imprisoned in the concentration camps for major crimes. They wore green triangles signifying they were murderers or robbers.

Each block elder had at his disposal one or two young thugs, called *pipl*. They were the elder's sex slaves and lived with him in his "boudoir" at the entrance to the block. He fed, clothed, and protected them, just as a lover would. It was too bad for anyone who dared say a bad word to a *pipl*. He was right next to the "king." He only needed to point out someone who had insulted him and that person was immediately removed from his bunk. He would be stretched out on the fireplace, and a rod would be placed on his neck. Then aides would step on each side of the rod until he choked to death.

The *pipl* were sadists and were always seeking victims to torture for their amusement. Every night the block elder would inspect the block with his *pipl* and the house aides, hunting for victims. If someone caught their eye, if they didn't like someone's face, it was enough: that person would be taken from his bunk and tortured to death. In particular, they looked for handsome, healthy boys; anyone who was stronger and more handsome than they was a special target.

Our very first night in our block, the block elder decided on a whim to put on a show. He gathered a few professional actors, singers, and musicians and commanded them to perform for him. There were a few actors among us from Berlin, and a few violinists and singers. The actors mounted a scene from the *Crimilonka,* a popular show in Berlin. It was a farce, and they made

94

the block elder, his *pipl,* and the house aides laugh till they held their sides. There was also a German-Jewish fiddler, a virtuoso. If I am not mistaken, his name was Schpitz. He played with sweetness and great feeling. It is impossible to describe the impression this made on all of us who were lying there in pain, despised and ridiculed, crowded like herring. It was a surreal joke on us. One of us fell asleep and started to snore. He was pulled from his bunk and dragged into a corner and made silent for all eternity. He had insulted "art." The artist had not yet been born who could paint such a picture: a few hundred slaves with shaved heads, broken bodies, aching stomachs, terrified eyes, feverish faces, looking out from three levels of bunks at a music hall farce.

The following morning before dawn, immediately on being awakened, we were herded out of the block. Anyone who was too slow was beaten with truncheons. Some of us were knocked to the ground in the rush to escape the beatings. Many of the fallen, those who couldn't rise quickly enough, were trampled to death. In a corner of the barrack were stacked the corpses of those who had died in the night. Now those who had just been trampled to death were added to it. Soon there was a shout.

"*Appell! Appell! Los, los antreten!*" (Roll call! Roll call! Line up!). We lined up in long rows and waited to be counted. Sometimes we had to wait for hours until the senior officer came and took the report. In the meantime, the block elder strutted around with *Kapos* and the block aides, all of them looking pleased with themselves as they guarded us. Anyone who was not standing straight in the row, who had slouched or was standing crooked, was pulled from the line and never seen again.

When the senior officer arrived , the block elder thundered "*Achtung, mützen ab!*" (Attention! Caps off!), and gave his report, which consisted of the number of inmates alive, the number who were dead, and the number of sick who awaited transport. If one of us was missing, we all had to remain standing until he was found, whether alive or dead. If he was still alive, he was soon dead anyhow.

34

The Work in Birkenau Camp

The Birkenau camp was supposedly a transfer camp, a sort of quarantine camp. Actually it was an extermination camp. Rarely did anyone come out of that hell alive.

Each day new transports arrived, often from Western Europe, full of finely dressed men, women, and children, all of the adults carrying suitcases as if they were tourists. They were greeted with stick beatings and humiliations. The *Sonderkommando* received them and escorted them to the selection. At each selection a few of young, healthy men and women were pulled from the crowd for work detail. The rest—the older men, the young, the mothers and their children—were taken immediately to the gas chambers. Between 60 and 90 percent of the arrivals were herded straight to their deaths. The rest were handed over to the *Kanada Kommando,* which was led by the notorious Pinkus.

All suitcases and clothing were taken from the new arrivals. These items were taken to special rooms for sorting. Those who were going straight to the gas chambers were placed in the charge of a Jewish workforce called the *Sonderkommando.* Those who had been assigned to work brigades generally did not live longer than three months. After that time they were liquidated and replaced.

The members of the *Sonderkommando* were kept isolated from the rest, in separate barracks surrounded by barbed wire. They were better fed, and their clothes were also better. They were not allowed to speak to anyone. They were directly under the political division.

There were eight hundred to one thousand people in the *Sonderkommando.* As soon as they knew too much and got a little wiser, they were rounded up and killed. If they wavered or refused to do the work assigned to them, they were led straight to the gas chambers. That is how one hundred Jews from Corse and one hundred from Greece were annihilated the very same day.

One day a rebellion broke out in the *Sonderkommando*. Its members tried to destroy the gas chambers and crematoria with explosives. Nearly all of them lost their lives in the attempt, but before they were defeated, they succeeded in killing and burning a number of SS troops.

In some *Kommandos* the Jews did skilled work—carpentry, bricklaying, farming, and so on—but most were occupied with nonproductive work, such as carrying sand and stones from one place to another. While doing so, they were beaten and whipped. They wore wooden clogs, which fit so badly that they developed blisters and their feet swelled up in the cold. Suddenly a gang of SS would arrive with truncheons, accompanied by attack dogs, and they would hurl themselves at the hungry and naked slaves. Some Jews were torn apart by the dogs; others were shot for sport.

One day a transport arrived with Jews from Italy. They entered the camp singing. Each one of them was tall and straight, handsome as a film actor. They stopped singing as soon as they came through the gate. In no time at all they fell like flies. Eventually only one Italian Jew remained in the camp: the son of the Fiume rebbe who came originally from Eastern Europe. The Eastern European Jews were used to hard times, so they were tougher. The Western European ones—those from Italy and Holland and so on, who were used to a more cultured and civilized life—broke down right away from the beatings and tortures, both physical and moral.

At Birkenau, the Germans applied all means available to put the people to death. After being in the camp a few weeks without food or sanitation, after suffering inhuman working conditions, after being tortured physically and mentally, of course they fell apart. Then every few days new selections would be made, and the weakest would be carted off to the gas chambers. Birkenau was not a labor camp. It was an extermination camp.

35

A Strange Meeting in Hell

People would by chance meet friends or acquaintances whom they could barely recognize. At Birkenau I met someone I knew very well from the shtetl of Opatow, near Ostrowiec. His name was Mordchelle Bernstein. Through his efforts, American Jews sometimes sent money and supplies to their relatives in the shtetls. Some of my own relatives had benefited from his work.

One day I entered the latrine and rejoiced greatly to see him. He gave me the tragic news about my mother. They had been deported together to the shtetl Tzoizmir (Sandomierz) when Ostrowiec and Opatow were liquidated. My mother was sent from there with a transport to Treblinka, where she surely perished after much suffering. He was sent, with a different transport, to Auschwitz.

Once, when the SS murderers came with their dogs and we scattered in confusion, I bumped into a man I knew very well—a neighbor of mine from Sosnowiec, Zendl by name, the owner of a large house and an extensive grocery business on Dekerta Street 2. He was very wealthy but a great miser. It was impossible to ever extract money from him for a worthy charity. He was always busy, never had time to talk to anyone. Before dawn, when we went to work, Zendl would already be busy in his warehouse. Late at night, when people returned home, we could still see him working in his store. Whenever someone came to ask for a donation, he chased them away: "Get away, you idle ones! Don't you see that I have no time?"

Later I learned that he had sewn into his clothes and comforters large sums in cash and gold, dollars, and jewelry. All this was later thrown onto the piles in the "sorting rooms." When I spotted this Zendl, running like a frightened deer, I became consumed with anger and burst out in a voice that seemed not to be my own: "So, Zendl, now you have time!" I immediately regretted my words, yet at the time I could not help myself. He heard me, and looked shattered. I never saw him again after that.

The "slaughterhouses"—the gas chambers and crematoria—were always near, but we were never allowed to approach them. That zone one entered only if one was never returning. All we saw was the smoke from the chimneys, which stank of Zyklon gas and cremated flesh. A friend of mine, Simon Foigelgaren, who was called "Max" in the camp, had come in 1942 with the French transports. He told me about something he had witnessed, a story I will never forget. I will try to tell it here as he told it to me:

"Coming out of Block 7, from which a friend of mine rescued me, I was assigned to Block 9. The block elder was Ludwig, and the house aide was Mietek Greenbaum. I was assigned to the planning *Kommando*. The *Kapo* was a Pole from Galicia whose name escapes me. There were more than two hundred of us in the *Kommando*. The foreman was a Jewish boy with only one hand. How they allowed him into the camp with only one hand is still a mystery.

"The *Kapo*, as I later learned, was—or at least believed himself to be— an honest murderer. His 'foreman' was this boy with one hand, who did everything the *Kapo* requested. Apparently they were both from the same town, somewhere near Krakow. The slaves of the *Kommando* were divided up for the various work: leveling land, filling up holes, leveling hilly ground, and so on. I ended up in the main division of the *Kommando*, where the *Kapo* could always be seen together with his Jewish foreman. The work divisions worked quite near one another, so when it was time to return to camp, everyone quickly gathered together. The *Kapo* always controlled the work itself; later, back at the barrack, his "lover" took over for him.

"This boy—I call him that because he was still quite young—had intended to become a yeshiva student. He always had a little siddur [prayer book] with him and a book of Psalms, which he was constantly studying. But he never neglected to supervise the slaves. If he saw someone stop working for a moment, he immediately called him over. In this way he collected ten to fifteen victims each morning. The victims were made to stand in one place until noon, when the *Kapo* arrived, and with him the cauldron of watery soup.

"I can never forget the scene: the pot in the middle, with the steam rising from it, and all the slave laborers staring at it as if it was the Messiah. The *Kapo* and his 'second to the king' stood near the pot, and around them all those who were lucky enough to be getting a bit of soup that day. In Polish and broken Yiddish, the *Kapo* pointed to the 'criminals' who were being sent to their death for not working quickly enough. That was why they had to be eliminated; why they were about to be choked to death with sticks pressed to their throats.

"The *Kapo* encouraged the *Kommando,* saying that today everyone would receive an extra portion—the portions withheld from those who were about to die. He also offered two liters of soup to any who would volunteer to help liquidate the condemned ones. The victims were standing in a state of shock, awaiting their execution. All the while the boy kept studying his sacred texts as if nothing was happening.

"What was in the hearts of the 'witnesses' I can hardly imagine. They felt sorry for the doomed ones, yet they certainly wanted the extra soup. Who can say which feeling was strongest? The Nazis had turned us into beasts without any human feelings.

"While all of us were thus standing, the camp elder suddenly walked by. He was a German, a political prisoner. He was also known as a heartless killer without redeeming qualities. He saw the *Kommando* standing in suspense and demanded that the *Kapo* explain what was going on. The *Kapo* replied that some of us had sabotaged the work and had to be liquidated. The elder suddenly shouted: *'Quatsch! Du Dreck! Sofort das essen austeilen'* (Shut up, you piece of shit! Start feeding them immediately). Then he added, 'You give me your word that nothing will happen to the *Häftling* (camp prisoners). If anything happens to them you go to the punishment block!'

"Dumbstruck, the *Kapo* and his boy started to dish out the soup. Maybe some of us regretted not getting the extra ration, but most of us were pleased with the outcome. A spark of hope had been lit in everyone's heart, that perhaps all was not lost. That time I ate the dirty soup with such an appetite, as if I had won my freedom."

My friend continued: "The following day I wanted to get into a different *Kommando,* but it was so destined that I was assigned to the same labor unit as before. The religious boy kept a particular eye on me. He watched me very carefully to make sure I was in the head *Kommando,* close to the

Kapo and him, so that he could observe whether I was working quickly enough.

"Nearly every day slaves in our *Kommando* perished. Our fate depended on the mood of the *Kapo* and the boy with the sacred texts. Many of us tried to save ourselves by getting into other *Kommandos*. If his labor units were short, the *Kapo* grabbed new victims right after roll call, straight from the most recent transports.

"Among the new arrivals were two men—a father and a son, I later learned. Everyone was curious about the treatment they got from the *Kapo* and his boy. They were constantly whispering to each other and pointing to these two with great respect. They were given light work assignments and extra-large places for sleeping, and were generally treated with respect.

"The *Kapo* ran off with a *Häftling* and ran back with a chapter of the Book of Exodus from the Hebrew Bible, which they had found near the latrine, where there were piles of Torah scrolls, Gemaras, phylacteries, holiday prayer books, and so on. The father and son stuck these pieces together, wiped off the dirt, and wrapped it up the way one wraps a newborn child.

"A profound change had come over the *Kapo*. He ran into the kitchen and brought back special food for the father and son: an onion, a carrot, a few potatoes, some boiled water—all of these things rarities in the camp. The father and son did not eat the camp soup, nor did they work. Instead they devoted their days to prayer. No one could approach them. The *Kapo* even mounted a special guard to ensure that no one could grab them and punish them.

"Furthermore, the *Kapo* and his boy were no longer selecting any of us for death. One day passed, and then another, and none of us died.

"I tried to get closer to the father and his son because this intrigued me, but the boy chased me away and began keeping a close watch on me. Days passed this way. In the camp the rumor circulated that our *Kommando* was the best in the camp. Suddenly everyone wanted to get into it. All of us were mystified. What had happened? What influence did the father and son have on these notorious ones? What sort of power did they have, that could cause these two to change so much for the better and conduct themselves so humanely?

"As it turned out, the father had been the rebbe in the Galician shtetl where the *Kapo* had lived. He had been greatly respected by the entire population, even by the Christians. He had been called 'the Holy Father,' and many Poles had gone to him when they needed advice. The *Kapo* had recognized him and his son in Block 16, the death block for children and Dutch Jews, and had brought them directly over to his *Kommando.*

"On their arrival, the *Kapo* had changed completely. He had become more humane and understanding and no longer drove his slaves so hard at work. Things lasted this way for some time. The *Kapo* supplied the rebbe and his son with food so that they would not have to eat the blood sausage and the nonkosher soup from the pot. No more people were killed in the *Kommando,* and no more people were consigned to death. To us, it was like the return of the Messiah.

"Then one day the *Kapo* received an order from the *Schreibstube* (office barrack) that he should prepare a section of a field near Tower 18, not far from the crematorium. The *Kapo* told us that anything we might see or hear from the crematorium we should keep to ourselves. We must not comment or tell anyone.

"Between Tower 18 and the gas chambers, before the crematoria were built, there had been large pits. Many people were shot beside these and thrown in, together with some who were still alive. These pits were later covered with quicklime. In places the hair of the buried ones could be seen sticking out of the ground. From time to time the earth would heave as if in an earthquake, from the gases escaping from the corpses. Later the dead would be exhumed and burnt in the crematoria. It was these holes that had to be filled and the ground leveled.

"Everyone in our *Kommando* watched and listened to learn what precisely was happening at the gas chambers and crematoria. It was not long before we had a chance to see things that even now shatter my nerves and make my blood rush to my head. Any of us who saw these scenes had his faith in humanity shattered beyond redemption.

"The *Kapo* suddenly vanished, leaving behind his boy, the religious boy with his sacred texts. But he soon returned and called the boy over. They whispered to each other and then ordered us to move back a distance, toward the guard tower. But from there we could still see the crematorium. Suddenly we heard the Nazi murderers approaching at a run, along with their Ukrainian, *Volksdeutsche,* and Gestapo helpers. They cordoned off the area. Soon after that, transport wagons began arriving filled with young children, whose cries immediately blended with the shouts of their murderers. A command was heard, and the Nazi murderers began heaving the children out of the first of the wagons as if they were bags of coal or sacks of garbage. The children—they were all between five and seven years old—were crying out for their mothers in Polish, French, and German. Their cries reached to heaven.

"We saw the Nazis and their helpers throwing the children into the furnaces, saw how their victims were silenced with blows from rifle butts. *'Schnell!'* the SS shouted, *'Schneller mit dem Mist! Schmeist rein den Dreck!!!'* (Quickly, faster with the garbage! Pack the filth in!!!). The ground actually shook from the screams of the children. The *Kapo* stretched out on the ground and told us to do the same, but still we could see and hear what was happening at the crematoria, and it froze our blood. Two more transport wagons arrived full of children, and the same happened to them. Their terrified screams will never be forgotten by all those who witnessed this. We also heard the beastly laughter of the tower guards, who watched calmly as this spectacle took place.

"Suddenly I heard a choked, mournful outcry from the *Kommando.* I looked around and saw that the rebbe and his son had risen to their feet. Now they stretched their arms toward heaven, and the rebbe called out with all his strength: *'Reboinoi shel olom, vo bistu? Vi kanstu tzukuken un shveigen?! Nein, nein, Yidn, es iz nishto kein Got!'* (Lord of the Universe, where are you? How can you witness this and remain silent? No, no, fellow Jews—there is no God!).

"His voice cracked with tears. The *Kapo* ran over quickly, trying to calm him and his son. Their words had shaken all of us, and none of us will ever forget them. The screams and wails we heard that day are burned into our hearts forever.

"Soon after, our world fell silent again, as if after a storm or an earthquake. The murderers went away, and the transport wagons left. A few members of the *Sonderkommando* could be seen sweeping up the children's shoes and clothing that had been cast aside.

" *'Aufstehen!'* (Get up!) called our *Kapo.*

"Even he was devastated by what we had just seen and by the rebbe's words. The rebbe and his son had fainted. With all his strength he tried to lift them, but suddenly the watchtower guard called down: *'Kapo, komm mal her! Was hat da passiert?'* (Kapo, come here! What just happened?).

"The *Kapo*, with his broken German, tried to calm the guard, but without success. He had to drag the two bodies to the tower and then step aside while a volley of bullets made an end to the rebbe and his son. The volley's echoes pierced everyone's heart. The *Kapo*, in a whisper, as if talking to himself, said: *'Boze, boze moj'* (God, my God). Then he broke down. The boy muttered some prayers and continued studying his sacred texts.

"The *Kapo*, in a broken voice, shouted, *'Weiter machen!'* (Keep working). To him it was nothing new to see someone murdered or a human life snuffed out, but he broke down this time. His humanity had been stirred awake. He handed over charge of the *Kommando* to his representative, the religious boy, and helped carry away the bodies of father and son. At the tower he announced, in a broken voice, 'Planning *Kommando*, two dead.'

"The watchmen at the gate cast a mocking glance at the two corpses. Then they laughed, and turned away, shouting: *'Weiter marschieren'* (Keep marching)."

36

I Break Down

Birkenau had a catastrophic effect on me. I was broken morally more than physically. I felt as if I had been turned into worthless garbage, to be walked over and crushed like a worm, and it shattered my psyche. As soon as we were awakened in the morning, it was hell on earth, with beatings and houndings.

I saw and felt that our work was not at all necessary, that they simply wanted to torture us until they liquidated us. The only purpose of our tasks was to hound us until we died. I was certain that none of us would survive this hell. Some sooner, some later, but the same death awaited us all.

The sanitary conditions were horrible. The lice multiplied and sucked our blood. We were never able to wash. It was rare that we were able to get even a handful of water. A lucky one who did get a handful could merely smear his face to freshen up a bit.

The food was miserable: just a bit of watery soup without fat or meat, which never filled our stomachs. There were never enough bowls for the soup. Spoons were not necessary, as there was no body to the soup, so each of us would wait to borrow a dirty bowl, into which the block elder or his henchmen threw a bit of soup. If someone did not have a bowl ready on time, he used his cap or got no soup at all.

Each day we got approximately two hundred grams of bread, which was mixed with sawdust. At first I told myself I would nibble this ration from time to time, to keep my hunger at bay, but the struggle within me—should I eat the rest of the bread or not?—was so powerful that it wore me out. I decided I would no longer hoard the bread for later, but eat it as soon as I got it. Besides, someone might steal the piece from my pocket. There were plenty of hungry people who could smell who had a piece of bread in their pocket and who would not hesitate to swipe it. So I decided to hide it in my stomach.

Once, going about deep in thought, considering how to end this horrible life, I heard someone call my name. When I turned around, I saw a good friend of mine from Sosnowiec, a man named Scharf, who had owned a cardboard factory. I had met him often in Sosnowiec, for we had traveled in the same circles. We rejoiced greatly. He told me he had been there quite a long time and had gotten somewhat accustomed to this life. He had been able to get into a good *Kommando*—the latrine brigade. There he got enough food to at least still his hunger. I confided in him that I was dying of hunger and that my pain had become unendurable. I was falling apart and wanted my life to end, the sooner the better.

Pitying me, he took me into his block, opened a straw bag, and took out a bowl of food, which was covered with dust and completely stale. When I saw this bowl of food, my eyes lit up like lanterns. He said to me, "Here's a spoon. Eat it quickly before someone comes." I started to eat like a wild man, tearing pieces from the stale mass and packing them into my empty stomach. The food was cold, tasteless, and half-spoiled, but who cared about such trivialities? I emptied the bowl in ten minutes. Then I left him, wishing him eternal life, and returned to my block contented and satisfied. I felt overstuffed and had difficulty breathing, but for the first time in months I was not hungry.

Night descended quickly. I could hardly wait for us to be allowed to lie down on our thin straw mattresses. My stomach began to churn, and I ran quickly to the latrine. I had just reached it when diarrhea started to pour from me. I also felt feverish. I looked for my friend Dr. Suchodolsky, but I could not find him.

Before I could get back to the block I had to run for the latrine again. As it turned out, I had to run all night. I could no longer hold back my excrement, which streamed from me continuously and stank terribly. I did not sleep that night. By around two in the morning, I could not stand the stench anymore and my neighbors were protesting loudly. Besides, everything was sticking to me. I went to the latrine to rinse my underpants so that I would not stink so much.

Outside it was snowing and freezing cold. In the laundry room were a few people who had come during the night when it was least crowded to wash up a bit.

I removed my pants and underpants and with my bare hands started to wash them and rinse the smelly filth from them. I was repulsed by it all. Having no other clothes to wear, I got dressed in the wet garments. When I went out it must have been four in the morning. Since I had a high fever, the frost overtook me. I started to shake violently. I had not yet reached my berth when the house aide began awakening everyone.

I heard blows and whippings as people started to run, tripping over one another. I couldn't move quickly enough, with my arms and legs as heavy as lead, so I was knocked over. The house aide ordered me to be thrown onto the pile of corpses that had been collected during the night. I was lying among the dead, waiting to be taken to the crematorium.

Suddenly, an acquaintance from Sosnowiec walked by, a horse dealer named Feitl Lenchner. We had been on the same transport. He recognized me and saw that I was still alive, and he could not bear to see me die. He pulled me from the pile and stood me up. I was upset with him for not letting me die. I wanted to die, to relinquish my soul, but he would not give up on me. He took me out to the roll call, supporting me the whole time so that I would not fall over. Later he took me back to the block, provided me with a white concoction to stop the diarrhea, and gave me pills to bring down the fever. He didn't leave me until he had saved me.

Later he sought out my friend, Dr. Suchodolsky, who helped me get on my feet again. I no longer had a fever but I was terribly weak. I could barely stand on my feet. Though my friends cared for me, I was sure my days were numbered. The atmosphere had a destructive effect on me. By now I was among the *Muselmänner* and becoming weaker and thinner every day.

My friends feared that at the next selection I would be selected out as no longer capable of hard labor. I was on the verge of breaking down physically and mentally. So they decided I should be listed for the next transport out of Auschwitz. Better that than to wait for a selection, when I would surely be chosen for the crematorium.

I got signed up for a transport, for which no one knew the destination. It was known that Polish Jews were not being allowed on this transport and that many of the privileged ones—those who had arrived with the French and Belgian transports—were signing up for it. Even my friend, Dr. Suchodolsky, had signed up for it.

The question was what to do about me, because I was a Polish Jew.

Then one of us discovered that in the central office, where lists were com-
piled for the transports, there was a Sosnowiec boy working, a little fellow
whom I knew because he had been the fiancé of the manufacturer Frankl's
daughter, who lived on Warszawska Street, and who was a friend of mine.

He was told about my situation—that I would die if I wasn't sent away
on the next transport. Could he make sure I wasn't documented as a Polish
Jew? He promised to do it.

My friends got me dressed, provided me with food for the day, fresh-
ened me up and prepared me as if I was a groom on his wedding day. I now
had to appear before a group of doctors, who would decide whether I was
physically fit for this transport. I presented myself before them, first pinching
my cheeks to put some color in them. Quivering with fear that they would
refuse me, I presented myself. Fortunately, they approved of me, and I was
registered. The joy of my friends was indescribable. Especially happy was Dr.
Suchodolsky, because we would be together again. Feitl Lenchner was also
able to change his nationality and sign up for that transport. So it was that I
already had a few friends with whom I felt secure.

Before departing, we were given new civilian clothes—an indication that
we were not being sent to die, but rather to a new workplace, though we still
didn't know where. I got a good, warm red sweater and a jacket, but a thin suit.
These were garments from people who had been sent to the gas chambers.
Before climbing onto the transport wagons we were given bread, margarine,
and blood sausage. It was snowing, and the freezing cold cut through my face
like a knife. I bundled myself into my new jacket, which warmed me up.

It had been a long time since I had such warm clothing. Sitting in the
wagon and seeing my good friends, I felt fortunate. First of all, I was happy
that I was leaving this hell. I had never believed I would leave that camp
alive. I did not care where we were being taken as long as it was away from
here, from the gas chambers and crematoria.

It was night when our transports started off. It so happened that on that
night fresh transports were arriving from somewhere else. We saw the
searchlights lighting up the place. We also heard the wild shouts of the SS
and their Jewish helpers: *"Heraus! Schnell, ihr Drecksäcke!"* (Out quickly, you
bags of shit!). The air resounded with the cries of children and women, fresh
victims for Auschwitz.

37

Warsaw

Our train was a slow one. The "goods" it was carrying were not top priority, so it stopped at many stations and waited on sidetracks to allow other trains to pass. The door never opened. Echoes of conversations reached us, calls and signals, but we had no idea where we were or where we were heading.

For the first few hours we were exhausted by the unknown and by our memories. We huddled together, each of us deep in his own thoughts, thinking back on our past and trying to imagine our future. As if in a nightmare, I saw the smoke rising from the chimneys of the crematoria, smelled cremated skin, and heard the cries of young children being murdered. I closed my eyes and tried to block my ears, but these memories permeated my whole being.

I fell asleep but woke again when the gray dawn filtered into the wagon through the cracks and through the tiny vent in the roof. The cold also got in and cut into our feet and hands. We had made a little space in the corner for our bodily needs. This area stank and polluted the air, and nobody wanted to sit close to it. This led to arguments and even to fights. People were upset, bitter, and in pain. Fortunately, the frost froze our waste so that it didn't run through the whole wagon.

After two days in these conditions, we reached our destination. In the middle of the night our train stopped at a station and there remained until daybreak. When the first bit of light started to filter through the cracks, many of us climbed to the little window to see where we were. We saw piles of glass and bricks. We tried to guess where we were, but nobody could.

The gray dawn light lit our yellowed and dirty faces. We stared at one another as if to ask: "What happens now? What surprise is next?" Our eyes had the look of lambs to the slaughter. Soon we heard movement outside,

109

the shouted orders that were now so familiar to us. We heard the clip-clop of wooden shoes, which sounded like piles of bricks crashing down. A little later the doors of our wagon swung open, and the SS stormed in with their helpers, the *Kapos,* and with truncheons and whips began beating us: *"Raus, raus, ihr Mist!"* (Out, out, you garbage!).

Quickly we assembled outside the wagon. Some of us were bleeding from being trampled on. Some had lost their shoes, others had had their clothes torn. Quick as lightning we were lined up in a row like soldiers.

We still didn't know where we were. We cast our eyes in all directions. Everywhere we saw piles of bricks, stones, and glass. In the distance we saw only ruins, pieces of buildings, chimneys and iron ladders that reached into the sky. We were afraid to ask where we were because for any unnecessary word or motion we were beaten and insulted. But one of us was able to learn from a camp inmate that we were in Warsaw.

Warsaw! Warsaw! This is what had become of the mother city of Israel—of the bustling Jewish streets, the lively courtyards, the synagogues and study houses, the clubs and organizations, the professional groups and political parties, the factories and shops, the restaurants and cafés, and Jewish schools and children's homes. Of all this there remained only ashes and rubble. This grand Jewish metropolis lay in ruins before us. I felt as if all these mountains of wreckage had landed on my head, had covered me with their steel arms and had cut into my limbs.

Later, when we were chased through the devastated streets of the Warsaw ghetto, I felt as if my blood was dripping. It was then that I understood why no Polish Jews were supposed to join this transport. It was we who knew the Warsaw of former days, the pulsating, bustling Jewish community. None of us were able to come to terms with the idea that this Jewish Warsaw had been utterly destroyed. We recalled the former Warsaw's learned men, its scholars and Hassidim, and the refined young men and hardworking older men, and the elegant ladies and working-class tradesmen, and above all the children, the Warsaw children with whose voices the streets rang, the Shloimelach and Yoselach, the Malkalech and Brochelech, those who used to play in the Warsaw courtyards, in the gardens and parks. Where were they all? This heap of bricks and stones was the mass grave of many thousands.

We could not tell where we were: there were no longer any houses, streets or neighborhoods, only hills of rubble and vacant lots. From the stone and rubble dangled wooden beams, pieces of wall, swaying doors and windows—a still-life picture of a dead city.

In another ruin I saw the remains of a child's crib, over which still circled childish dreams of angels; unfortunately, it was devils that materialized. We had no idea at all which streets we were passing: we were wading through a sea of destruction. But at certain intersections someone had placed the old signs where Muranow had been, from which extended the Nalewki, the narrow Mila and the wide Mila, then Nowolipki, Twarda, Gesia, Krochmalna. All these streets had contributed gloriously to Jewish history. Now all was erased, pulverized into ashes and dust. It was as quiet as a cemetery, yet from this silence rose the wail of the thousands of dreams, hopes, and fantasies that now lay buried in this mass grave.

We were chased into a *Lager* (camp) on Gesia Street near the former military prison. Here a slave labor camp had been established and filled with thousands of Jews "released" from the concentration camps. These slaves had been set to work cleaning up the destruction. Wherever houses were still standing, the rubble was to be cleared away. If a house could be rebuilt, it was to be done. Polish foremen were in charge of this work. They arrived every morning from their own side of the city and left in the evening.

We were housed in barracks and divided into contingents. At first I was assigned to clear away bricks and pile them neatly. We worked outdoors all day with frozen feet and hands in heavy snow and extreme cold. Walking back and forth over the rubble in wooden clogs twisted and scarred our feet. Our shoes quickly fell apart in the damp. When my shoes fell apart, I wrapped my feet in rags that I had scavenged from the ruins and tied them on with wire. At night it was hard to remove the rags, and in the morning I would not have time to tie them on again. On being roused in the morning we had to dress quickly, grab our few sips of black water (so-called coffee), and get out for roll call. If we were slow, we were beaten. So I slept in my rags.

38

The First Day Amongst the Wreckage in Warsaw

After a night of horrible nightmares in this hell that was the Warsaw ghetto, we were awakened before dawn and rushed out for roll call. This was conducted at half past four in the morning, earlier than usual, because we newcomers had to be counted, registered, and assigned to *Kommandos*. It was a cold, damp day that we felt in our bones. Finally, shivering, we were sent out to work.

The clatter of thousands of pairs of wooden clogs echoed through the mountains of debris. We felt as if we were disturbing the peace of a cemetery. The mouths and eyes of the wrecked homes gaped at us as if beseeching us to leave them in peace. The shouts and orders of the *Kapos* echoed loudly in this tormented and devastated world.

We arrived at the headquarters of the *Kapos* and foremen, where work tools were distributed to us—picks, spades, and ropes—and we were assigned tasks. Here I saw free Poles for the first time. They entered the ghetto every day to help clear the wreckage. I stared at them in bewilderment: it had been a long time since I saw free civilians who were clean and decently dressed. Another thing that surprised me was that the Poles could communicate best with the Greek Jews, with whom they had developed a sign language. With the Polish Jews, who spoke the same language, they avoided contact.

I noticed one of the Poles staring at me. I approached him and asked, in Polish: "Why are you looking at me like that?"

"Oh, so you speak Polish?" He seemed glad to hear this. He stared again, tugged at my red sweater and said, "Sell me this."

When I heard this, I was completely confused but at the same time astounded: I wasn't used to words such as "buying" and "selling." Did business go on here? As it turned out, the Greek Jews were keen entrepreneurs, even though they did not speak Polish. They had arrived here a few months earlier than us and had been able to establish contact with the Polish foremen, with whom they did business on a grand scale. Whenever they found anything of worth, they traded with the Poles for food. They offered gold, diamonds, and jewelry for a piece of bread, an onion, a few potatoes or cigarettes, or sometimes a bottle of liquor. The Poles made a fortune out of this.

Yet I froze when I heard this offer to trade my sweater for bread. The magic word "bread" immediately flashed before me, but then I started to think more logically. If I gave away my sweater in this weather, I would freeze. I would grow sick and die. This thought sent a shudder through me. But the Pole would not leave me alone until I agreed to sell it to him. I told myself that if I kept the sweater and did not freeze to death, I would die of hunger, and how would that be better? Either way I wasn't going to last long here, so let me at least once have my fill of bread. The mere word "bread" grew in my mind, out of all proportion, into something immense. Bread! Fresh bread!

I agreed to trade my sweater for half a loaf of bread and forty zlotys. For Poles, a kilo of bread cost five zlotys. The next day, when I came to work, he would have both the bread and the cash.

I did not sleep all night. My empty stomach was already reacting to the smell of the bread. My stomach growled all night long. I beheld in front of me only one thing—bread! Bread in all its many forms and shapes. I could hardly wait until morning. As soon as the night guard shouted *"Auf!"* I was on my feet. I looked at my sweater with love and longing, knowing I would soon have to part with it. I pressed it to my heart, cuddled it and kissed it the way one parts with a lover.

When we came to work among the ruins, I searched in all directions, looking for my customer. He finally appeared and gave me a meaningful wink that I should follow him. We descended into a bunker, where he pulled out a fresh-smelling loaf of bread, counted out forty zlotys and said, "Hurry up so we don't get caught." I quickly took off my jacket and removed my red sweater and handed it to the Pole, who quickly rolled it up into his suitcase and disappeared.

I started tearing pieces from the fresh bread and stuffing them down my throat. With each mouthful I felt my entire body reviving. Never in all my life had I tasted anything so delicious. It was as if the gates of paradise had opened. I quickly hid the money away deep in my pockets and tied the ends of my trousers with wire so as not to lose the "treasure." Then I returned to work feeling like the luckiest fellow in the world.

My blessings did not last long. Perhaps an hour later I made sure no one was looking and sneaked another bite, chewing it with pleasure. I had been looking for my friend, Dr. Suchodolsky, with the intention of sharing some of my prize with him, but he didn't happen to come my way. He had disappeared among the ruins. While I was working away, knocking bricks from their mortar, I felt a hand grasp my shoulder. I turned and saw a Greek Jew leering at me.

"The *Kapo* is looking for you," he said.

"The *Kapo*? What does he want me for?" I shuddered, though not from the piercing cold. I saw trouble coming, but when told to go one had to obey. I was led up to a wrecked house. A fire was burning on the first floor. There was the *Kapo* with a truncheon in his hand, surrounded by his servants—the foremen, the top informers, and the *pipls*. I knew well what their stares were telling me: these "royals" regarded me as a fool and a victim. An evil kind of joy was lighting their eyes. The *Kapo* looked me up and down and then roared:

"Where is your sweater!?"

I blinked and stuttered, "I don't have it. I was never given a sweater. I don't have one."

The beating began immediately. I fell, all bloodied. When I rose again they began anew with sadistic pleasure, using their hands, their feet, and their truncheons. Then they started ripping my clothes off. When I was naked, they robbed me of my forty zlotys and the rest of the bread. Having done that, they chased me out into the snow again, still naked, my clothes in my hands.

I fell to the ground, bloodied, bruised, and desperate, again praying to die. Now I had no sweater, no bread, and no money. Blood and tears poured from me. Soon after, another *Kapo* came along. He too began cursing me and beating me with his truncheon: "What are you doing here? Why aren't you going to work, you son of a bitch?" I tried to explain and to beg for his mercy, but to no avail. While he beat me, I jumped into my wet clothes and ran to work with my last bit of strength. At that moment I was crying too hard to feel the cold, hot tears of anger and desperation. Only later did I feel the penetrating cold. I shivered that whole night.

Later—too late for me—I learned that the Poles had an agreement with the *Kapos*. The Poles bought things from the newcomers and then informed the *Kapos* who they had bought from and how much they had paid. The "marks" were then taken to the *Kapo* "headquarters," where they were questioned, beaten, and robbed of their bread and money. Then the *Kapos* and the Poles divided the spoils.

39

Work in the Ruins

We were set to work among the ruins of the Warsaw ghetto. The first days were terribly difficult: we had to dig into the wreckage and tear down the last vestiges of Jewish Warsaw. To us it was like taking apart human limbs, the limbs of our own community, the greatest Jewish community in Europe. Every house, every stone was a piece of the history of the Jewish people.

In cellars and bunkers we came across the bodies of Jews, entire families that had been shot or gassed or that had died of starvation, thirst, and sickness. Many of these bodies had been robbed or disfigured by whatever beasts had extracted their gold teeth. These bodies, decomposed, putrefied, rotting, were taken away immediately to reduce the threat of epidemic.

In Warsaw there were no crematoria yet. Such ovens were being built while I was there, but fortunately, they were never completed. So we gathered the corpses we found in the bunkers, and the corpses of those who had died in the night in the camp, and stacked them in piles, just as one stacks lumber, in the yards of Gesia Street 43 and 46. Gasoline was poured over them and ignited. After that the ground was covered with quicklime.

When the foreman turned his back, we often took advantage and went down into the cellars. There we could rest a little, safe from beatings. We would poke around the cellars for anything we could find, such as linens, clothes, and perhaps even gold and silver valuables. These held no interest for us, except as they could be traded for food. The Poles bought these things from us for next to nothing—for a few potatoes, a few cigarettes, or a piece of bread. When they could, they often tricked us into giving them something for nothing. They themselves were forbidden to bring in food for us, and often they were searched when entering or leaving the ghetto.

116

Sometimes they were even arrested. That was their justification for demanding so much gold for so little bread.

The Poles scavenged for treasure on their own. The *Kapos* also had their "sappers," whom they released from work specifically to seek buried valuables. Furthermore, they had their enforcers and *pipl,* who spied on us slaves and reported anyone who found anything so that the *Kapos* could "requisition" it for themselves.

One of the most sadistic of all the *Kapos* was a fat little man, power-drunk, with bloodshot eyes. Once, while running through a labyrinthine cellar, I ran into him just as he was raping one of us slaves, a young Belgian boy with blond hair. It was too late for me to duck back, as he had already seen me. The *Kapo*'s face was flushed, the young boy's pale as the wall. I quickly fled to avoid the *Kapo*'s revenge. Fortunately for me, we were not in the same *Kommando.*

In the basements we found Hebrew books of Holy Scripture, secular books, documents, and business records. Some of the companies in the ghetto had been powerful corporations and had played a vital role in Poland's industrial life. All of this enterprise had turned to dust and ashes.

In a bunker in a courtyard on Twarda Street, we found a diary in which a young boy had recorded every episode he had witnessed from his bunker during the siege of Warsaw. We took it back with us to the camp and read it together. The diary somehow got lost during the transports.

Once, when we were marching out to work, we met a survivor of the ghetto in one of the ruins. He had climbed to the top of a wall and was threatening our guards with two revolvers. Frightened, the SS guard marched us off in another direction. We never learned what happened to this man. Another time, a mother and her daughter were dragged out of a bunker. Both were white as ghosts from lack of sun. Their hair was tangled. Their rotting clothes hung from them like dirty rags. Their eyes were blank, apathetic, as they stumbled over the rubble of bricks. An SS guard, accompanied by an attack dog, escorted them at machine gun point to who knows where.

◆　　◆　　◆

The ruins were not dynamited. This was probably to avoid destroying whatever could be salvaged from the walls of the wrecked houses. On one occasion we tore down a "false" wall, part of the home of the well-known *Rivka di ku* (Rivka the cow), and found an entire wall full of fur and leather coats.

We would tie ropes to the highest part of a wall, hack away the foundation, then pull until the wall came down. Those who weren't quick enough got buried in the rubble. One day, Dr. Suchodolsky and I were given the job of destroying a foundation in this way. This was back-breaking work to which neither of us was accustomed. With the tools provided we chopped away at the concrete. For this job strong men should have been used, ones who were well fed—not emaciated weaklings like us.

As a doctor, my friend was accustomed to using delicate tools, and was not used to any kind of heavy labor. For me also it was exhausting, but it was my friend who collapsed first. Soon he could no longer stand on his feet. Then I saw a foreman passing nearby, a Yugoslavian Jew, a tough brute who must have been a butcher or a horse dealer back home. I thought to ask him to assign my friend to easier work, perhaps cleaning and piling bricks. As soon as he heard my request, and my reasons for it, he flew into a murderous rage.

"Who is he, that one? So he's a doctor? He's a *Dreck!* And who am I if he's a doctor? He's a son of a bitch! And who am I?"

He began beating my friend viciously with his truncheon until he was bleeding on the ground. He did not spare me either. Then he told us that if the wall doesn't come down in three hours he would transfer us to the punishment *Kommando,* where the slaves were brutalized constantly while they worked, supervised by sadistic *Kapos* who wore them out as quickly as they could beat them. No one lasted more than a few days in that *Kommando*: every day, it carried a few corpses back to the camp.

Dr. Suchodolsky cried with bitter tears. I helped him rise and washed his wounds with a damp rag, and we got back to work. He did not last long. His tool fell out of his hands, and he collapsed.

"It's all the same to me," he said. "Let him send me wherever he wants. I can't survive any longer."

Fortunately, the Yugoslav never came back. We dragged ourselves home, utterly finished, and fell like the dead across our plank beds.

All the *Kapos* were brutes and sadists. There are two reasons why. First, most of them had been selected from among the criminals and perverts and had police records for robbery and murder. Second, they themselves were slaves, who like the rest of us had been insulted and degraded, robbed of their freedom and honor. This affected them morally. They revolted against their fate by unleashing their worst instincts, taking out their anger and bitterness against the weaker slaves. Over the rest of us, at least, they had power; over the rest of us they had strength and superiority. And so they showed those things to reduce their own pain. That is why any slave in their *Kommando* who was wiser, wealthier, or more educated, and who made the mistake of showing it, became a special target. It wounded the *Kapos* not to feel superior to the rest of us in every way.

Intellectuals and men of wealthy families they hated with a special passion, hounding them, working them to the ground and lower, torturing them till they died. They did the same to good-looking young men, with whom they also could not compete. They could "organize" fine boots, fine suits, fine clothing from those who had been liquidated or from the bunkers in the ghetto. They could even arrange for slaves who had been tailors before the war to fit their clothes for them in return for a bowl of soup or a piece of bread. But they could not change shape or wear a different face or nose, so they could not tolerate those who were bequeathed by nature with personal charm and a handsome build. That is why they took revenge on the "luckier" ones.

In our *Kommando* there was a very handsome boy—tall and slim, with beautiful eyes, a slim nose and a face that glowed like the sun. Even though he was in rags, he looked like a prince. The *Kapo* was always picking on this boy. No matter what he did, it was never good enough. He sent him to do the worst, dirtiest work. He beat him with all his strength and was after him like a devil, possibly because he did not want to become his *pipl.* One day, on the way to work, he took him out of line and beat him to death. My heart cried with sorrow, but what could we do? The *Kapo*'s sadistic fury wouldn't have spared us either, had we dared say a word. We carried the boy into the camp and quietly grieved over him. The *Kapo* announced to the guards, *"Aufrämung Kommando*: seventy-nine and one body."

40

Destiny Gives Me a Chance

Fate is always blind. It did not help us much to be wise or strong. In no way could any of us change what lay in store. Often it was the wise and the strong who broke down most quickly and the weak and the foolish who escaped all dangers and misfortunes. True, good instincts could help one avoid trouble, but generally, it was a matter of luck whether one lived or died.

One morning, when we were lined up in the dark for roll call, a senior officer of the SS came out and called to us: "Whoever is a tradesman in construction—bricklayers, locksmiths, welders, glaziers, tinsmiths, please step forward."

At that moment a thought flashed through my mind: I will be a glazier. Why not? Who was to say I wasn't? An inexplicable force gave me a push and I stepped forward with a few others. I informed the officer that by trade I was a glazier. I knew as much about this as the village idiot, but I had owned a large glass business in Sosnowiec, where I had watched tradesmen cutting glass and large display windows. I knew about glass, its varieties and qualities. I had even imported huge mirrored glass from Belgium and shop windows from there and Czechoslovakia. Many times, for a lark, I had taken a diamond cutter or cutting wheel and cut large panes. I hadn't been very good at it, but I was the boss so it was permitted. I had also watched the glaziers in my shop cut and install windows. All that aside, about glazier work I really knew nothing. But now I decided to take a chance. It was a matter of death or bread.

When the foreman approached and asked me once more if I knew the trade, I decided to risk everything. He pointed out to me that if I was fooling him, it would mean the end for me.

The SS led me to a large wooden hut in which I saw an oven, a large table for cutting glass, and various plates of glass. I was scared out of my wits. But I also felt the oven's warmth in my bones just as if a ray of sunshine was warming me. The SS turned to the Pole who was standing by the table. He gave me a cold-eyed stare. The SS told him that he had brought him a helper to try out. If I didn't know the trade, I was to be returned: he would know what to do with me.

When the SS left, I fell to my knees in front of the Pole and begged him not to send me away. I told him the truth, that I did not have much practical experience, that I had worked with glaziers and understood the trade but was not a qualified glazier. I promised him "paradise," that if he rescued me perhaps we would both survive this war. Also, both of us were Poles so we should help each other. If he helped me now, I would repay him more than double when the war ended. I looked at my savior with tears in my eyes and asked him for mercy.

He stared at me coldly, with a pair of murderous eyes, so I tried another approach, telling him I would bring him the valuables that my many friends were finding in the bunkers and that he would grow rich through me.

When he said he was ready to try me out, I wanted to hug and kiss him. I felt as if someone had thrown me a life buoy in midocean. It meant, first of all, that I wouldn't have to work outside in the frost and snow. I would also have a safe *Kommando,* away from all the *Kapos* and foremen, away from the beatings and punishments. In addition, I hoped the Pole would provide me with enough food to stave off hunger.

Now I had only one worry: how was I to secure some valuables to show the Pole I was "behaving well" and that keeping me was worth his while? I began inquiring among my friends, who brought me some valuables—gold and silver brooches, earrings, and various coins. My Pole was not pleased— he wanted things of greater value than this.

I sought out Feitl Lenchner, my friend from Sosnowiec, who had saved my life in Auschwitz-Birkenau, and was able to bring him in as a coworker in the glass shop. I had two motives for this: I needed to return the favor he had done me, because if not for him I would have long ago gone up the chimney; and this Feitl was a very capable scavenger who also had good connections with the gold traders. He always knew who had something to sell and how to make contact with buyers. Besides, it was nicer to work with a friend.

The Pole exploited us terribly, earning fat sums and providing us little, but it didn't matter much to us. We had a roof over our heads, near a warm stove, no less. We were able to boil a few potatoes, make a bread soup, boil a little water. The Pole provided us with a few potatoes, a piece of bread, an onion, garlic, and a piece of margarine, a few eggs, and some schnapps.

We were not the only ones in the "market." Every day a hundred or so Poles would enter the ghetto to work at clearing away the ruins, and they all did business with the slaves of the Warsaw camp. They brought in food and carried off riches. The biggest "merchants" were the Greek Jews, most of whom came from Salonika. They were especially talented at "organizing" what they called *"klepsi-klepsi"*—that is, articles from "nonkosher" sources such as thievery. They also knew how to deal with the Poles.

41

Relations Between the Camp Inmates and the Poles

After the war I used to hear and also read about Jewish leaders bragging that they had provided food to the Jewish slave laborers though arrangements with those trustworthy Poles who had access to the camps in Warsaw. I can state categorically that this never happened. We received no support from the Poles. In fact, they often cheated us by taking our valuables, promising to bring us food in return. Later, when we asked them to keep their part of the deal, they would mock and insult us. Not only that, but they often reported us to the *Kapos* and even to the SS, who took everything from us and beat us severely, such as the beating I took in my first days.

In the camp I used to talk often with a Parisian friend, Fenigstein, a politically astute fellow who was later the editor in Paris of the communist *New Press,* for which he wrote under the pseudonym A. Vilner. We often commented sadly that we had no contact with the outside world and that no one thought to send food to us through the Poles, and not even a written word of encouragement.

It pained us deeply that the whole world had forgotten us. Had we had any contact with the outside world, had there only been someone who was willing to hide us outside the camp, some of us might have been able to get out somehow, in spite of the close guard.

Once a Greek boy ran away. He had been working in a *Kommando* near the Vistula. It was the Poles who betrayed him. They caught him and brought him back to the camp, and we all had to stand and watch his execution. It tore our hearts out to witness this. The Poles prospered by exchanging Jewish treasure for a little bread. None of them ever helped us, nor did they show us any compassion. They only used us for their own advantage.

42

I Belong to the Privileged Class

My situation definitely improved. I became adept as a glazier and soon became a top man in the enterprise. Our task was to replace the shattered windows in the ghetto houses that were being rebuilt. So it was that we reglazed all of Nowolipki Street 44, where the Germans were establishing many of their storerooms and offices.

Our work meant we could meet with friends in other *Kommandos,* to see if they had found any treasures we could trade for them. In this way we also met Poles with whom to do business. While renovating various buildings, we developed contacts with a number of Poles who could bring in food by the sack. Soon we were the middlemen between them and the camp inmates.

Our friends gave us the things they had scavenged from the cellars, and for these we found buyers. We were able to get the best prices for our friends, because we were not limited to one buyer. Their items were safe with us because no *Kapos* or foremen were watching us and because we had secure hiding places. Even better, we were able to go anywhere we wanted in the ghetto. We could pick up a window and start carrying it and go wherever we wanted. If the SS stopped us, we had a perfect excuse: we were on our way to install a window.

We did not want our Pole to know anything about our transactions with other Poles. Very soon, however, he simply disappeared. Probably he was caught smuggling goods in or out of the ghetto. One morning we came to work and he wasn't there. A little later a senior SS man entered, the one in charge of all construction, and asked us, "Will you be able to carry on alone without the specialist?" I immediately understood that something had happened.

I promptly answered that if the specialist was employed elsewhere, we would be able to carry on the work ourselves, provided we were supplied with enough glass and putty. The SS took out a notebook and wrote my name and number. He also noted what we needed and added, "Beginning today, you are in charge, and you will answer directly to me for all the work. Make sure everything runs properly! Understand?"

I clicked my heels and replied, "Jawohl!" (Yes, sir), while my friend, Feitl Lenchner, smothered a smile. After the man left, Feitl hugged and kissed me.

"We've gotten rid of a despot!" he said.

From that moment on I was in charge of all glazing in the Warsaw ghetto. I was also in charge of the wooden hut. The stove there kept the putty warm, but it served other purposes. First of all, we no longer suffered from the cold. Outside there was snow and frost, but in here we didn't feel it much. When there was a snowstorm outside, even the *Kapos* used to come in to warm themselves. One day, when a *Kapo* was sitting at the entrance, the SS man in charge of all the *Kapos* stormed in.

"What are you doing here, *Kapo*?" he demanded.

The *Kapo* knew how to reply. He covered his mouth with his fist and began to groan: "Oh, my tooth! I have a terrible toothache."

"You're pretending! Come on, go where you should be."

The *Kapo* vanished. His commander watched to see that we were working, and told us to work faster, and left us.

Since we had our own warm hut, it was easy to establish ties with the "strongmen" of the camp. The *Kapos* and foremen needed favors from us— often a hiding place, or help getting food, schnapps, and cigarettes from the Poles. Naturally, we always took our cut.

We were also able to cook for ourselves—some soup, a few eggs, or a piece of meat. Whenever we provided something for the *Kapos* or block elders, they gave us some soup, a piece of sausage, or a little marmalade, which they received as special rations.

I wanted to take Dr. Suchodolsky into the shop, but he could not adjust to the work. For the tasks at hand one had to be quick on one's feet, running through gutters, hauling windows, and this was beyond him. But through my connections, I was able to find him a position as a doctor. I also supplied him with food.

Our position became good. We had enough to eat and could even help others. My Polish contacts brought me newspapers—German ones, *Warsaw*

Zeitung or *Krakower Zeitung*—and I would read these for war news. I would read between the lines for what was actually happening. As a result, I was always the best informed slave in the camp.

I had a group of friends who waited for me every evening so that I would tell them the war news. I described the situation in rosy colors. At the end of 1943 and the beginning of 1944, the Germans were being defeated on all fronts. Rommel's Afrika Korps had been defeated by the Allies. The Russians were advancing after their fierce winter offensive. Germany itself was being bombed heavily. Though the German papers said little about these defeats, I could glean what was really happening and tell my friends about it. I was the camp's acclaimed political commentator.

Often I would embellish my commentaries with fantastic predictions, to instill hope in the despondent hearts of the others. Looking at the thin faces and protruding eyes of the desperate camp inmates who were hanging on to life with their last bit of strength, I wanted to instill in them new hope and fresh strength. For them, I described the situation to make it seem that we would soon be free. This was even though I knew that freedom was still far away. Who among us knew which of these living dead would survive until the liberation? Yet I believed I was instilling in them a new spirit. On nights like these, more than one of them fell asleep dreaming sweetly that freedom was already flying toward them with beating wings.

One of my listeners was a young Moroccan boy from Paris, George Sheba. A brilliant fellow. He always listened carefully to my commentaries. Though he did not understand a word of Yiddish, he saw the hope in the eyes of the others and gathered that I was telling stories worth hearing, so he asked the others to translate.

One day after the war, I was walking through the streets of Paris when someone grabbed me and started to hug me. It was George. He would not leave me alone until I agreed to come home with him and meet his family. That evening, we entered his home in a wealthy district of Paris and I found a whole crowd of people, among them the brother of Leon Blum. He introduced me as his savior, telling them that I had saved him and many others in the concentration camp of Warsaw by giving them the courage to endure those treacherous and bitter times. Everyone drank to my health. I left feeling deeply satisfied.

43

Block Elders

The block elders of the Warsaw camp were mostly criminals, sadists, homo‐
sexuals, and underworld scum. But because there were "trading opportuni‐
ties"—that is, goods to exchange or to use as bribes—"good brothers" could
sometimes be smuggled into the system. That being said, most of the
"strongmen"—the block elders, the *Kapos,* the foremen—were still bandits
and murderers. They had the power of life and death over us and often took
out their bitterness and frustration on the slaves in their *Kommando* or block.
Often they were simply power-hungry and wanted to show their strength—
to prove to themselves that they were rulers, not slaves.

They often tortured the weaker slaves to death. Human life had no value
to them. In fact, human life had little value anywhere in the camp. The bod‐
ies of those whom the strongmen had murdered in the night would be
tossed out the block's front door as if they were rats, to be picked up by the
corpse wagon whenever it arrived. An accurate record was kept of the num‐
ber of dead. The Germans were very precise about this. They insisted on
order . . .

The block elders were responsible for keeping the blocks clean on the
outside, although inside they were utterly filthy and neglected. It was diffi‐
cult for any of us to stay clean; not everyone had the privilege of an occa‐
sional wash. In our camp there were more than four thousand inmates, yet
there were only two wash barracks. In the morning we had barely enough
time to pull on our dirty clothes, grab a drink of the black water that was
called "coffee," and run to roll call so as not to get beaten. After roll call we
were immediately marched to work. As a result, each morning the wash bar‐
racks were besieged by people hoping to get a handful of water to rinse their
faces.

First in line at the wash barracks were, of course, the strongmen, the privileged ones. They would chase everyone else away from the taps, so the ordinary slaves had no time to get water for themselves. Almost right away the shout would be heard— *"Appell! Appell!"*—at the sound of which everyone ran like crazy.

Most slaves slept in their clothes, for several reasons. First of all, it was warmer in winter. Second, many of us had to urinate as many as ten times a night, probably because of our watery and totally fatless diet. Outside the barrack door there were pots to which we were running constantly. Another reason was that some of us had things to hide—a piece of bread, or a find from one of the cellars. To keep them safe in the night and to avoid tipping off the block elder, we slept in our clothes with our goods tucked inside them. In addition, by sleeping in our clothes we improved our chances of getting water in the morning.

There were no baths or showers in the camp. Such things were only a dream. Sometimes we were taken to Pawiak, a local prison, where there were communal showers, and there we could at least rinse off some of the dirt. The prison supervisors would tease us as if we were dogs. Through the windows they would wave chunks of bread at us, pretending to want to share them with us. When we approached, someone from above would pour down on us pitchers of water.

So it was that we went around dirty, infested with lice, covered with boils and sores. The suffering drew from us our last reserves of strength.

Feitl Lenchner and I were able to wash from time to time. I would heat a container of water in the glazing shop and wash with a bar of soap I had bartered from the Poles. Then Feitl would stand guard at the door to make sure nobody was coming. Later it would be his turn. We were also able to wash our clothes, but what help was that? When I lay down on my plank bed, I would only be attacked again by my pesky neighbors. At night in the barrack, a small lamp was kept lit and we could watch the hoards of lice marching over us in processions.

By now there were Hungarian and Dutch Jews among us. Their bodies broke down quickly. So did their minds: hope of salvation drained from them almost instantly. The Polish, Russian, Lithuanian, and Yugoslavian Jews did not succumb as quickly as this because they were used to living hard lives. They were the ones who struggled to keep faith. It was the "refined" Jews who gave up. They let themselves go and soon died. What made the camp even worse for them was that they did not know Yiddish, German, or Polish, the camp's three spoken languages. No one could understood them or talk to them. Their lives, therefore, were extremely bitter.

It was the block elders who distributed the food in the blocks. Those among them who were criminals always divided the bread so as to hold some back for themselves. When distributing the soup, they gave us the thinnest portion in which floated a few beans or a piece of potato; the thick part they kept for themselves and their helpers. If anyone dared complain, their soup was taken away and they were beaten.

With the soup and bread they withheld from us the block elders would barter for sausage, cigarettes, and schnapps, which the slaves smuggled in for them from the construction sites. Most smuggled goods entered the camp tied to the sleeves or pants of slaves. This was terribly risky, because the *Kommandos* were regularly stopped and searched. It was just too bad for anyone caught with contraband. Whenever such a "search" took place, the slaves threw any articles they were carrying on the ground. If the guilty one could not be established, everyone in the group was deprived of his next food ration. In this way the innocent suffered through no fault of their own.

It was the block elders who had the means to buy contraband, it was they who had the "surplus" of food—sometimes bread, sometimes thick soup, sometimes marmalade. And of course they could trade the various articles they had confiscated from the slaves or bought from them.

A few of the block elders were clients of mine. They would give me their articles and I would bring them whatever they wanted. Mainly this was schnapps—Polish "vodka." As a result of these dealings I had good relations with the block elders; this in turn meant I could arrange improved conditions for my friends.

One day something very painful happened. While I was walking among the barracks I heard someone calling me, "Glazier! Come here!" I turned and saw the block elder we called Yupe. His face was brick red. It seems he had consumed a few too many. He waved me into his room and showed me a pair of good leather shoes.

"Take them. They're for you!"

It so happened that I very much needed new shoes—my present ones were torn, water damaged, and completely rotten. Rejoicing, I immediately put them on. But when I went out I suddenly saw someone lying on the ground, dead and without shoes. I shuddered.

"What's this?" I asked.

"I knocked him dead, that *Schweinhund*. He stole from his comrades."

He just could not put up with such wrongdoing, with the notion that someone other than him should steal. So he had killed the man. I walked on those shoes on tiptoe after that. I returned to my block, sought out one of my friends, and exchanged shoes with him, telling him these ones were too tight for me. When I met that friend with the shoes, it reminded me of that shattering scene.

Among the block elders were a few half-decent ones—the ones who had got their positions through pull. Some of them had been important and worthy people before the war and had played important roles in Jewish life. So ways were found to place them in charge of a block, where they wouldn't have to do hard, cold labor.

Being a block elder had its own dangers: these men were, after all, responsible for those in their blocks, among whom there were all sorts of types. There were lazy ones among us, who tried to evade work, and there were thieves who did not scruple about stealing their neighbors' bread.

One of the "good" block elders was a Jewish artist who had got his posting through the influence of his friends from Paris. One day in his block I witnessed a scene I will never forget.

It was Sunday, and the artist was dishing out the soup while those in line waited anxiously. Far down the line stood a Hungarian Jew, ragged, dirty, and hungry. The smell of the soup must have made him so crazy that he could no longer contain himself. He broke from his place in the line and ran up to the soup pot and tried to scoop some into his cap. This placed the block elder in a dilemma: if he permitted such disorder, everyone would start running, the pot would spill, and there would be no food for anyone. The block elder could pay with his life for allowing such chaos.

So he put down the ladle, walked up to the deranged man, and slapped him so hard he fell down with blood running from him. When the block elder saw what he had done, he turned white as chalk and sat down on a bench. One of his helpers finished portioning the food. If it had been any other block elder, the episode would have ended tragically. But it seems the artist had retained some of his humanity, and for that reason the incident pained him.

44

My Luck Runs Out

It seems I was not meant to enjoy for long the good fortune that had chanced to come my way. My mother would have said that the "evil eye" had got me. I had established myself nicely. I felt neither hunger nor cold, the two greatest enemies of camp inmates. I also had a good reputation in the camp and belonged to the so-called privileged class, because no *Kapo* or foreman ruled me. The block elder was protecting me because he often relied on me to bring him contraband. As a tradesman in strong demand, I was an "independent." I was able to wash from time to time and to dress better. There were tailors in the camp who for a piece of bread or a bit of other food would alter slaves' striped clothing so that it fit properly.

I was also exposed to danger, because I was always hiding articles and smuggling things into camp. One day a notoriously cruel *Obersturmbann-führer* entered the glazing shop. Perhaps one of the *Kapos* pointed him to me. To this day I cannot guess who sent this killer. He began to search and found two bottles of schnapps, a few eggs, a few packs of cigarettes, and some onions and garlic. (The latter two were especially important in the camp because they protected us from microbes, which were so prevalent.)

He showed me these things, and I started to tell him that a Polish supervisor had once worked here and must have left them, and that I had never seen them before. He grabbed an iron rod and began beating me without mercy and kicking me with his boots until I had collapsed in a puddle of blood and broken glass. Then he knocked out a few of my teeth and left me half-dead. He took the contraband with him and probably would have arrested me if there had been anyone to help him. Instead he told me that if ever again such things were found on my premises, he would shoot me on the spot.

So it was that I had to stop doing business for some time. I knew this guard was watching me. Eventually he disappeared. I heard from someone that he had been transferred to the front. He did not die there, however, because right after the war I encountered him at the Dachau trials, where he was sentenced to death. I was a witness against him.

Once he had left, I again started doing business, though very cautiously. But as the saying goes: "If trouble is fated, it will come right in one's door."

In the spring of 1944 one of the block elders gave me a few gold coins and a few rings and asked me to bring him a few bottles of "vodka." That Sunday a few friends were going to help him celebrate his birthday. I sought out my Polish contacts and placed the order. I would give them the gold on Saturday when they brought me the bottles. They brought the schnapps on that day, along with a piece of Krakow sausage. They also brought me the day's newspaper, the *Krakow Zeitung*. I rejoiced at this last item, because I always wanted to know what was happening in the world. My friend and I stuffed the contraband in our clothes, and with God's help we finished our week. When I brought the goods to my block elder, he wanted to kiss me, he was so happy. He even gave me an extra piece of bread and some sausage for my trouble.

The afternoon of the following day, Sunday, the block elder got his friends together and they started to party. They got drunk and began getting rowdy. Just then the camp's senior SS officer, whose nickname was *Umshmis* (he came from Danzig and was extremely cruel), came to inspect the camp. He rode through the gate on his motorcycle directly to the block where the "party" was taking place. He dismounted, looked through an open window, and saw what was going on. Naturally, he hauled everyone away and began an investigation. He beat the block elder into disclosing that he had bought the schnapps and other things from someone in the building compound.

The block elder's breakdown soured the mood in the camp. Never before this had a "strongman" snitched on another inmate. I was told right away that *Umshmis* had smashed the party, hauled off all those involved, and forced the block elder to reveal the source of the liquor. A chill ran through me.

Soon after, it was announced through the loudspeakers that a roll call of the entire camp was to be held immediately. This was never done except in unusual circumstances—when there was an uprising or when a prisoner had escaped. I immediately understood that the point of this roll call was to find me. I sought out my friends to distribute all my belongings, then I bade them a heartfelt farewell because I was sure I wasn't going to come out alive from this predicament. I begged them, if they survived this hell, to find any of my relatives still living and tell them how I perished. I also gave one of my friends my shoes. Let him enjoy a decent pair: I no longer needed them.

The whole camp was lined up by *Kommandos*. All the SS staff were there, with *Umshmis* at their head. Beside them stood the block elder, his eyes downcast, his face pale. One by one the other *Kommandos* were let go until only the construction workers and the craftsmen were left. Finally only the glaziers' *Kommando* was left, and the block elder pointed me out. I was taken away; the others were let go. As I was led to headquarters, all eyes followed me. This was a march to the scaffold; they were certain just as I was that my end had come.

During questioning, they tortured me to try to make me tell them where I got the goods and how much I had paid for them. I denied that I had brought the goods in from the construction sites, and insisted that I had bought them from people in the camp. But I also insisted that I didn't know their names, or which block they were in, and that I had only been paid a piece of bread and some marmalade.

They stretched me out on a bench and administered twenty-five lashes. When they undressed me, they found stuffed into my pants the *Krakow Zeitung*. While I was giving away everything that morning, I had forgotten to take it from its hiding place. But now a miracle happened: none of them noticed that it was the most recent edition, that I had an interest in politics. Had any of them done so I would have been shot immediately. But they simply assumed that I had stuffed my clothes with paper to protect myself from their beatings.

They beat me so viciously they tore my skin off. The strap they used was of leather with a piece of lead at the tip. They stood me up and started to question me again. I continued to give the same answers: that I had bought everything *inside* the camp, from a Greek whose name I did not know. In truth, I had bought one of the bottles from a Greek. But in no way did I want to reveal his name, though the torturers promised to free me if I told them. I knew that was a lie, that if I gave them the Greek's name they would only torture him too and it wouldn't help my situation at all. Again they stretched me out on the bench and gave me twenty-five strokes. When they found they could not break me, they beat me again, chopping at me as if I was a head of cabbage, so hard I stopped feeling anything.

Finally, they told me they were letting me out, but only so I could find the Greek and bring them his name the next day. I don't know how I walked from that room. My legs had no strength. They had crippled me. I was barely able to drag myself to the block. When my friends saw me, they were overjoyed: battered as I was, I was still alive. I told them what had happened. They started to nurse me, applying cold water to my wounds. Dr. Suchodolsky brought me a salve from the medical supplies. I told them to tell the Greek to have no fear—I wasn't going to give them his name. All night long I sobbed. I could not lie on my back, so I lay on my belly.

The next day I did not go to work; the block elder had been ordered to bring me back to SS headquarters. My friends said good-bye to me and kissed me because they were sure they would never see me again.

While the block elder was escorting me to SS headquarters, he told me that everyone in the camp, including all the "strongmen," condemned the block elder who had betrayed me. All considered that a despicable thing for him to have done. To them I was a hero, because I had not succumbed to the SS tortures.

When I entered the headquarters I saw only two officers. They were slightly older and more reserved than the ones of the day before. They asked me whether I had brought the name of the Greek, and I told them I had looked for him but hadn't been able to find him because all the Greeks looked so much alike. I had gone up to one, thinking it was him, but he did not know the first thing about the matter, and I was not going to drag an innocent person into the process.

They stared at me in disbelief, knowing I was lying, but they had run out of ways to make me speak. They smiled and winked at each other, conferred in another room and returned shortly after with my sentence: half a day on my knees and sixty days in the *Strafkommando* (punishment brigade).

I was led straight out and made to kneel with a brick in each outstretched hand. Across from me kneeled the block elder in the same position. Neither of us looked at the other—he because of shame, I because of disgust. The half-day of kneeling was worse than death. Several times I fainted. Each time I was revived and made to kneel again until the torture ended.

When I returned to the camp that night, my friends were ecstatic. Everybody came running, and even the block elders and the *Kapos* praised my behavior and condemned the treachery of the block elder. They all went to the *Kapo* of the *Strafkommando,* who looked like a young boy, and asked him to treat me with care because I had endured such hard questioning without giving in. The *Kapo* said he would do all he could to protect me. Dr. Suchodolsky bandaged my wounds.

He sat beside me all night, applying salves, and in this way he saved my life. He even took me into the infirmary for two days, having received permission to do so from the head doctor, so that I would not have to go straight to the punishment brigade in such terrible shape. Yet in the infirmary I felt even worse—the ambiance had a depressing effect on me. I looked at the sick, the *Muselmänner,* who were covered with wounds and struggling with death. They were pleading for death but the Angel of Death took no pity on them. They lay three or four to a bed, with high fever and in great pain, each infecting the next. I wanted to escape this place despite the great pain I was in because I could not stand the foul air.

On the third day I left the infirmary and reported to the *Kapo* of the *Strafkommando.* I had to appear before five in the morning because at six we were to leave for the village of Stara Wies, on the road to Otwock. There we were to clear a woodlot and prepare the ground for a sanitarium.

The *Kapo* would keep his word and treat me decently. I was to be one of his servants—to tend his fire, prepare his food, and guard his things.

45

The First Day in the Strafkommando

I had lost my independent post, where I had survived in peace without being beaten much by the *Kapos* and where I had had enough food. Even so, I was glad I hadn't been sentenced to death, and the *Kapo* here had promised me good treatment. I was happy as well to be leaving the crowded ghetto for a place where I could breathe fresh air.

My first day in the *Strafkommando* was a terrible one for me. Before dawn we were loaded onto a transport wagon on a branch track that ran alongside the Umschlag Platz of terrible fame. Here, amid scenes of unbearable heartbreak, hundreds of thousands of Jews from Warsaw region had been loaded onto cattle cars for shipment to the death camp at Treblinka. Even today the earth there is soaked with blood and tears. No signs linger of those heart-shattering days: the area has been cleared and is covered with grass. One even sees wildflowers swaying in the spring breeze. In the blooms of those flowers I see the staring eyes of children, eyes that were shut so cruelly by the Nazi murderers.

Outside, it is the eve of Passover, 1944. The door of our wagon is half-open. Outside stand SS guards with machine guns. We are forbidden to stand near the doors, but from a distance we can admire the free world. We watch people move about freely, enjoying the spring sunshine, and we envy them. The sun is melting the last snow of the harsh winter, and its warm rays are reviving the earth. The trees are beginning to bud as the world turns green again. In the Polish forests, the young needles of pine trees are shining in the golden light. But this sun here does not burn for everyone. It has a golden smile for the German children we see playing with all the joy of life. It is shining for the fat, stout Germans who are striding across all Europe, stealing for themselves all the joy of life.

137

The sun hardly shines at all for the Jewish slaves in the ghettoes and camps, and when the sun sometimes did penetrate the ghetto and camps, it was only to shed light on their tragic abandonment. For them, the sun is lighting the graves at the camps where hundreds of thousands of slaves have struggled with pain, suffering, and death. Jewish children, pale and exhausted from their lives in the cellars, ask with bitterness when they see the sun: "Is it shining just to tease us?" Too often the sun is serving as the partner of our tormentors, pouring its hot rays on us while we carry heavy loads, driven by the Nazi murderers. At such times the sunlight drains our last bit of strength. Instead of a pleasure, a blessing, the source of all life, it is a curse, something we have learned to hate.

As the wagon carried us through the forest of Swider, Michali, Otwock, there awakened in me memories of earlier times when these forests were full of Jewish summer cottagers, when the air rang with the laughter of Jewish children at play. On this day the forest was quiet as death itself. The only sounds were of the chirping birds and the steaming locomotive.

We had stopped at the Otvotsk station. Gentile girls were walking along the platform selling bread rolls, cigarettes, and lemonade. Our SS guards bought provisions for themselves. One of the girls came to our wagon, her head in a peasant's kerchief. Even from a distance I was sure I had seen her before. When she came a little closer, she saw me and turned white as a sheet. Now I knew: she was the youngest daughter of my downstairs neighbors in Sosnowiec. She was disguising herself as a gentile, staying alive by selling snacks at Otvotsk station. I forced myself to stay back from her, not to utter a word. I was barely able to contain myself. The girl walked away quickly. Probably she could sense the panic I felt. All day and all night I was haunted by that chance meeting.

At the work site, the *Kapo* noticed my bewilderment and asked me if I was all right. I replied that I was still weak from the beating I had taken. He told me to sit by the fire and prepare his food and help the cook prepare the watery soup for noontime. While he was my *Kapo,* that would be my task.

All day the other slaves carried and piled up felled trees, driven by the foremen. The crackle of falling timber and the snap of breaking bones were the only sounds. An SS guard was beating all the slaves on the head with a tree branch to make them work faster. It was a pitiful scene. The slaves were pouring with sweat, and many of them collapsed. Those who did were forced to rise quickly. Those who could not were beaten to a pulp and left for dead.

This *Kommando* left at six each morning and returned to camp at eight each evening. The slaves were made to work at a frantic pace to the beatings of the SS and the *Kapo* and his foremen. They came home each night utterly exhausted and despairing, carrying with them their dead.

My body was aching worse and worse. I couldn't sit because my buttocks were one big wound. Nor could I stand without help; I had to lean against a tree. It was a miracle I didn't have to do hard labor and that I was permitted to keep warm by the fire, to which I kept adding branches. The fresh air also had a soothing effect on me and helped me clear my lungs. I was in great pain, yet I could still enjoy the fresh, fragrant air, the smell of pine needles and the warmth of the sun.

The *Strafkommando* became for me a place to heal. This was entirely thanks to the influence of my friends and those whose respect I had earned. Each evening when we returned they were waiting for me in my block to ask about my health. Each of them brought me some little thing to strengthen me and encourage me. They also hoped to hear a good word from me. They missed my political commentary.

Unfortunately, I no longer belonged to a construction *Kommando,* so I had no way to "organize" newspapers. But my friends still were able to find me scraps of newspaper, the bits that had been used as wrapping for the parcels received by the German foremen and the Poles. These I would read for any news. Later I would comment on what I read, letting my imagination run free. I described the situation in the rosiest colors, feeling that I was giving my listeners new hope. I could see in their eyes that my words were a balm to them.

In fact the news *was* good. The Germans were being pushed back on all fronts. According to the Poles we talked to, and from our observation, the Germans were becoming demoralized. They all seemed to know that their advances had been halted, that the Wehrmacht were being pushed back everywhere. They were beginning to lose their faith in victory. Only the fanatics among them believed that the Führer would be able to reverse the war's course, pull them out of the swamp into which they had sunk and establish for them the "Thousand Year Reich."

Rommel's armies had been driven from Africa. The Allies had landed in France and were threatening Germany itself. The Russians had taken back Byelorussia and were marching toward Poland. I described all this to my friends. Then, extrapolating, I predicted what would happen next. With considerable accuracy, as it turned out . . .

46

Jews Bake Matzo in Hell

I rode every day to work with the *Strafkommando* to the forests of Stara Wies. I gradually recovered from the beatings. My skin was still bruised and bloody, but it had started to heal. I was very satisfied with this *Kommando,* though food was scanty here. The only thing I could not stand was that my friends in the *Kommando* were suffering so much and being driven so brutally. They were never given a chance to catch their breath but were constantly rushed: "Get going, get going!" The SS guards in charge of the *Kommandos* had been chosen especially for their sadism, and they rejoiced at others' suffering. The setbacks at the fronts had little effect on them. They were bloodthirsty, and they believed blindly that their Führer would prevail. I still shudder at the memory of them.

Unfortunately, I could not help my friends at all. I had no influence on the *Kapo* or the foremen, and certainly not on the SS. The beatings I watched them administer depressed me terribly. More than once I wanted to shout: "Leave those people alone!" But I bit my tongue because they might well have killed me. So I kept all this inner agony to myself for the sake of my own survival.

In this *Kommando* the worst days for me were the Sundays. According to the "statutes" of the *Strafkommando,* that was also a workday, but it was also the day my "guardian" *Kapo* was not on duty. The SS guards oversaw the work on Sundays and made certain that the foreman never gave any of us a moment's rest. On that day I had to work with the others, loading wagons with bricks, hauling them to various places, and stacking them in piles. The work was arduous and dull, but I had no choice but to get used to it.

All the snow had melted, freeing the earth from its iron shackles. Foul odors began rising from the ruins of the ghetto. Meanwhile the days of

Passover 1944 arrived. Some of my friends had kept a reckoning. One of them was Maier, a Slavic Jew, who was observant. He was tall and broad-shouldered, with a pair of bright, sharp eyes. He never lost his faith in the Creator and served him with all his body and soul. Whenever he had a spare moment he prayed, recited Psalms, and praised God for the good he had bestowed upon him.

This Maier succeeded in "organizing" some flour, which friends of his had found in a cellar. He hid it until Passover eve, with the intention of baking matzo so as to fulfill the commandment of eating matzo.

A day before Passover a few shadows, my own among them, found their way into an empty storage closet. We placed two friends outside as a precaution against the Germans. Then we lit a fire and on it placed a tin pan that had been scrubbed and koshered. We kneaded and rolled the matzo dough and placed it in our "oven." We had to do this in the dark so as not to attract attention.

The flames under the pan cast a soft glow on our faces. We stood by the fire as if around an altar, each of us absorbed in the holiness of the preparation: here we were, a few young men risking a holy service in a concentration camp. When I close my eyes I can still see those moments perfectly. If only I had a talent for drawing, I could produce from this memory a unique and precious sanctification of God.

On the first Seder night we came home from work and gathered in Block 3, where Maier had his bunk. We placed a couple of boards on two boxes, covered the boards with a piece of white sheet that someone had brought from a cellar, and began to perform the Seder. Maier had also brought *Hagadot* that we had found among the piles of holy books in the ruins. Besides being Passover, it was the anniversary of the Warsaw ghetto uprising. That bloody drama had taken place less than a hundred meters from us. This camp was on Gesia Street where the Polish stockade once stood, and extended down to Smocza Street, and on the other side to Zamenhoff Street, where the Judenrat headquarters once was. During the uprising this latter building had been the command post of the resistance. There had taken place bitter fighting between a few isolated and desperate martyrs and the most powerful military force in Europe. Here, in this place of Jewish martyrdom, a few slaves were able to perform one year later a new act of Jewish holiness, continuing the tradition of generations.

The words of the *Hagada* ring out: "In every generation there arise those who want to destroy us, but the Holy One, blessed be He, rescues us from their hands." Maier speaks the words with great intensity, and we repeat after him. The pale, thin faces peering down from the wooden bunks watch closely. At that moment a spark of hope lights their hearts and their pale lips utter: *"HaKadosh, Baruch Hu, Matzileinu M'yadam"* (And God, blessed be He, rescues us from their hands).

We have no wine because it would have come from a Pole, so it would not be kosher, and we do not want to stain the holiness of the holiday. So instead we distribute to each man there a piece of matzo the size of an olive. Then, with great intensity and tear-filled eyes, we say the words: "And we shall cry out for our God, the God of our fathers, and He will hear our voices and will see our troubles and our suffering and will save us."

The world of the largest Jewish community in Europe lies in utter ruin. From Gesia Street 43 and 66 we smell the smoke of burning human flesh. Hell is aflame on all sides of us and is swallowing up the last remnants of Europe's Jewish community. Yet here, in the very midst of our sufferings, matzos are being baked and Passover eve, the time of our freedom, is being celebrated.

It was for me a great honor and a very emotional experience to participate in this sanctification of God. This scene is engraved in my memory and in my heart.

47

Typhoid Breaks Out in the Camp

As long as the ground was snow covered, everything remained frozen. Once the spring sunshine melted the ice and snow, everything started to come apart. The corpses that were buried in the ruins began rotting and disintegrating and filling the air with a foul stench. Extra *Kommandos* were established to gather the dead and burn them in piles, but some bodies were missed, so the warmer it got the more foul the air became.

In addition to this, the slaves became filthy and infested with lice. We could gather lice by the shovelful. They covered our bodies and sucked out our last bit of blood. We would take off our clothes and shake the lice out as if shaking out a dust cloth. We developed boils and infections from scratching our wounds.

Procedures were established for disinfecting and delousing our clothes. All of us also did what we could to kill the lice by our own methods. But nothing helped, because the blocks were also infested. To rid ourselves completely of them, we would have had to burn the blocks down. Sleep was impossible; each night under the glow of the electric bulb we saw clouds of lice crawling over our covers, heads, faces, and skin. We could scoop them up by the handful without even looking. There was no escaping them, no matter what we tried.

We were seldom able to change our clothes, which hung from us like disintegrating rags. Those who worked in the outside *Kommandos* brought rags back with them from the cellars. These smelled and were full of germs and other dangers.

It did not take long for the consequences to manifest themselves. A typhus epidemic broke out and quickly assumed catastrophic proportions. At first, typhus was only a rumor to us, but within a few days the whisperers were packing the infirmaries. There was no room in the sick bays for so many. Five or six shared a bed, never mind what illnesses they had, and in this way they infected one another. The straw mattresses had rotted long before, so people were placed directly on bare planks.

There were no medicines. Infirmary aides sold the clothes of the sick and stole their rations of bread and margarine—after all, what use did they have now for food? Very often the dying lay together with the dead because there was no time to remove the latter. Besides, these aides told themselves, better to keep them around and continue collecting their food rations. But these aides themselves were hardly immune: fate sought them out too.

Each day the epidemic grew worse. It swallowed people without cease. Each morning, when we woke, we watched our friends being carried out, never to return. In the morning I would be talking to a friend; in the afternoon he would be dead. All my neighbors in the block, those who slept above me and those who slept beside me, the epidemic seized them all. By a miracle I myself did not get sick. Perhaps this is because I had started to eat raw onions and garlic, which my friends brought to me from the construction sites. These foods killed the germs and enabled me to resist the epidemic. The epidemic did not spare the healthy and the strong—in fact, these succumbed even faster. The *Kapos* and foremen were not spared either. The corpse wagons were constantly being hauled away.

In one of the wagons I recognized my tailor, Applebaum, from Modrzew near Sosnowiec. All the *Kapos* and foremen had gone to him for alterations. He had not suffered from hunger in the camp, because his trade provided him with sufficient food, but even so he succumbed as well. The dead lay everywhere. In front of the blocks there were piles of naked bodies covered with sores. They lay like garbage, waiting for the wagon to pick them up for burning.

The SS immediately quarantined the camp. Roll calls ceased because the guards were afraid to enter the gates. For those who were still healthy there were still *Arbeitskommandos* and the *Kapos* and foremen still ran them; but these were assigned now to cleaning up the camp. Anyone, who could stand, still had to work for his meager rations.

The rumor spread that the SS was planning to burn the camp down so that the epidemic would not spread to Warsaw. They might even have done it—to the Nazis, a few thousand slaves didn't matter much. But before they got around to it, we slaves on our own took radical measures to halt the epidemic. We burned all the rags and straw mattresses. We started scrubbing and cleaning the blocks. For this purpose we were provided with quicklime, matches, and disinfectants.

I was horrified when someone was sent to tell me that Dr. Suchodolsky was among the sick and was lying with high fever in the doctors' infirmary. I immediately ran to see him. I was not allowed to enter but was able to send in some food for him, including onions and garlic. Each day I returned to the infirmary window to find out what he needed. There was no limit to my joy when I saw him outside one day, walking on his own two feet. I provided him with strengthening foods and with medicines that I had "organized" from my contacts among the *Kapos* and block elders. I finally restored my friend to good health.

48

After the Epidemic

At the end of May the epidemic finally ended. The roll calls and *Kommandos* resumed. At the roll calls the rows were far shorter than before, and the ranks were much thinned out. Over half of us had died: twenty-five hundred victims.

Blocks 7 and 8 had been converted into sick bays during the epidemic. Afterward they remained empty because there were no longer slaves to occupy them. But very soon after new transports arrived full of Hungarian and Dutch Jews to fill the empty places.

These newcomers told us about the situation in the outside world. The Wehrmacht was on the defensive everywhere and falling back. Deserters were being shot en masse, and the mayor of Breslau, a man named Spiegelhagen, had been shot for attempting to evacuate his post. We ourselves could tell from the faces of the SS guards that the situation for the Germans was not good. They had lost their bravado and their arrogance. On the quiet, many of them were hinting to us inmates that the war wasn't going to last much longer, that we might soon gain our freedom.

At the beginning of June 1944, we heard that the Allies had crossed the English Channel to Normandy in a massive invasion by sea and air and had breached the Germans' coastal defenses. This infuriated many of our guards, who let their anger out on us. But the news had given us the strength to endure these difficult days. Among my friends, I used all my journalistic skills—and all my imagination—to describe the political and military situation in the rosiest colors. I spoke so enthusiastically that I myself started to believe what I was telling them. My satisfaction was great when I saw how my words encouraged my audience. Many of them dreamed sweetly after hearing me, in the belief that if they survived the dark night they would awaken to peace and freedom.

One day toward the end of July, the entire sky lit up with slowly descending flares, almost as if it were Christmas. We began to hear shooting. Soon after, an alarm was sounded in the camp. The block elders and house aides were ordered to make sure we didn't show ourselves. We were ordered to lie on the ground until the alarm ended. We got down from our beds, stretched out on the ground, and looked up at the sky with love, courage, and hope. The prospect of liberation seemed very close.

We later learned that it was the Russians that had been firing the flares. They had already reached the opposite bank of the Vistula but would remain there for a good time yet without attempting to cross. This delay was for political reasons. They wanted to crush the Germans with one blow, together with the Polish National Movement that was grouped around the AK (Krajowa Army), so they wouldn't end up fighting two battles. Better, they judged, to defeat both enemies at once. But we didn't realize it at the time. Even so, their flares that had illuminated our night had given us new strength and hope.

49

We Await Evacuation from Warsaw

Some of us were still going to work, though under close guard. Only those *Kommandos* that had vital work were being sent out. The *Strafkommando* was disbanded: the Germans were afraid to take us out of the camp because the Polish partisans were preparing an uprising.

The SS leaders did not know what to do with the Warsaw camp. We slaves—more than four thousand of us—might well join the Polish revolt when it began. Besides that, the Russians could cross the Vistula any time and take over the camp. Faced with these threats to their position, at the end of July 1944 they decided to evacuate us from Warsaw.

On July 27, 1944, the air was sweltering. The earth lay quiet under the blue sky. The broad, deep roll call square of the Warsaw camp was packed with tired, exhausted slaves. We had been chased out of the blocks and told to wait. We four thousand slaves—95 percent of us Jews, from every European country—lay roasting under unrelenting sun, waiting to hear our fate. We clustered in groups, conversing only with our eyes. None of us had the strength to speak after a day without food. The strain on us quickly became unendurable.

A roll call was announced, and every living creature in the camp assembled for it, including all the SS and the entire staff of the camp. The SS all came in their parade uniforms as if to a gala performance. This roll call stretched out interminably. The SS probably did not want to rush this last one. We slaves knew by now that this was our last roll call in Warsaw and perhaps forever.

Our hearts pounded, our souls rose and fell in torment like the sea in a storm, our eyes and ears strained to catch every sight and sound. We already knew that the order had come down to evacuate us. But where would they

149

take us? If there was nowhere for us to go, they would finish us off right here since the Russians were already at their heels and they had to act quickly. The night before, they had set fire to their headquarters, burning all documents they didn't want to take with them. They had also doubled the guards on the watchtowers and encircled the entire camp with heavily armed soldiers. The guards were nervous.

We became even more restless when all the Aryans among us were ordered to assemble separately. Many of the Aryan *Kapos* and block elders, when they left our ranks, cast pitying glances on the rest of us, as if to say, "You poor lost bastards." Many others looked pleased, as if to say, "It's true we're criminals and jail birds, but we belong to the master race." I looked at my friends' faces and understood we were all certain that death was at hand: that the last act of our lives was almost certainly being staged.

A rumor spread through our ranks that the Greeks were planning an uprising. We all knew what the consequences would be, yet in our hearts we were ready to support it. We knew we had nothing to lose, and we weren't going to be sheep to the slaughter. At least we would die fighting. With nods to one another, we gathered our resolve to act.

A voice bellowed into the loudspeaker: "All those who feel weak, who have weak legs and cannot march more than one hundred kilometers, should step forward and they will be transported by truck." All the veterans among us, the ones who well knew the tricks the SS played, winked to one another. We urged the greenhorns among us not to step forward: this was certainly a trap the SS was setting. To our regret, many of the older and weaker slaves did come forward, certain they couldn't walk so far. They had given up on life and didn't want to fight any longer.

I myself tried to prevent a Hungarian Jew from stepping forward. I pleaded with him: "Man, what are you doing? At the last moment you're going to throw away your own life? Maybe you will be able to endure this last crisis."

But he tore himself from my grip. "I've had enough," he insisted. "I'd rather die than live like this. With my swollen feet, in these clogs, how can I march a hundred kilometers?" He and 240 others formed a line, and the SS escorted them to the transport, which lifted them to heaven before the rest of us.

The roll call ended, but we were ordered not to return to our blocks or to leave the square. Instead we were to await further orders. The SS was having great difficulty arranging our evacuation. No rail lines were open to us, and no trucks were available. They were going to have to walk us out of the city—a dangerous tactic, with the Poles on the edge of revolt and the Russians just across the Vistula. The only open road was the one through Lowicz-Kutno, but that one was packed with German troops and civilian evacuees. Furthermore, it was going to be dangerous to guard and keep together four thousand slaves in the midst of so much upheaval, with the Russians on one side and the partisans on the other. On top of all this, the SS were looking to save themselves. That meant leaving as quickly as possible, before the Russians overpowered them, which could happen at any moment. For all these reasons, the SS attempted to provoke us into revolting so that they would be justified in murdering us on the spot.

They withdrew most of their guards, leaving only a handful in the watchtowers. Then they made us stay all day on the roll call square under the broiling sun without food or water, hoping this would drive us to revolt. Later, in another attempt to provoke us, they led us off in groups of one hundred without telling us where we were being taken. We were supposed to think we were being led off to be shot. When we heard machine gun fire, all of us shook with fear. Then, in a last attempt, they cordoned us off so that we couldn't move at all. They hoped we would lose patience and throw ourselves at them. If we had, they would have been able to say they had shot us because we had revolted.

But we were convinced these were provocations—that they were simply looking for a pretext to liquidate us—so we gritted our teeth and stayed put. We agreed among ourselves not to react, knowing that if we did we would be jeopardizing all our lives. At the last moment, if we saw they were leading us to the Judenrat building on Zamenhoff Street, near the new crematorium, we would fall upon our guards and at least die with honor.

Meanwhile we baked in the sun. Each of us was deep in thought, making a personal reckoning. Into my mind there sprang scenes and episodes of my life, of my youth. I closed my eyes and saw people passing by, faces and figures whom I had long forgotten. I saw my father, may he rest in peace, gazing at me with all his love and tenderness. I saw the steadfast look of my mother, from whose eyes tears were flowing. She was showing me her prayer book, Korben Minchah Siddur, from which she was praying and offering a prayer for me. As if through the lens of a camera, all these scenes and pictures unfolded for me, pieces of my life that was about to end. Then I awoke from these dreams and beheld a mass of shriveled bodies, skin and bones, desperate and bitter, with the fear of death in their eyes. We had been condemned and were waiting to be executed. Our hearts ached for all the years we had suffered so much, gone through such hell. Now, with the end so close, with freedom in sight, we were about to lose our lives.

"You know what," a friend told me that day, "I would like to live at least one day after the end of the war, to live to see the day of revenge! Our lives will be ruined anyhow because after all we went through, all that we saw and endured, after having lost all our near and dear ones, what sense will our lives have? The only thing that keeps me going is to see the day of revenge, to see our hangmen get publicly judged, to be able to slit their throats and see how their blood runs—not ours but theirs—to be able to spit in the faces of the murderers." These words he spat out from his tortured soul. His eyes burned with a strange fire. "Revenge!" he sputtered. "Revenge! It is that day that I want to live to see and then I can die." These words echoed symbolically through the ruins of the largest Jewish community in Europe. The shattered walls of the Warsaw ghetto overlooked the tragedy of the last remnants of European Jewry, breathing their last breaths before their extinction.

In the evening came another command: "Everyone in the blocks! Tomorrow at three in the morning everyone is to get up and be on the march from Warsaw." Breathing easier, we returned to our blocks. That night was a stormy one. Once more the *Stalimtkertzen* (the Russians' flares) lit up the sky. We were not allowed to approach the windows, but from a distance we could watch the spectacle and see and hear the flak batteries as they lit up the sky. It looked like magic to us, like fireworks at an amusement park. We clasped one another's hands and rejoiced. "With God's help," we encouraged one another, "we may see our liberation this very night."

But our joy did not last. The shooting soon stopped. We lay on the hard boards and waited for a miracle, until the wake-up gong halted our dreams. Once more we were hurried out for roll call. There, three hundred of us were selected to stay in the camp to do cleanup and various work. Dr. Suchodolsky was dragged out from my row to remain as camp doctor. He wanted to leave with the rest of us and did not want to be separated from me. I asked to stay behind too, to be with him, but this was forbidden. Parting with him was unbearable. I had lost my dear friend forever. I learned later that he perished in the Warsaw uprising.

50

We March out of Warsaw

On July 28, 1944, before dawn, we march out of the Warsaw camp. We can see a clear blue sky through the wreckage of the ghetto. We march in groups of one hundred, ten to a row, led by a *Kapo* or block elder and guarded on all sides by heavily armed SS and their attack dogs. They make sure we stick together and keep a steady pace.

For the last time I look at the destroyed Warsaw ghetto, which had once been the Mother City of Israel. More than once I had enjoyed myself in the Jewish-Polish metropolis. I had known all the streets very well. All of them have been destroyed now: Dzika, Gesia, Nalewki, Smocza, Pawia, Twarda, Nowolipki, Zamenhoff, and many others. This had been the glorious heart of Poland's Jewry, which once had numbered three-and-a-half million. Now all is rubble and the last remnants of European Jewry are marching out from the wasteland. I stare at collapsing walls that point to heaven as if to protest their destruction. The sun's golden rays penetrate the ruins as if to lick their open wounds. To me the ruins are alive and waving to us: "Farewell, farewell, my children."

As we march out the gates of the ghetto, we see for the first time in years a place where people are living in freedom. The streets are alive with people walking freely, strolling along, eating, and sleeping wherever they wish and as much as they like. It all looks alien to me. White bread and rolls in every street, and people too indifferent to buy them. A woman passes wearing clean clothes. How often I have dreamed of such things: white bread, clean clothes, a soft bed, and to be able to sleep, sleep forever. We march past the Warsaw streets. Doors and windows open, and people come onto their balconies in their night clothes to stare at the spectacle of our passing, at this caravan of slaves. Some of them have tears in their eyes, others are wringing their hands, still others look happy to see us suffering. Words of scorn can be heard: *"Zhidi, Koti"* (Jews, cats).

I turn to look one last time. The ghetto's ruins stretch heavenward like captives beckoning from behind a wall. They cast a shadow of fear over all of Warsaw, over the whole world. This destruction will not end at the Warsaw ghetto boundaries. It will extend much farther, to cities and countries, to large and wealthy boulevards and streets, and will destroy everything that human civilization has created over countless generations. Those who caused all this destruction will soon be destroyed themselves.

From the other side of the ghetto, smoke is rising that stinks of burning flesh. It pierces our hearts when we remind ourselves that in ovens they are burning the corpses of fresh victims, those who were still alive yesterday morning, dreaming about and hoping for freedom, who felt they were too tired for the march and chose to be transported by truck. A poke from a gun wakes me from my thoughts and shoves me back into line. The push makes me drop my eating bowl, which falls with a clatter to the Warsaw pavement.

Anyhow, who at such a moment thinks about eating? None of us has an appetite as we reflect on the ruined streets that were once so familiar to us. As dawn breaks, more than four thousand pairs of wooden clogs clack along the streets of the Polish capital. Groups of Poles gather at street corners to watch our caravan of skeletons. We move like robots in our striped clothes. We look to either side, hoping in spite of everything that the Polish resistance will attack our column and offer us a last chance to be free. We know very well that for quite some time the Russians have been on the opposite bank of the Vistula. We also know that our evacuation is common knowledge in Warsaw. The Poles who worked with us in the ghetto knew exactly what was going to happen. The day before, a woman on a balcony we could see from the camp had signaled to us with her hand that the city had been encircled. But the miracle never happened. All the help that Warsaw will extend us is a few sympathetic glances and a few drops of women's tears.

Warsaw soon disappears from sight. The suburbs give way to green fields. The road is blocked by soldiers and by evacuated German civilians and their loot. They are fleeing as if from a fire, back to their country. The right-hand side of the road is reserved for us. Jammed together as we are, we are forced to trample one another to avoid the beatings of the guards. We are being driven like sheep. The chief "drover," Kramer, follows, standing up in his car in a Führer pose, driving us on, roaring at the top of his voice:"You gang of swine! You Jewish rabble, I'll show you how to march!" *Umshmis* on his motorcycle is fluttering about us like a bird, hounding the weak, frightened mass of us to move faster. Whoever cannot hurry up ends up under his wheels.

Each of us, feeling the Angel of Death perched on his shoulder, marches as quickly as possible with his last bit of strength. Whenever the senior officer feels like it, he commands,"Run!" So we run on rubbery legs, losing our clogs on the way, just to get away from the murderers.

By noon the heat is unbearable. The sun burns relentlessly. The SS guards take off their helmets and unbutton their shirts. We slaves begin throwing away our excess belongings. Anyone who has two blankets throws away at least one, but this barely helps. The sun is unbearable, and our four thousand pairs of clogs raise a cloud of dust that covers our clothes, our faces, and our lungs and glues our tongues to our mouths. The beatings we take no longer have an effect. The shouts of "Lift your legs higher!" do no good: no one has strength any longer to lift their legs. Everyone is pleading:"Water! At least a sip of water!"

We march past villages, peasant cottages, rivers. We continue to plead for water to wet our leathery tongues, but a blow from a truncheon is the only response. "Keep marching! You'll get that further on." Peasants come out with pitchers of water, but they are not permitted to approach us. The SS drink this water themselves and give none to us. They also take turns visiting the cottages, to feed and wash themselves, strengthening their courage to drive us faster.

Our legs cannot carry us any longer. Rivers of sweat run down us. The many of us who can no longer keep up are pulled from the column and shot by the roadside. Near me is a friend, Nechemya Neier from Modrzew. He has a strong build, broad shoulders. In Warsaw he had a very good *Kommando*—*Friedhof* (cemetery), the metal scrap yard near the Gesia cemetery. That was where the iron and steel scavenged from the ghetto was gathered. He was the *Kommando*'s clerk, and has kept himself very fit. But he can no longer endure this march.

"I cannot keep going any longer!" he tells me with glazed eyes. "My feet can't carry me any longer."

"What's happening to you, Nechemya?" I appeal to him. "You want to kill yourself? Keep going. Hang on to me. Strengthen yourself. You can't give up at the last minute."

My pleading doesn't help. He wrenches himself away. "I can't go on any longer," he groans. "It's all the same to me. Whatever will happen, let it happen now. I don't want to suffer any more."

He remains on the ground awaiting death. A bullet puts an end to his young life. I will never forget his last look. His eyes expressed so much sorrow, bitterness, and desperation. Once more I have lost one of my closest friends; we had been in the camp together from the very first minute. Together we had spun dreams, together we had made plans and prepared ourselves for the struggle. Often he would tell me stories of his life, of his youth. For me he opened all the chambers of his soul. Often he would show me a smuggled picture of his wife and child—a beautiful young woman and a darling little child—and tell me that was what gave him strength and courage. "Because of them," he would say to me, "it's worth struggling and hoping. I know they're alive and waiting for me."

They will not see that day. This death march has swallowed him up and spat him out. If his wife and child are alive, I can only tell them about his last look.

His death shocks me deeply. I feel as if a piece of me has been torn away. I gather all my strength and march on. Military columns tread by. Officers stop and look at us as if we were ghosts. Our skeletons limp past them, looking less than human. They ask our guards what sort of criminals they are accompanying. When they learn we are Jews, they nod their approval: the Führer's plan is unfolding as it should.

We drag ourselves on like this until sundown. Our blackened lips spit out bitterness and curses. Our last shred of energy is leaving us. Then, miraculously, a command: "To the right, take a rest!"

We struggle to a piece of open ground, which is immediately encircled by SS guards with machine guns and attack dogs. No longer able to take another step, we fall to the ground like sacks of bricks. The ground is warm, heated by the sun. At last our legs can rest. We sink down with our faces toward the ground to benefit from the moisture, to cool our sunburnt faces. The sun is setting in red-hot flames, as if dipped in blood.

Gradually night covers us. We are forbidden to stand up. We would not have the strength to do so anyhow. Bread is distributed, but only to those who have the strength to form the line for it. Most of us lack the will to rise, since we could not eat anyway. Our mouths are too dry. Only later is some "coffee" brought.

Though I am dead tired, I cannot fall asleep. My bones ache too badly, and I have seen too much that day to risk dreaming about it. My mind is flooded with terrible images. In my ears there still ring the wild shouts of our guards, mixed with the tearful pleas of the dying slaves—"Water, water, a sip of water"—and the last words of my friend—"I can't go on any more." As if he was pleading for my forgiveness:"I *can't* any more." In the night, I see the Warsaw streets. I open my eyes and stare at the canopy of the sky across which a full moon is traveling like a sail. A cool breeze brushes my face and hair and lulls me to sleep. I sink deeper into the night and embrace it as if fearing that someone will grab it back. I shudder at the thought of how brief the night is. Daylight will soon appear with the sun's strong rays to scorch us and drive us farther on our march.

51

The Second Day of the Death March from Warsaw to Dachau

When the alarm woke us, night had already vanished. The bright new day uncovered thousands of crippled, dusty, dirty bodies. We greeted the new day with fear and suspicion. Everyone got up quickly—the SS guards were already carrying on wildly, hurrying everyone to line up for roll call. They counted us and also counted how many had died in the night. Bread and black water were again distributed, and then we were made to march again.

On this morning we were made to march at a quicker tempo to take advantage of the cooler morning hours. We marched past houses and villages where the people were just waking up. The sun soaked up the dew on the fields and sported with the stalks of wheat, which were heavy with grain. A group of *Hitlerjugend* (Hitler Youth) in crisp new uniforms marched past us, looking arrogantly at us, the slaves of the Third Reich.

Once more the sun began to burn with all its might. I took a bit of bread in my mouth but couldn't swallow it—my mouth and tongue were too dry. My only desire was for a sip of water. By noon it was again unbearably hot. The heat began to bake my whole body. I licked the salty sweat that ran down my forehead to moisten my burnt tongue. That helped very little. On the horizon something sparkled in the sun—the spire of a church. All eyes turned in that direction. With pleading eyes we whispered: "Water . . . Water . . ." Our eyes started to burn feverishly. Everyone wanted to be closer to the river, if not to drink then at least to look at the shining surface.

As we neared the shtetl we read a large sign: SOCHACZEW. This name left us speechless, for it was famous throughout the Jewish world. It was associated with the Sochaczew Rebbe, whose thousands of Hassidic followers had once come to him on the three religious festivals. The Sochaczew dynasty was world famous. The grandfather of the last Sochaczew Rebbe had been a son-in-law of the rebbe from Koch, and had himself been a great scholar. Only the most promising scholars were admitted to the Sochaczew yeshiva—the brightest and most disciplined.

When I saw the sign I trembled, remembering what the name represented. This was a "mother city" of Israel. I knew this shtetl was already clean of Jews, like so many others, and I wanted to see what this archetypical Polish-Jewish city looked like when the Jews had been driven out. A shudder ran through me when we encountered, right at the entrance of the shtetl, a division of Russian Cossacks. These were Wlasowcy, the notorious Russian Cossacks, who were fighting on the side of the Nazis. What an appropriate coupling . . .

This shtetl made a horrible impression on us. Every house, every stone, reminded us of Jewish life. The streets and houses remained, but no Jews had survived. Through the windows of the houses peered red, ugly faces, and in the streets blond gentile children were playing. The Shloimelech, Berelech, and Yoselech were no longer present: Hitler had murdered them all. It was as if I could hear the choking sobs of those who perished. Their weeping stabbed at my heart. We, the last remnant of European Jewry, continued marching past the defiled streets of what had once been a traditional Hassidic community toward an uncertain tomorrow.

52

The Third Day of the March

The most dreadful day of our march was the third one. Beginning before dawn we were herded nonstop. The SS guards were completely wild that day. They themselves were exhausted, even though they were spelling one another every few hours, with the tired ones riding in the vehicles that were accompanying us. All any of us could see were the sticks and truncheons over our heads. Now people were constantly falling out. Every guard stepped on the collapsed ones as he passed, and finally a special guard finished off those of us who had fallen by the wayside.

Every little while we heard the shouted command: *"Lauf!"* (Run!). Then the guards would chase us with clubs. It was of no help that all of us had thrown away our shoes and discarded all unessential belongings. We couldn't stand it any more. The greatest number of victims were swallowed up this day. We were soaked with sweat and stifled by thick clouds of dust. Our legs buckled. It seemed to us that the entire world, heaven and earth, had ganged up against us. Nature and humanity tormented us without pity.

For the first time, I broke down completely. I felt I could not continue any longer, that my life was about to end. The terrible thirst, the heat and running, had drained me completely.

My mouth was parched. My leathery tongue was stuck to the roof of my mouth. My eyes were beginning to pop from their sockets. I ran up to a guard and opened my heart to him: "Look, I'm completely parched. Give me a sip of water or kill me!" For a reply, I got a blow with a club. I reeled back into the line, unconscious. My friends caught me so that I would not fall. They wiped my sweat with dirty rags and revived me and supported me. I awoke, regained my senses somewhat and, supported by my friends, was able to keep marching.

When all our energy was gone, when we were dragging ourselves as if not on our own feet, truly with our last bit of strength, we heard the command:"Everyone left . . . Rest . . ." This was salvation for us all. Like a bolt of lightning the command flashed through the column. Our glazed eyes suddenly brightened. To rest, beside a river! It was as if the Messiah had arrived. We went crazy with joy. We were led to a large field bordering a wide river. We were told to sit down and wait. But many of us became restless, wild at the sight of water. Flowing water! The water cast a teasing spell on us. People threw themselves down to drink without permission. At that moment we heard machine gun fire from all sides. As the first victims fell, the water mingled with their blood. Even as they were falling, the victims continued trying to lap up water from the moist earth. They wanted their tongues to be wet so that they could utter their last curse:"May you be cursed forever."

We were ordered to start marching again. Our pleas and cries did not help. The *Kapos,* who despite everything had got some water, beat us back into formation. We were led out onto the road once more. As we passed a ditch, I threw myself down and scooped up a mouthful of dirty, stagnant water, just to wet my tongue and mouth. Other friends did the same. We scrubbed our heads and faces with mud. When the SS guards saw what we were doing, they began beating us viciously with their clubs. The *Kapos* helped them push us back into line. The sand in our mouths immediately burned. A disgusting residue remained in our mouths. Still, the moisture had revived us a little. The guards were angered by our breaking the line and began driving us harder than ever, with such madness and cruelty that we barely had an instant to breathe. Those who lagged behind were shot immediately.

When we reached our night's resting place, we collapsed like a pile of bricks. We stretched out on the ground, our souls crushed by the fact that the magical river had been taken from us. Neither could we fall asleep—we were too thirsty. Our organs had nothing to function on. Dried up and burnt, we lay like the living dead.

53

The Miracle of Water

Night had descended on the mass of exhausted bodies. The moon made its way across a cloudy sky. On all sides, guards surrounded us with their light and heavy machine guns. Lying this way, people started to move slowly. Whoever had a spoon, a knife, or a bowl started to claw chunks of soil from the ground. The dark soil gave way under thousands of hands. It grew softer, until water began seeping from it. "Water! Water!" people started to murmur, and everyone's eyes began to glow. We hugged each other with joy. Word spread from mouth to mouth, from row to row. Half-dead though we were, we suddenly came alive. We arose and started to bless the water. The smell of water stirred our despondent hearts. Something miraculous, something Godly was appearing before us. Religious people, with their broken bones, rolled over to see with their own eyes this miracle, and with their dry lips uttered a prayer of thanks to the Almighty for providing it.

All over the field we slaves began digging feverishly. Every few meters water began seeping from the ground, reviving us and instilling new energy in our fragile limbs. It was as if Mother Earth had uncovered her breasts to quench the thirst of her hungry children. The sun broke through the dark clouds, lighting up the field, reflecting in the water, adding splendor to the *Yomtov* (celebration) of a few thousand slaves who celebrated the "great miracle of water."

By the time the guards realized what we were doing, it was too late to stop us. Surely they did not want to provoke a revolt. When the SS officers arrived shortly before dawn, they shrugged their shoulders, smiled ruefully, and went away. They understood they were helpless to fight nature.

◆　　◆　　◆

On the fourth day we were approaching Lowicz. The traffic along the way was much lighter. We encountered many peasants rushing to church in their Sunday clothes and carrying beads, crosses, and prayer books. The peasant girls and their boyfriends were strolling on the edge of the forest. We remembered it was Sunday, and this awakened in us a longing and a sadness: we recalled our old, idyllic life, our girls, our blessed rest. We passed peasant huts and observed signs of the calm, peaceful life—curtains, tablecloths, comfortable beds, and sufficient food. I immersed myself in thoughts and dreams, recollections and longings, until a heavy blow to my head brought me back to reality. This was compliments of the *Kapo*, who cursed me: "*Mensch, du spürsts?!*" (Hey you, do you feel that?). I cradled my head in my hands, so my hands also got their share. I ran, crying bitterly: "God, make an end to this dog's life . . ."

That night we rested in a valley between Lowicz and Zychlin. The moon was entirely hidden behind dark clouds. Chunks of bread were distributed to us, along with pieces of horse sausage and again the black water. We lay down on the ground to rest. Near me lay a Jew in his forties who looked like sixty. He raised his two bony arms heavenward, grinding his two remaining teeth, which looked like gravestones for a broken life. "Oh, God," he croaked, lacking the strength to shout, "when will our suffering end?"

Exhausted, worn out, and desperate, we had just fallen asleep when the earth began to shake. Thunder and lightning tore the sky open. It looked and sounded like the end of the world. We clung to the earth, and the earth to the night. As one man we shuddered with fear and raised our heads to watch. Our eyes lit up, shining diabolically. It was such a joy: let the earth founder together with us.

Our joy did not last. Soon a cold wind began to blow, growing stronger and stronger until it tore our rags off. An icy rain started to rip madly at our bones, growing more and more powerful. There was no place to hide. We could not get up either because we would have been shot immediately, so we clung to one another, covering our naked skin with whatever we could: a rag, a scrap of blanket, a few branches. But nothing helped. The rain pounded down and soaked us through. Soon the entire valley turned into a river. In the cold, relentless wind, we shivered with fever. The water flowed over us as if wanting to drown us. This continued all night. By morning the storm had moved off a little, though the sky was still filled with black clouds. Sometimes it started to thunder again, like the sound of distant artillery, and a flash of lightning shot through the gray dawn. We were shivering like wet cats from the damp and the cold.

Soon the staff arrived, rested and dry, dressed in proper raincoats. They watched us shiver and smiled, content with themselves. Soon came a command: "Line up!" Everyone was crying and groaning. We could barely walk because of all the mud that was clinging to us, but the SS guards and the *Kapos* with their truncheons soon reminded us not to expect any pity. They lined us up and began a strict inspection. We turned our pockets inside out and were beaten until we gave them everything. On this day the SS stole a huge amount.

We were led out to the road again and taken to the train station at Zychlin. Here, empty freight trains awaited us. We were packed in like sardines: as many as one hundred of us to each wagon designed for forty. The doorway had to remain clear because that was where the SS guards and the *Kapos* sat. Even today, I still can't remember what happened to me after I was shoved and hounded into the wagon. I must had fallen down. I was stepped on. People sat on me, but I did not feel anything. It was as if I was actually dead. A few hours later, I started to hear something, as if someone was sobbing and groaning from very far away. I awoke and saw for the first time this new version of hell. The wagon was still at the station; it hadn't moved since we boarded. We could not understand why. Later we learned that in the commotion while we were being loaded and while the previous night's dead were being buried, some of us had escaped. Some were caught and shot immediately. Others disappeared. I do not know what happened to them.

Among those who ran away was Rosenzweig, from Paris, originally from Ozero in Poland. Among those who were caught was Alben, from Paris, a very good friend. He was captured and brought back half-naked and shot. No intervention helped. Every last one of us mourned him. In the Warsaw ghetto he was known as one of the few decent *Kapos*. He never hit anyone and even helped some of us. He was one of the few humane *Kapos* any of us ever encountered, and each of us had good memories of him. May this be a comfort to him on his journey to eternity.

There is one other *Kapo* I want to mention here: Fenigstein. He wore a

Kapo's armband, yet he never lost his decency or humanity. I was far removed from him ideologically—he was a passionate communist—but he never did anyone any harm, nor did he torture anyone. Perhaps he was one of those who was made a *Kapo* to save him from being crushed by work. Whatever the case may be, I never heard anyone complain about him.

54

The Hellish Scenes in the Locked Train Wagons

We were allocated two days' rations—half a loaf of bread each, a bit of margarine, and a piece of sausage. Then the wagons were sealed shut, the train whistle blew, and the wagons began to roll. The SS guards sat near the doors. They started to curse us: *"Wie es stinkt von der Jew Bande"* (What a stink from this Jewish gang).

The senior of the *Kapos* began waving a thick belt in the air, each time slashing it down on whoever dared say a word. "I warn you," he lectured us, "there must be complete order and quiet here! Anyone who breaks discipline will die." As he spoke he kept glancing at the SS guards to see what impression his speech was making on them. Noting that they were pleased, he continued: "You must remain for the whole time exactly where you are sitting, even if you need to crap. Stay put. Naturally it's not as comfortable as your former homes or the theater, but you lived well long enough. It's no loss if not all of you reach our destination. They don't worry about it. We'll simply save some food because you're eating for free anyhow. *Ihr Jew Bande!*" he thundered, winking to the guards. "You're no good for work anymore anyhow, and it's taking you too long to die. You filthy race, you Jews. You think Truman and Stalin will help you? We'll finish you and them off together."

As we listened to him, we choked on the curses we had to keep to ourselves. We felt like spitting in the blood-red face of this "noble" German criminal who had been appointed our overseer. He had spent his entire adult life behind bars. His hands were smeared with the blood of his victims, and now he was feeling superior with his green triangle, which marked him as one of the "master race." The entire Nazi movement was made up of murderers and killers, so he was in his element.

We sat crushed against one another, unable to change position. The air

was so dense we could have cut it with a knife. When one of us groaned because his neighbor pressed on his leg, the *Kapo* jumped up: "Who did that?"
When he saw the face of the one who had made the noise, he immediately
tore into him with his belt, screaming, "You *Schweinhund!* You old *dreckig
Rabbiner!* You dare disturb the peace here?"

He lashed the poor man's head and neck with his belt buckle until blood
began to run. Then he rested for a moment before starting on a new victim.
"And you! What's wrong with you?! I'll blind you!" he roared, foaming at
the mouth, his belt slashing, his eyes flaming like a wild beast's.

The guards smiled with satisfaction. Their sadistic thirst was being sated.
The silence and stillness became absolute except for the sound of our breathing. No one noticed that in the corner there sat a person who no longer saw
or felt anything. He sat squeezed among the mass of open-eyed men with an
ironic grimace on his face and a sarcastic look in his eyes. No one realized
that he was no longer breathing until his neighbor noticed he was supporting his friend's entire weight. He looked over and saw his friend looking up
at him with a dead man's smile. At the *Kapo*'s command, the corpse was
shoved into a corner and covered with a blanket. At the next station he was
removed, together with another two who had died on the journey.

The air in the wagon stank like poison. Our wet clothes hadn't been
able to dry in the night, and now the moisture in them began to clot the atmosphere. Sitting in this condition became more and more intolerable. The
lower parts of our bodies were becoming scorched from the heat and steam.
Our feet cramped and we could not stretch them. All of this was an unbearable torture. We were racked with thirst and could barely breathe. Some of
us stripped off our clothes, but this was no help. We had to perform our bodily functions in the wagon, from which we were never let out. At the second
door, human waste began to accumulate, then run off in all directions. All
this, together with the breath of close to a hundred people, and the foul odor
of a few decaying corpses, left no air for us to breathe.

The train continued chugging through Polish territory. We knew we
were heading for German territory, the very jaws of the beast. None of us
knew what would happen in the following days. We knew the war was
about to end and that the Germans would be the losers, but as far as our personal destiny was concerned, none of us had any illusions that we would escape this hell with our lives. Once the Germans accepted that they had lost

the war, they weren't going to let us live; they weren't going to leave any witnesses to their atrocities. So we all assumed. Yet we also wanted so much to live and see the end of the war, to live for at least one day after the downfall of the Nazis, to see that with our own eyes and know they were paying for their bestial sins. Then we would be able to die in peace.

Dusk was followed by darkness, which covered the mass of living dead with a blanket of shadows. The only light was from the cigarettes of the guards near the door, who smoked constantly, probably to keep our stench away. It was getting worse by the second. Every minute another uproar broke out in some corner because the people could not stretch their cramped legs and free themselves from the agony. The *Kapos* came right over and restored "order."

It was impossible for us to sleep because of the sharp, needlelike pains in our buttocks. Because the air was so foul, our mouths felt as if they were on fire. Our thirst was unbearable. We were squashed together in one lump, without any possibility of turning around. Some of us started to whimper, groan, and cry. This disturbed the peace of the *Kapo,* who was lying on a pile of blankets. He got up and ran around like a mad bull, lashing out blindly with his truncheon. Our nerves were shattered. Many of us became hysterical and started to scream. At that point the SS guards intervened, shooting into the human mass and killing some of us at random. Then we grew quiet again and lapsed into utter despair. A bullet whizzed past my ear, damaging my eardrum. During all this commotion I drew myself closer to the wall. From it I took a rusty, cold screw. I placed it in my mouth and licked it, hoping to freshen my mouth with something cold. Soon the screw got warm from my breath. Some of us put their heads close to the cracks in the walls to catch a breath of outside air.

During the day, conditions deteriorated even more. The sun penetrated the cracks in the walls and the small, barred windows. The heat transformed the foul air into a thick, choking miasma. Our bodies were dehydrated and our mouths were stuck closed, so that we could not even eat our ration of bread. We could neither chew nor swallow.

"Water! Water!" everyone pleaded. Had any of us been able to forfeit ten years of his life for a scoop of water he would gladly have done so, especially when life had such little value. The *Kapos* and the guards beat us pitilessly, and the numbers of dead grew steadily. We wanted either water or to be put to death.

In front of me sat a man, pale and faint, who gave away his portion of bread to a Hungarian Jew for three-quarters of a cup of urine, which looked like beer. He himself could no longer produce any, so he bought it from someone else, just to be able to moisten his tongue and lips. He poured it down his parched throat, making a sour face, as if he was swallowing bitter medicine. But this liquid did not help him much. He turned completely yellow and lost consciousness. He was dragged closer to the door, where he struggled with death. Someone else, a Greek Jew, constantly wiped his forehead and face with urine. From time to time he also dampened his parched lips.

So it was that people were transformed into beasts. All had enjoyed high social rank before the war and had played an important role in their communities, in trade, in commerce and industry; here they had been degraded into beasts. They fought tooth and nail for what was left of life. With all the resolve they could summon, they tried to live through these harsh, fiery hours.

At the first station, already somewhere in Germany, the door was opened. The dead were removed and the filth was cleaned out a little. Some black water was brought along with fresh rations of bread. The "coffee" did little to quench our thirst. Everyone was afraid the doors would quickly shut and that hell would resume. We convinced the SS guards to bring some water. They insisted on being paid for it. Unfortunately, nobody had anything any longer; before we had got on the train everything had been taken from us. So the SS agreed to bring some water in exchange for gold teeth. People tore out their gold teeth and dental fillings and gave them to the guards for a bit of fresh water. When one of us got a cup of water, the rest of us fell on him like madmen and tore the liquid out of his hands. Understandably, each cup of water cost a few lives, because the *Kapos* and guards had an opportunity to throw themselves on us to restore order.

Among us was a Dutch Jew, who must once have been quite stout from the way his double chin hung down. He became crazy from thirst. His eyes were protruding, and his pupils were racing back and forth. He crawled and stepped over people because he no longer knew what he was doing. When anyone got a bit of water, he threw himself on that person, stuck his hands in the water, and licked them lustily, just the way a hungry dog licks a bone. Naturally, he took plenty of blows. Whoever could reach him struck him.

The guards got hold of him and began making sport with him, telling him to get down on all fours and run and bark like a dog. I will never forget watching him change into a dog. He jumped and barked, all at the command of the guards, who were proud of their idea. Drool poured from his mouth as he carried out their commands for the hundredth time: "Get up! Get down!" When he did not get down properly on the ground, a guard stood on his back and in that way straightened him out. The victim stayed on the ground like a slaughtered cow.

There is a second memory I will keep with me as long as my eyes remain open. One of the guards suddenly declared that it smelled too much near him. "What happened here?" he demanded. No one answered, but all eyes were cast in the same direction. Soon a Jew in his forties got up and like a shamed child with his toothless mouth and face, declared: "I'm sick, *Herr Wachtmann*. I couldn't hold it any longer till I could reach—"

The Nazi started to scream: "Why did you do that, you *Dreck??!*"

The man shriveled, feeling the Angel of Death on his shoulder. He started to stammer: "Because . . . Because . . ."

"What did you say, you filthy Jew?" the SS said as he went over to him with his club. "Clean up right away with your bare hands."

The poor Jew gathered his feces with his own hands. When he did not manage to clean up completely, the Nazi murderer grabbed his head and wiped the waste from the floor with it. A second Nazi and the *Kapo* observed the scene and rolled with laughter. The spectacle obviously pleased them.

55

We Reach Dachau

The horrible journey from Zychlin to Dachau took three days; the pain and suffering would have sufficed for thirty years. Such horrible things took place that it is impossible for me to recount even a small part of what we endured. This journey took many lives. Many of us choked to death from the polluted air, many of us were squeezed to death, and many of us fainted from hunger and thirst, our tongues hanging out like leather belts. Many of us broke down physically and mentally. Near me one man died, but he had nowhere to fall because he was pressed in. The whole time he swayed back and forth with a knowing smile on his face, as if to say: "I'm already laughing at all of you. My world, my suffering is finished."

Finally we reached our destination, Dachau. We got down from the train like crazed, wild people, half-naked, filthy, our skin covered with wounds. The air affected us like alcohol. We stumbled as if on strangers' legs. Our eyes cast wild, scared glances. We did not know what to do with ourselves. At roll call we regained some of our senses when we started to be counted, to be recorded. We were given new numbers. My number in Dachau was 88724.

Half the area was covered with bodies. Everywhere, people were lying like corpses—sick, half-dead, and dead. I did not have a mirror in which to see how I looked, but looking at the other faces I could well imagine my appearance. These were not human faces but masks. One felt like crying, but the wells of tears were dry. Near me lay a living-dead young man of around thirty who already looked like an old man, all gray. Blue veins in his temples throbbed. His thin lips moved as he tried to say something. He was actually praying and thanking God for His mercy in letting him survive.

Suddenly it was as if everything exploded. We heard a voice: "Coffee!"

Two pots of black water were brought. Soon *Kapos* and block elders appeared in clean clothes, looking very human. They accompanied the pots of coffee and came to get acquainted with us. I heard one say to another: *"Mist"* (garbage).

When we saw the pots of coffee, we got up and stood in line for it. We went back three or four times for more, which created a revolution in our stomachs. But it did revive us somewhat, and we began to free ourselves from the horror that was the journey from Warsaw to Dachau.

We stayed in Dachau only a few days, only until the dirt was washed from us, our hair was cut, and a selection was made. We were sorted like livestock and parceled out to different branches of the Dachau camp, which were scattered over a wide area of Bavaria. I was loaded onto a wagon headed for Ampfing-Mühldorf, where I had been assigned to slave labor.

56

Mühldorf and Waldlager *(Forest Camp)*

Mühldorf, approximately eighty kilometers from Munich, had two camps: the *Stammlager*, which was the headquarters of the slave workers, and the *Waldlager*, so called because it was in the middle of a forest, roughly fifteen kilometers from Ampfing. The camp was under construction, and it was our job to complete it. I was assigned to the *Waldlager*. I was happy that a few good friends were coming with me, among then Feitl Lenchner, who was so good at "organizing" things to eat. At the *Waldlager*, however, we were deep in a forest, far away from any settlement, cut off from the world.

We were housed temporarily in windowless wooden barracks. Later, tomblike bunkers were dug for us. Only their roofs, which looked like animal humps, were above ground. The roofs were covered with sod to keep out the cold and rain. In the middle of each bunker a passage had been dug, and on the ground on either side were our "beds"—narrow straw sacks. The only window was in the entrance. These bunkers were spread over the whole camp. Ten of them, five on each side, constituted a block. Besides these bunkers there were wooden barracks in which only the "prominents" stayed. The SS guards and their commander were installed outside the camp on the other side of the forest. The kitchen and clothes storeroom were inside the camp but separated from the bunkers by barbed wire. There was also a stable for horses, donkeys, and oxen, which were looked after by the slaves.

Our main task was to build an underground airplane hangar and installations to mount V-1 and V-2 rockets, which were to be aimed at London. The work was very hard and sapped our strength. Just getting to and from work tired us out. We had to walk eight kilometers on foot, through dense forest, in wooden clogs that twisted our feet. On the way there we walked with more pep after a night of rest; on the way back, after a day of back-breaking work, we barely dragged ourselves forward, rushed along by SS guards who were in a hurry to get back to their warm, comfortable barracks and canteens.

The work consisted of hauling sacks of cement and iron beams and rods. The rods were placed in wooden forms, which were then filled with cement to form reinforced pillars. I preferred to haul iron and bricks rather than sacks of cement; the former work was harder but also cleaner. The cement dust got into one's mouth, eyes, and nostrils and settled in the lungs, making it hard to breathe. Often we felt like vomiting, but the *Kapos* and foreman did not let us catch our breath. They were constantly driving us forward with blows and curses.

Thousands of slaves were working in the hangar complex. Every fifty slaves had their *Kapo,* foreman, and SS guards. Anyone who misbehaved was taken into the forest and simply tortured to death, with no bullets wasted. It was like building the Tower of Babel, so many languages were spoken in the camp, so many curses from different nations were heard. But all beatings were given in one language, and everyone cried with the same tears.

There came a time when we could not cry any more. It was as if our well of tears had dried up. Our hearts sank and our feet gave out. The hunger became unbearable. The fresh air of the forest gave us a healthy appetite, and our stomachs ached for food. Instead of food, though, we got cement dust. Once more I began losing strength, till I feared that I was breaking down completely. At this camp as well, selections were made every week. The ones incapable of working were sent to Dachau, where they were expedited to heaven in the quickest possible manner.

I will never forget the time I accompanied a group from the camp to Dachau. Among them were some Lithuanian intellectuals, advocates, judges, who once played an important role in their country. Their gazes were blank, their cheeks sunken, their faces bitter and desperate. They knew where they were being taken, but they did not protest, did not complain. They just wanted it to be over. It tore at my heart to watch them being taken to their death after having endured so much. Now, with freedom not far off, with the terrible war nearing its end, they were having to say farewell to life.

When I returned from work, my friends waited for me to tell them some news, to offer some commentary on the political and military situation in the world, to predict how much longer we would have to suffer; but I came back tired, exhausted, and demoralized, so much so that I could not even gather my thoughts to evaluate the immediate situation, which was growing worse from day to day. Besides, I had no opportunity to read a newspaper, though my friends brought me pieces of newspaper from their places of work among the German tradesmen, the pieces in which the Germans wrapped their sandwiches and other items. I was so tired and exhausted that I had no strength or patience to read even these. Besides, my eyes burned like fire after absorbing cement dust all day long, and I could barely open them.

There were no wash barracks at the *Waldlager.* From time to time we were taken to a wash barrack in the middle of a field not far from the *Stammlager,* to rinse off and to get rid of the lice. They would take us through the town of Ampfing. All the shop windows, with their displays of dresses, suits, and accessories, did not interest us at all, but when we passed by the bakery and smelled the aroma of fresh bread, we went crazy with desire to bite into a fresh loaf. Our eyes lit up like flashlights, and everyone's eyes sought one thing only . . . Bread! Bread!

57

A New Trial

My friends sought to improve my situation and boost my morale, which had completely deteriorated. They truly wanted to help me so that I would not have to work in *Hauptbaustelle* (construction), doing so much hard work. One day they came to me with a suggestion. A block elder had been punished for smuggling in "luxury" items—cigarettes, better clothing, fruits, and so on. He had also been corrupting young children, abusing them and then paying them with bread and soup he was stealing from the rations. My friends intervened with the camp leader, who was a political prisoner, to arrange for me to take his place.

The slaves of that block were overjoyed with the suggestion that I become their block elder. However, I was to bitterly disappoint them. I thanked my friends for their efforts and for their friendship but added that I could not accept the post. I told them why: I had resisted many similar temptations and would resist this one, too. For four war years I had suffered from hunger and had been exposed to great danger, but I had persevered. I could not allow myself to be ensnared by all the temptations to reduce my suffering—temptations that the position would bring. I had never served the Nazis and certainly would not do so now, just as the war was ending.

My friends started to argue: "You're wrong. Everyone here wants you to become block elder. We used all our influence and connections to help you so that you would survive this critical moment when the end is near. You don't have to be a bad block elder. You'll be a good one who will help your brothers in this difficult time."

I tried to convince myself that my friends were right, that they sincerely wanted to help me. They wanted me to be freer, to be able to read and delve more into politics, to be able to offer commentary about the situation. But my good inclinations won out over the bad. They warned me: you will not be strong enough to resist temptation when you apportion the food; you won't be able to resist leaving the thickest soup for yourself. And when you apportion the bread, you won't be able to resist carving a larger portion for yourself. Besides, you will be responsible for the misdeeds of others. There are bad elements in the block who will try to avoid work, who will try to steal bread from their friends, and you as block elder will be the one who has to punish them.

So I decided emphatically that whatever happened, I would not accept such a position from the Nazis, even if it meant my death. I had survived until now without besmirching my name, and I would continue to withstand temptation no matter how hard it was for me.

The night before I came to this decision I could not sleep—the decision wrenched my heart. Being a block elder would mean no more dragging myself long kilometers to and from work, no more sacks of cement, no more dust in my lungs, no more iron frames and cement blocks, no more blows and curses from the *Kapos* and foremen. It would mean a peaceful life in the block after the *Kommandos* marched out, the chance to eat in peace and to rest after eating, the possibility of "organizing" food supplies to supplement our rations, the chance to make contacts with the camp leadership, and the possibility of getting better clothing and other things.

But then I thought of the suffering in the eyes of the starving slaves waiting in line for a bit of soup, for a piece of bread. I thought of the block elders who tortured them at the behest of the SS guards. I thought of my helpers, the house aides, who struck and tortured the slaves and made them go to work even when they had high fever, and who punished them severely for the slightest misdemeanor. I did not want the suffering of all the mistreated ones poisoning my conscience.

By dawn I had decided that I would not become a block elder. It was a bitter disappointment for my friends; yet personally, I was relieved that I had resisted the temptation. I went to work that morning in a calm mood, feeling peace of mind, as if I had won a battle.

58

Destiny Offers Me a New Chance

My friends did not give up. It hurt them that I had to work so hard on the main construction job. They saw how I was collapsing, how I was getting thinner by the day and was barely able to walk. They regretted that I no longer took an interest in politics and no longer talked about public affairs. Every evening I collapsed in exhaustion like a rag doll; every morning before dawn I had to rise and drag myself to the construction site.

My friend Feitl Lenchner had a friend in the kitchen, a butcher from Chrzanów. I regret that I can't recall his name, because he was a good, quiet fellow who did a lot of favors for his friends and whose name should be immortalized. Feitl used to bring me unpeeled potatoes from him or sometimes a carrot or a bit of soup. These restored my soul, and I enjoyed them very much.

One evening I returned from work very despondent. The *Kapo* had it in for me and had assigned me to pour cement; this arrived loose so that we had to fill sacks and boxes with it; as a result my nose became blocked and my eyes stuck together. But on this night my friends had good news for me. With the blessing of the camp leadership, they had succeeded in convincing the head of the *Stallkommando* (stable brigade) to take me in. According to them this was a "golden" *Kommando* because often one rode out with the horses and oxen, so opportunities arose to "organize" something to eat.

I rejoiced at this news. Not long before, I had passed by the stables and seen sacks of dry beets outside. They were meant for the cattle. Some friends tore these sacks open with their nails and we all helped ourselves. The taste was still in my mouth. Now I would have even more chances to steal from the cows.

The following day I was taken to the stable and handed over to its *Kapo*.

He was a horse dealer from home named Krakovsky. I was also introduced to my colleagues in the *Kommando,* all of them healthy specimens with firm muscles and ruddy complexions. They saw I knew nothing about horses, so they made fun of me, cracking jokes at my expense and asking whether I knew how to muck out the stalls.

"If he doesn't know yet, he'll learn!" Krakovsky shouted, scattering them. He took my hand and led me to an old donkey with a huge pair of ears and said, "You'll stay by this one. He's an old one, a quiet one, so you'll groom him, keep him in shape, and ride out with him. I'll teach you what you have to know."

He handed me a brush and a metal comb. The *Obersturmbannführer* often came in and brushed this donkey with his glove. If he noticed dust in the hair he would be furious and dish out punishment. No German can stand it when an animal isn't clean and well kept . . .

When I was introduced to the donkey, he turned his old head toward me and snorted at me, blinking one eye and swishing his tail. I suppose I did not make a good impression on him. Still, he let me comb and brush him when I offered him something to eat. I quickly felt comfortable with him and even gave him a name—Shlomo Natan. This creature was no longer wild and did not revolt or protest when I harnessed him. He shook his head like a Jew (let us make the respectful distinction) at prayer. He was very lazy, though, and did not like to pull any loads. From time to time he would stop and say that he wasn't going any farther. Out of pity for him, I chose not to whip him. Doing so never helped anyway. He would turn his head toward me and wink at me with his blind eyes as if to say: "It won't help. If I say I'm not going, your blows won't make any difference—I'm not moving." So I would beg it: "Shlomo Natan, may your mother be so well, take a few steps. Why make trouble for me? After all, I'm your friend." That helped. He would turn his head toward me as if to say: "Now that you're talking like a *Mensch,* I'll listen to you."

Slowly I got used to my new trade and became a genuine teamster. Shlomo Natan did not last long, though. One cold, snowy winter night, when was I using him to haul a load of wood, he stood still, started to bray, and refused to continue. The whip did not help, nor did my gentle voice. He tried to pull the wagon but then stood still again. Night fell. The SS guard who was accompanying us began to shout, pouring out curses, and started to whip him himself because he was in a hurry to get home to the warm canteen. But Shlomo Natan refused to take another step. After another few lashes he lay down in the snow, his eyes staring blankly, his mouth foaming. He threw his head back in resignation as if to say: "I've had enough. Let whatever must happen, happen." And it happened that shortly thereafter he expired. The guard stopped whipping him and said to me: "It's no use. The beast is dead."

I pitied Shlomo Natan when I saw him dying. True, he was only an animal, but he had become my friend. I used to pour out my heart to him. Sometimes I would cry with bitterness in his presence, and sometimes, when I succeeded in "organizing" some food, I would share my joy with him. He would listen in silence to my chattering, expressing his "feelings" with twitches of his long ears. At the moment of his death, he opened his misty eyes as if wanting to be sure I was there at his side. Then he closed them again, this time forever.

Meanwhile, I made friends with the other animals, with the horses and oxen. Krakovsky helped me a lot in this respect. He respected me as an intelligent man who happened to be a poor teamster; in things in which he was not very knowledgeable, he understood that he could depend on me. He liked to talk with me more than with the others in his *Kommando*. "What do the horseheads understand?" he would complain to me. He told me he came from a long line of horse dealers. His grandfather had been the employee of a Polish count. When talking with me, he looked for nice, descriptive words, "intelligent" words, not words such as he used with the "guys." When he needed something brainy to say to the chief guard, he would look me up and ask me for something intelligent to say to him.

I grew even more in his eyes when he saw how the "in group" came to talk politics with me and paid attention to what I said. He was proud to have such a "wise one" in his *Kommando*. So he protected me and did not let the others make trouble for me. He himself taught me how to handle the horses and oxen, how to harness them, how to slip on the bridles and adjust the cinches. If there was food to be "organized," he let me know and then shared it with me. The others gritted their teeth, resenting my special treatment. But they could do nothing about it as long as the *Kapo* was my patron.

One day the *Obersturmbannführer* came in and asked if anyone in the *Stallkommando* was capable of keeping accurate records of the animal feed we were using. He needed someone to prepare weekly reports about how much feed we were going through and how much it cost per animal per week, and estimate how much would have to be ordered for the following fortnight. The *Kapo* immediately pointed to me, indicating that I was quite knowledgeable in such matters. The *Obersturmbannführer* studied me for a moment and asked:

"You know mathematics and bookkeeping?"

"Jawohl," I said proudly, standing tall.

I must have pleased him, because he told me to come to his office at noon. That was outside the camp, across the road. The *Kapo* was very proud of my appointment, of how I had answered, and of how I had impressed the *Obersturmbannführer.* He was especially pleased that he would now have his own connection with the camp's high command. This would open the door for special influence. I was also pleased to have found a good post in the camp administration. This would make it possible to alleviate my constant hunger. Also, I was now seen by the other slave laborers as a privileged one—one in regular personal contact with the *Obersturmbannführer* himself. Even my colleagues from the stable looked at me differently, as one "close to the royalty."

When I arrived that afternoon in the administrative office, the guards waved me in; they had been told that I was a personal appointment of the *Obersturmbannführer.* When my friends saw me leave the camp without a guard and walk directly into the administrative barrack, they envied me. It was no small thing to be able to do this.

The *Obersturmbannführer* was waiting for me. He sat me down at a table, placed all the papers in front of me, all the debit and credit notes, and explained what I had to do. My fingers were no longer used to handling such delicate items as pens, typewriters, and adding machines. He told me to prepare the calculations, balances, and statistics. He arranged for me to come twice a week with all of those things prepared and present the accounts to him.

This *Obersturmbannführer* was not a typical soldier, a stiff and stuffy military man. He seemed to be an intellectual. He was short and thin, with a pair of mild blue eyes and a soft voice. He rarely wore his shirt buttoned up, and the leather belt of his uniform was not fastened but hung down loosely. His face was pale and he always had a worried expression. He treated me strictly, but not the way a soldier or a despot would—rather as a strict uncle. He never confided in me, though in his instructions he was always proper and courteous.

I worked in a room that was close to the canteen where the SS, the O.T. (Organization Todt) men, and some officers of the Wehrmacht hung around. Many of them, when they passed through my room and saw me in my camp clothes, cursed me under their breath, knowing that I was a Jew and a camp inmate. But there were also some who smiled and sometimes even tossed me a piece of bread or fruit, or a cigarette, making sure no one saw. From time to time, the *Obersturmbannführer* himself told someone to give me something to drink or eat—just like a dog is thrown the remains of a meal.

59

The Klausenburg Rebbe

My bookkeeping for the animal supply occupied me only twice a week, a half-day at a time. The rest of the time I continued to work in the stables, grooming the horses and oxen. From time to time I would ride out to fetch various supplies. In the camp this was enough to earn me status as a "prominent." I resumed my political commentaries, but now for a select group of friends. I now had more opportunity to read the German newspapers, which I came across in the *Schreibstube*. I would gather up pieces of newspaper and use them to wrap up my ledgers. Later I would read them and compose my commentaries, which I would share with my friends. This brought me status and respect.

I helped my friends as much as I could. I had many friends among the French and Dutch Jews, fewer among the Greek Jews. Many of the Greek *Kapos* were especially false and brutal. That said, among the Greeks there were also decent and intelligent people. I found it hardest to get along with the Hungarian Jews because we could not understand each other. Most of them spoke only Hungarian and did not understand any other language. They were often isolated because of this. I often felt sorry for them—they walked around as if deaf and dumb, unable to participate in our discussions. As a result they suffered doubly. They felt lonely and abandoned in a strange and hostile world.

There were two sorts of Hungarian Jews: the highly religious and the highly assimilated. The religious ones—especially those from the regions bordering Romania, Hungary, and Slovakia—understood some Yiddish, which was the Esperanto of the camp. Yiddish bonded together the Jews of the various countries. Even the Dutch and Greek Jews learned to chat in Yiddish.

The Hungarian Jews who were religious were profoundly so, as this anecdote shows: One day I was ordered to drive a group of twenty or so women and girls to a village to pick some vegetables for the camp kitchen. Two SS guards, a man and a woman, accompanied us.

I sat on the wagon and looked after the horse while the girls filled sacks with vegetables. Most of the women were Hungarian. The guards, meanwhile, went into the peasants' huts to do as they pleased. I noticed that in the distance one of the girls was standing straight the entire time without moving. When I saw the SS woman coming, I became afraid she would grab this girl and beat her harshly. I ran into the field as if to pick up a filled sack, with the intention of warning the girl that the "devil" was coming, that she must bend down and pretend to be working. The girl did not answer me, but instead quietly moved her lips. A friend of hers then told me she could not answer me because she was saying the *Shmona-Esrei*.

The Klausenburg rebbe was a wonderful personality who suffered terribly both physically and mentally. His beard had been shaved off, probably forcefully. He absolutely refused to eat his ration of soup and sausage, and as a result he lost strength and became thinner with each day. Many people resented him for carrying on in this "foolish" way. Here, everyone had to save himself any way he could, and not try to keep the dietary laws of *kashrut*. Some accused him of trying to attract pity. Still others mocked him and even tried to strike him. Personally, I thought he was sincere—he truly was prepared to die of hunger rather than eat nonkosher food. He would trade his soup and piece of sausage for a dry piece of bread. In this way he was letting himself be cheated—the soup was worth far more than the bit of bread he got for it. When there were no takers for such a trade, he gave away the soup for nothing, without touching it.

From time to time I would supply him with a piece of bread or a few potatoes, sometimes even raw ones. I had some pull with the leader of the kitchen staff and would beg of him a few potatoes, a carrot, or a beet for the Klausenburg rebbe. I believed I was helping him stay alive. His townspeople told me he had lived through a great tragedy: his entire community had been destroyed, and his wife and children had perished. Still, he did not complain. He accepted what had happened as a punishment from God, and accepted his suffering with love. Yet one could see the tragedy reflected in his dark eyes: they were always soaked with tears. He spoke little, and never to complain. He prayed aloud and read Psalms. In prayer he found hope and comfort. He would stand in a corner or in front of a tree so that nobody would notice him, and pray his prayers.

One day I took a chance on his behalf and asked the *Kommando* to remove him from the hard labor in the *Hauptbaustelle* and let him work in the block as a house aide. He used to go around the block and sweep with a broom, straighten things out a bit, and return to his prayers. He was grateful to me for my intervention. Whenever he had a problem, he would ask me for help, and I always helped if I possibly could.

During the high holidays of 1944, we set up a minyan in the *Waldlager*. We arranged it in a round barrack, one of the older ones in the camp. Some of us were "calendar counters" and so knew when the holidays were. On the face of the Klausenburg rebbe, we could see that the high holidays were approaching. His face became deeply earnest. His eyes looked back endlessly to a time of long ago, and his lips were constantly murmuring. He looked like someone preparing for a great trial.

A few slaves had decided among themselves to conduct prayer services on Rosh Hashana and Yom Kippur. Since there were no high holiday prayer books in the camp, the Klausenburg rebbe offered to pray on everyone's behalf; after all, he knew almost the entire prayer book off by heart—without the later poetry, of course. So he would pray out loud and the others would repeat after him. During the day it was, of course, impossible to have a minyan because everyone had to work, but at night we gathered in the barrack and prayed. It is interesting that at Kol Nidrei there were Jews from all the blocks. They had learned that prayers would take place in this barrack and had arrived from all over, filling the barrack to overflowing. No one who experienced that Kol Nidrei night in the *Waldlager* would forget it for the rest of their days.

With a gently echoing voice, the rebbe began Kol Nidrei. The assembled ones accompanied him with a deep hum that developed into a lament, as if all hearts were letting everything out. From the lament, the voice of the rebbe continued: *"V'asurei, V'shevuei, V'charumei."* Now the well of tears could no longer be contained. We reminded ourselves of Kol Nidrei night in our former homes, in the circle of our families, in our synagogues, recalling at the same time what had happened to our homes, families, and synagogues, and not knowing what tomorrow held for us—whether we would ever be liberated from this hell. So all of us wept. The only one who did not break down was the rebbe, whose voice grew stronger and stronger. When he sang out *"M'yom Kippurim Zeh, Ad Yom Kippurim Haba Aleinu L'tovah,"* it seemed to us all that he became hopeful and that he had eliminated an evil decree. He continued with a clear, encouraging voice: *"Sh'vikin, Shvitin, B'-talin U'mvatalin, Lo Sh'ririn V'lo Keiyamin."*

So absorbed were all of us that even the one who was standing guard outside did not notice when the camp elder came along and asked, "What's going on here?" When it was explained to him, he understood, because he himself was a prisoner, but he asked us to disperse since the SS guards might notice and consider it an act of rebellion, which could have tragic consequences. We stopped and returned to our barracks, each with a deep pain in his heart. Our wounds had opened and our suffering was sharper than before. We stole back to our blocks, lay down on our hard boards, and tossed and turned for a long time before falling asleep.

60

The "Good Germans"

Much has been said about the "good Germans." It has been suggested that not all Germans were degenerates who supported the Nazi murderers. Possibly there were some "warm-hearted" Germans who could not stand the bestiality of the Nazis, but they did not show themselves to us, nor were they ready to fight against this evil. In the first years of the war, while the Wehrmacht was achieving spectacular victories, conquering country after country, all the Germans—even the "good Germans"—blessed their Führer, who was wiping away their humiliation and turning them into a *Herrenvolk* (master race), a great power in the world. They gladly forgave him all his sins and covered their eyes to many of his crimes against humanity, in particular against the Jewish people. After the war, all the Germans had a ready answer: they'd had no idea what the Nazis were doing; they had not protested or rebelled because they hadn't known the facts. But this is not true. If they did not know it was because they did not want to know. It was worth their while not to know. The fact is that it was common knowledge what was happening inside the concentration camps and what was happening to Europe's Jewish communities. It was not only the SS troops who participated in the actions; so did Wehrmacht divisions and even O.T. battalions. The families of these soldiers most certainly knew what was happening. I want to tell about one such case.

While in the *Stallkommando,* I was often assigned to the sewage wagon. There was a tank with a pump. I would pump the waste out of various latrines and spread it on the fields as fertilizer. An SS man always accompanied me. Perhaps the peasant woman who saw me working all day without eating had some pity for me, or perhaps she was arranging some sort of alibi—that is, she wanted to be able to say she had helped a Jewish slave. By this time it was obvious that Hitler had lost the war, and many Germans were trying to do good deeds so that later they would have witnesses for their kindness toward us. This peasant woman left three apples at the edge of the field and signaled that they were for me.

On the way back I picked up the apples and ate them. The O.T. man noticed this. Back at the camp, even before I had unharnessed the horse, I was called to the SS headquarters, where I was accused of accepting food from the civilian population, which was against the law. For this "sin," I deserved a bullet in the head. Fortunately for me, the *Obersturmbannführer* needed my technical work, so he protected me. I was simply warned that if it happened again I would get my due penalty.

I also pumped out the toilet waste in the main *Kommando* of the O.T. This was a large roll call square surrounded by barracks. In these barracks were the camp offices. The windows looked out on the open lot. Every time I came there to pump out the waste, a gentile woman stood by the window and watched me work. She would also call over her friends to come and look at me as if I was an exotic animal, yet she never dared send something out for me to eat. She merely liked watching a Jewish slave empty her toilet. About this woman, more later.

Yes, many Germans felt for us, and looked on us with pity, but they did nothing to ease our suffering. They knew what was happening in the camps. They watched us slave away at the *Hauptbaustelle*. Early in the war they perceived our suffering as necessary to fulfill the Führer's vision of a "Thousand-Year Reich." Later, once they realized they had lost the war, they felt sorry for us, but they still did nothing to help us. It was convenient for them to say that they heard nothing and knew nothing.

61

The Last Winter in the Concentration Camp

The last winter in the camp was a harsh one. The cold and snow penetrated our bones, causing sickness and often death. The Germans could no longer steal food from other countries, and there weren't enough people to work the fields. Since the harvest from German soil was barely enough to feed the army, the civilian population was also suffering from hunger. As a result, the camps were left without provisions and slaves were dying like flies.

The weak and sick were no longer being transported to the gas chambers and crematoria. They were left to die in suffering. The infirmary was crowded with cases of tuberculosis, diarrhea, anemia, and blood poisoning. There was a shortage of medications and bandages, so the sick and injured simply wasted away until they died. We slaves yearned to live at least until the day of liberation, simply to know that our enemies and torturers had been defeated, but death showed not even this much mercy. It was often my task to carry the dead to the camp's mass grave, a large pit deep in the forest. Here the dead were dumped the way garbage is dumped and then covered with quicklime. Every few days another wagonload of dead was taken out.

We in the *Stallkommando* were the best off of all the slaves because we were able to swipe food from the horses and oxen. In the horse and cattle feed was mixed dry beet; we chewed on this and also smuggled some out for our friends. Whenever we went to the villages for supplies, we "organized" for ourselves a few potatoes, carrots, and beets.

The SS kept pigs in their own sty. One day I returned from the *Schreibstube* with the news that one of the SS piglets had fallen sick. The *Obersturmbannführer* told me to ask the *Kapo* of the stable, a specialist in cattle and livestock, what should be done with the sick piglet. This news brought joy to the *Stallkommando*; we quickly made plans to "liberate" the sick pig for food.

The following day I took the *Kapo*, Krakovsky, with me to the pigsty. The piglet lay on the ground with milky eyes, breathing heavily. The other pigs stood at a distance, gazing at it. Krakovsky looked at the piglet as if he was an expert, examined it from all sides, and declared that it must not remain there even one day more because there was a chance of contagion. It should immediately be killed and buried. The *Obersturmbannführer* then asked the *Kapo* to take care of the matter. We brought it into our stable and slaughtered it that very night. The *Kapo* himself took care of this mission, with the help of two of the butchers.

The next day, I rode out with the horse and wagon to pick up coal for the camp. When I returned, I found a festive mood. Preparations were being made for a feast. Someone rinsed out a horse bucket, and the cut-up meat was placed in it. The bucket was then filled with water and put on the fire. From time to time we stopped by to have a look at how the cooking was coming along. The *Kapo*, though, would not let anyone get close; in his view, such a "holy" duty belonged to him alone. When the meat was ready, we sat on the ground and the *Kapo* gave everyone a portion. It is a pity there was no artist among us to paint the scene. We looked like cavemen. Our faces shone with fat and our eyes were lit with ecstasy.

Even in the stable, though, things were not good. Often there was difficult and painful work to be carried out. Once I was transporting a wagonload of bricks through the forest to the camp. By the time the bricks were loaded, it was already night. I was rushing the oxen because I myself was also very hungry and cold. The *Kommandos* had already returned to camp, and night had already descended. The SS guard was simmering with anger and cursing the damned weather. He wanted to be back in the warm canteen all the sooner so he was shouting: *"Mach, mach Junge, das soll schnell fortkommen!"* (Hurry up, get going quickly!).

Apparently the oxen did not understand German, for they did not respond to my pleas or to the prompting of the guard. They were also hungry and tired, so they moved slowly. When I whipped them to go faster, they stopped completely and refused to budge, no matter what. Maybe it was my fault, too—I lacked experience with oxen. I had not given them enough to eat all day and had not sheltered them from the cold. I tried pleading with them. In return they tossed their heads as if to say: "Don't bother us."

Now the SS guard flew into a rage, unable to bear the hunger and cold. He grabbed a branch and started to thrash the oxen so brutally that they broke away from their yokes and ran deep into the trees. Except for the trees they would have ran much farther; as it was, they went only so far and then stopped. From their mouths, steam came out and drool ran down. They showed all signs of being pleased with their accomplishment.

The situation was serious: at this late hour it was impossible to call for help. The SS went wild, but what could he do with such rebellious oxen? We discussed the situation, and decided we would have to leave the wagon where it was and bring the oxen back to the camp. We returned to camp very late that night, hungry, cold, and shaken. Also, I was afraid of being punished, since the oxen could not be. Animals were much more important to the Germans than human beings. When a human being died, the Germans paid little attention, but when an animal was hurt, God have mercy. Luckily, this time too I escaped with only a good scare.

I was not a trained teamster, so I did not know all the habits of the animals. I did not know, for example, that donkeys are stubborn animals and can attack from behind. One day I went to take off the harness, and one of the two donkeys gave me a ferocious kick with his hind legs. Another five centimeters to one side and he would have killed me. My friends, the experienced teamsters, saw this and laughed at me—at the fool who didn't know the first thing about handling a donkey.

62

News from the Front

Though I was inexperienced with animals, my colleagues from the stable treated me quite decently, regarding me as a "better person" who knew little about horses and donkeys but a great deal more than them about other things, cultural and political. They respected me mainly because the *Kapo* was on my side and often consulted me. Krakovsky was proud that "prominent" ones from the camp came to his stable to learn what was going on politically and to discuss news about the war.

I worked several times a week in the *Schreibstube,* so I was able to gather up old pieces of newspaper that had been used as wrapping. Later I would read these scraps to learn what was going on outside the camp. The German newspapers did not tell the whole truth because they did not want to demoralize the civilian population. Even so, I could read between the lines.

By August 1944 I knew that the Allies had landed in Normandy the previous June. When the Germans wrote about fierce battles and "heavy losses inflicted on the enemy," I understood they were in grave trouble. When they wrote that thanks to the good relations between the Swedish consul general and the German general Von Scholz, the destruction of Paris had been avoided, I understood that the French had retaken Paris. In September 1944 I found a scrap of newspaper on which was written: "In accordance with that which was clearly announced a few days ago, the dramatic and total *Kriegein-satz* [war effort] is now taking place. All theaters, circuses, concerts, exhibitions, and congresses, all cultural life is ceasing." The same article noted that no more books were to be printed except textbooks. Even the popular Nazi publication *Kraft durch Freude* (Strength through joy) was ceasing publication. It was then I knew that the German economy was collapsing.

I later told a group of friends about all this, people whom I could trust.

193

I then commented that the Wehrmacht would soon be defeated, even though it still had scores of well-armed divisions, including armored divisions, because it lacked reinforcements and because the Germans had no skilled workers left to supply the war. Besides, the Allies were relentlessly bombing Germany's industrial regions and its ports and railroads. This was paralyzing German transportation and isolating the front-line troops from vital war supplies.

In December 1944 a military report announced: "Strong German forces are on a wide front on the Western Front, after a short but powerful battle and are now on the offensive to chase the enemy out of German territory." But the Germans no longer believed such stories. They knew they were being fabricated to strengthen morale and the will to fight on. They no longer believed they were going to win and were losing their faith in the Führer. Their gloomy eyes and their sour faces became more and more noticeable. Only the most fanatical Nazis still believed in a miracle—that the Führer would pull the Germans from the jaws of the enemy and lead them to final victory.

The Nazis were bitter, and let out their anger on the camp inmates, beating and torturing them. The food rations shrank even more. No more meat was provided, and fats and bread also started to become scarce. At the same time, we slaves were forced to work harder than ever on the underground hangar. The bombing grew heavier with each night and day, and the Germans were anxious to finish the hangar as quickly as possible to protect their few remaining bombers from attack. Under the tougher regimen, slaves began dropping like flies. The infirmary overflowed; some were sick with serious illnesses, while others had simply broken down. There were no medical supplies for anyone.

Word spread through the camp that the war was nearing its end and that liberation was not far off. Sadly, many of us who heard this news would not live to see the day. We learned through the grapevine that Yugoslavia and Greece had been liberated. In December I brought the news that Budapest had been surrounded by the Russians. When the Hungarian Jews heard that the Nazis were about to be driven from their proud capital, their patriotism stirred once again; they sang patriotic songs and whispered, "Pest . . . Pest . . ." with joy in their eyes.

I was there when a French Jew was in his death throes, letting out his death rattle. One of us wanted to give him encouragement, to awaken in him the desire to live, so he reported to him that Paris had been liberated. At this news his eyes brightened and with a feverish whisper he uttered: *"Paris, Paris, le coeur du monde"* (the heart of the world). Immediately after, he died with a smile on his lips.

On the last New Year's Eve of the war, December 31, 1944, the Führer—may his name be erased—and his propaganda minister, Goebbels, spoke to the people, trying to instill in them the spirit to fight on. At that time the Wehrmacht still had around two million soldiers. In Austria and Italy alone there were twenty-two divisions totaling roughly nine hundred thousand men. V-2 rockets were being launched at England, although they were doing only sporadic damage there. Germany's soldiers no longer had the will to fight. They understood that defeat was looming and that everything was turning to dust. By this time the German air force had collapsed. Its fighter planes could no longer prevent Allied bombers from carpet bombing Germany's cities. The Allies were also targeting military targets, railroads, airfields, and munitions plants. With their new radar technology, they were able to aim their strikes precisely, even in the worst weather conditions.

63

The Rescue Operation to Munich

One day our camp got an urgent call to send a *Kommando* of slave laborers to clean up the train station in Munich, which had been heavily bombed. Quickly a *Kommando* was formed. I thought this might be interesting work, so I arranged to go. We were dispatched by train to Munich.

This was a wonderful spectacle for us. We reached Munich at dawn, while people were hurrying to work. There were no young people to be seen and very few men—only old folks, most of them women. The young ones had all been sent to the front. The faces we saw were gloomy from too many nights in the cellars. When they saw us, the slave laborers, fear stabbed them, because they now saw their defeat.

We were delighted with what we saw: bombed streets, gutted high-rises cluttered with bent iron beams and with ceilings hanging down. It reminded us very much of the Warsaw ghetto. Our thirst for revenge was somewhat quenched—this was payback for the destruction of Jewish streets and houses.

Dead and wounded were being carried out of the wrecked buildings. Women were crying and wringing their hands. Their homes had been destroyed, their nearest and dearest ones killed or injured, their possessions turned to dust and ashes.

The train station had been bombed the previous day. We saw wrecked trains with their wheels in the air. Red Cross ambulances were speeding past. Badly injured people were being taken out. On the tracks, goods were scattered: flour, sugar, potatoes, machine parts, and so on. We were told to start gathering the scattered supplies, to fill boxes and sacks with them and carry them to a storage area. We did this with great satisfaction. I went straight to the broken bags of sugar and stuffed myself with it, and then filled my pockets. Others among us headed straight to the scattered potatoes and ate them raw. Thus we were doubly satiated, from the sight of the destruction and from the food. All of this was sweet in our mouths and in our souls.

We remembered then that every sin is punished. It was a shame that for millions of victims of the Nazis, it was too late to see what we saw then. Their aching hearts would have been soothed. In these ruins our murderers had once lived, the ones who had destroyed our own homes. Now God was making them pay. We worked quickly all day, as if a new strength was stirring within us. We couldn't talk among ourselves because we were too closely watched, but our shared glances spoke more than enough.

At night we were supposed to return to camp, but before we could board the trains, sirens began sounding, the signal that another attack was starting. The Germans fled in panic to the bunkers. Our guards also raced for shelter, but we slaves refused to hurry: we wanted to see what would happen here at the station. The guards shouted curses at us, but we took our time. We felt like shouting back: "Leave us alone. These are ours."

◆   ◆   ◆

In the days that followed, the bombing raids became more and more frequent, more and more intense. When it was foggy, we only heard the roar of plane engines and the explosions of bombs. For us this was the most beautiful music because we knew these engines were bringing our liberation closer. On clear days we could see the silver birds in the sky by the hundreds. They ruled the sky; the Germans lacked the planes to repel them. Antiaircraft guns tried to shoot the Allied planes down, but their range wasn't great enough—the silver birds soared too high. As soon as they saw where the ack-ack was coming from, they immediately swooped down to silence it. This was the most beautiful sight I ever saw, and to this day I remember it perfectly. To us, the Allied squadrons looked like God's own white angels, sent by Him to punish our torturers, who had tried to annihilate our people. In the night our souls rejoiced as we listened to the explosions. Our huts and bunkers shook with them.

It was obvious to us that the war was ending, that the Germans had lost it, and that freedom was close. As I sank my head into the dirty straw mattress, I prayed to God to let me survive the war, even if only for one day, so that I would be able to see with my own eyes the total defeat of Hitler's

Reich. I prayed for the chance to leave the camp as a free man, to eat my fill and sleep on a clean bed. I was terrified that the bastards would not let us live, that they would finish us off so as not to leave any witnesses. The rumor was spreading in the camp that the SS had a contingency plan: when the situation became critical and the end grew near they would march us into the forest and finish us off. We wanted badly to live.

Some of our guards understood the situation and changed their attitude toward us. They began to show a little humanity in an effort to rehabilitate themselves in our eyes. Sometimes they uttered kind words to us, and sometimes they gave us a piece of bread. But there were other Nazis who still considered the Führer a god and believed he would perform a miracle and lead them to new victories. The Russians had benefited from a miracle at Stalingrad, so why not the Germans at Munich or Frankfurt? These guards let out all their bitterness and frustration on us. They tortured and beat us. They insisted that they were losing the war because we weren't working hard enough, that we were the reason they were powerless to do anything against the steel birds who now ruled the sky. They could not defeat the Allied air force, but they still had the strength to beat up the unprotected slaves.

64

Mercy, or Fear for the Future

As I mentioned in an earlier chapter, I often rode out with a horse and wagon, accompanied by an SS guard, to neighboring villages to pick up food for the camp: flour, potatoes, beets, and hot soup. One day I rode to a village called Yetenbach or Gittenberg, I can't recall which. I remember, though, that we had to cross the river Inn to reach it. This river flows from the Swiss Alps to Austria. We rode into the large estate of a landowner to load the wagon with potatoes.

At lunchtime, my guard and I got hungry, so he ordered me to unhitch the horse and feed it. I myself was to go and sit in the barn. Inside this barn was a door that led directly to the owner's house. Another door opened onto a large, rectangular yard. In the barn were bins of grain, potatoes, and fruit, and also stables for the cattle and horses. The lofts above the stables and storehouses were filled with straw and hay; here were also chicken runs and pens for geese and ducks. Outside were kept wagons and plows, which were covered so that the rain would not soak them.

The guard was afraid to leave me alone in case I tried to escape, so he asked an old servant woman to watch me while he ate lunch with her master. I sat there, thinking about my fate and how I might survive until the Allies freed us. The servant woman watched me closely the entire time. Through the open door she saw that the SS guard was deep in a discussion with the owner and into his second mug of beer. Seeing this, she moved slowly toward me and placed beside me two apples and a piece of white bread.

"Hide these," she said. "They're for you."

I hid them right away. Instead of leaving immediately, as I expected, she looked at me with glistening eyes and said: "The war won't last much longer."

I stared at her in astonishment, knowing that she wanted to say more. To give her courage, I replied: "May your words come true, ma'am."

She moved even closer to me, pulled another apple from her apron and handed it to me.

"You are so young," she said in a teary voice. "You haven't lived yet but have suffered so much. It would be a great pity if you were to die while you're still so young, with the war about to end."

Her words touched me deeply. It was the first time since the war began that I had encountered such empathy from a gentile. Tears appeared in my eyes. The woman summoned her courage and told me:

"Save yourself, young man! It would be a shame for you to perish. I know from a reliable source that you're all going to be murdered, shot, so that you won't live to be freed. Save yourself. Run away."

I was stunned by this talk. I choked on my tears and replied as if she were my mother:

"I would run away, but where could I run in my camp clothes? I would immediately be discovered and caught. Then I would be sent to death for certain. I've already lived through so much, endured so much, so now, when we're so close to being liberated, should I risk my life and try to escape, not knowing where to run or who would help me?"

"Run away and come to us in the village. Find a way onto this property. Go right up to the haystack and hide there. Later you'll find a way of letting me know you're hidden here, and I won't let you go hungry. Perhaps that way you'll get through this dangerous time. Did you understand me?"

As soon as she had spoken, she hurried back into the house as if afraid of her own words. Right after that my guard came out, red-faced from the beer. He threw me a few pieces of stale bread and butter.

"You've lazed around long enough," he said. "Load up the potatoes."

I loaded the potatoes, hitched up the horse, and rode off. The servant woman followed me with her sad eyes. *"Auf wiedersehen,"* I told her with a friendly smile.

I left the estate in shock, because of the old woman's offer to help me and because of the warning she had given me, that our end had been planned. I could not stop thinking about her suggestion that I hide in her haystack. I wondered how it could be done. On the drive back, I began spinning all kinds of thoughts and plans. I was so engrossed in my thoughts that I did not even notice that our horse had taken a side road. The guard noticed before I did and started to curse me. However, he soon calmed down after we heard sirens and saw several squadrons of Allied planes approaching. He jumped off the wagon and dragged me into the forest with him. I very much enjoyed watching the planes and had no desire to hide, but the guard pointed his gun at me and demanded I follow him. After the raid was over, I saw how wise it had been for us to hide in the forest; the potatoes in our wagon had been shot through with machine gun bullets.

When I returned to camp I did not tell anyone what had happened to me. That night, my mind would not rest. I lay awake making plans for my escape. I wondered whether it would be worthwhile to bring someone along. I also wondered what the servant woman's motives were. Was she only trying to establish an alibi for after the war? Why would she want to save a slave from death? If hers was truly a humanitarian act, why weren't more people like her? Why had no German helped me before this? Where were they hiding, these "kindhearted" people? On the other hand, I believed in the woman's honesty and decency; she was willing to risk her own life to help me.

Perhaps when Hitler's armies were achieving one victory after another, when it seemed he might conquer the entire world, these same "good" people pretended they did not see anything and were not willing to risk their lives. Now the end of the Nazis was approaching, and the German nation was about to be destroyed the way it had destroyed others, and the "little people" were prepared to take risks to help us, if only to prove that they hadn't been Nazis. And perhaps by saving a few slaves from annihilation, they would be protecting their property from being plundered and themselves from being murdered.

Whatever the servant woman's motives, the fact remained that for the first time someone had offered to help me. I had to somehow use the opportunity to save myself. I considered plan after plan to escape from the camp. The surrounding area was packed with soldiers, Gestapo, and SS, and more so every day, with the front getting closer. On my supply runs to the local villages, I often encountered foreign workers—Poles, Yugoslavs, Romanians, Ukrainians, and Hungarians—who had been imported by the

Germans as slave labor. They also wanted to free themselves and return to their homes and their families, so perhaps it would be worthwhile to establish contact with them and escape as a group. These "outside" slaves were already half-free. They had more freedom of movement. Perhaps we could establish a partisan group!

All night these ideas kept spinning through my mind. Nightmares and dreams began to torture me. I dreamed that I had run away, that I was being chased and shot at, and I started to scream. My bunkmates shook me awake, asking, "What's wrong with you?"

"Nothing," I replied. "A foolish dream upset me."

65

The Front Gets Closer

The spring of 1945 started very early, as if to order, so that the Allies would be able to carry out their operations all the sooner. In the *Schreibstube* I continued preparing the balance sheets, but I barely thought about what I was doing—my ears were trained on the news from the fronts. I could tell from the faces of the Germans that the situation was grim. They were going around anxious and distraught. The *Obersturmbannführer* looked exhausted and depressed. He probably listened all night to the radio and probably had other contacts, so he was not rested. He was angry and sad.

In the *Schreibstube* they kept the doors shut so that I couldn't hear the radio, but from the body language of the guards, and from their faces, I could sense that the Germans' prospects were bleak. Since December 10, 1944, the Germans had been hanging on to the Hungarian capital despite massive assaults by the Russians. Then in the new year I found a scrap of newspaper in which I read that on February 13, 1945, the Germans had "cleared" Budapest and withdrawn to other defensive lines.

Long before, Hitler had issued an order that whatever the price, Budapest must be held. He intended this city to be the second Stalingrad; every house was to be fought for. To prevent the Russians from breaking through to Austria, which was his birthplace, he had assigned his best troops to the defense of Budapest. But on February 13, the Russians broke the German lines there. This effectively ended the war. On the Western front the situation was no better. The Allies now ruled German airspace. In March the British began a bombing campaign that utterly destroyed German factories, industrial centers, and fuel depots, thus crippling the Wehrmacht.

The largest German cities were subjected to constant air attacks, both day and night, that killed German civilians by the tens of thousands. The

German high command tried to mount a counteroffensive and salvage something. But nothing they developed—not V-2 rockets, and not new fighter aircraft—was able to reverse the situation. The Germans had lost the Romanian oil fields and their refineries had been destroyed by bombs, and this had knocked their airplanes and tanks out of the war. That left only antiaircraft guns to protect the Fatherland. Then in January 1945, the Russians launched their final offensive. Marshal Koniew started his march in the south from Poland, Marshal Zukow in the center, and Marshal Rokozovsky in northern Poland. From these three directions they met on German territory. By January 19, the main arteries of Poland were captured: Radom, Warsaw, Lodz, and Krakow. Rokozovski, supported by the army of General Czerniakowski, cut through to eastern Prussia and reached the port of Danzig. And Marshal Koniew and his forces broke through Oberschlesien and Unterschlesien and reached the gates of Breslau.

At this point the *Obersturmbannführer* saw no point in keeping track of feed supplies, and that ended my bookkeeping duties. I regretted losing my source of information but was also glad that the end of the war was at hand. While working in the *Schreibstube,* I used to bring back information to the camp, where it was eagerly awaited, as were my commentaries. Often my friends would grab me and start to kiss me because I gave them new hope. Though the treatment we received kept getting worse, the news I brought fed our souls by reminding us that the troubles would soon be over.

The work on the *Hauptbaustelle* became harder each day. The Germans were anxious to finish the hangar to protect their remaining planes from air raids, but the Allied commanders had learned about the project. The steel birds flew in groups of one hundred, in symmetrical formation as if they were a host of angels. One day we were watching them when one of them broke away and swooped down. It seemed as if it was descending right on our camp, but soon we heard a powerful explosion not far away. The bomber had targeted the construction site and blown up everything that had been built up until then. Many Germans who were working there were killed that day, and so were many of my friends, who were buried in the rubble.

The Germans wanted to establish a strong defensive line along the rivers Oder and Neisse, and in the Tatar and Carpathian mountains, but they could no longer stop the rain of fire that was pouring down on them. The Russians had broken through on all fronts. From Budapest they pushed forward into Slovakia, then Prague, then Vienna. From Warsaw and Radom they pushed east toward Breslau, Opole, and Frankfurt am Main. From Danzig they punched their way into Stettin and continued toward Hamburg. Meanwhile, the British and Americans were taking the Ruhr, the center of German industry. Coming from France and Belgium, they quickly advanced to Düsseldorf, Bremen, Hamburg, Hannover, and Frankfurt am Main. They crossed the Main and marched toward Nuremberg, Stuttgart, Ulm, and Munich. The armies of Generals Patton and Hodges circled the German divisions, which were forced to surrender. On March 2, 1945, General Patton's Seventh Army occupied the Trier fortress and quickly proceeded to Koblenz, where they crossed the Mosel to attack Worms and Ludwigshafen, encircling the German troops in the Saar and the Pfalz. Immediately following, they crossed the Rhine and took Mainz and Frankfurt. With this, Germany's fate was sealed.

After I was sent away from the *Schreibstube,* I no longer had exact information about the front. We saw how angry and worried the SS were, but we did not know how far the Allies had penetrated. In the camp, rumors began to spread once more that the Germans intended to evacuate us deeper into the country. It was also whispered that huge pits had been prepared in the forests, where we would all be shot and buried. Everyone came to me, asking if this was true, as if I knew. I tried to comfort them, saying that now, with the end of their regime at hand, the Nazis were unlikely to increase their guilt—which was already so great—by killing us en masse.

Yet in my own heart, I trembled. I believed that the Nazis were capable of such bestiality if it meant leaving fewer witnesses. I also believed they were bitter enough to revenge themselves on us. Now I thought in earnest about fleeing the camp. But when I confided my secret to my closest friends, and asked if they wanted to accompany me, they discouraged me from trying. According to them, it was better to wait. Perhaps if the Germans tried to evacuate us, that would be the right time to try a run. They argued that the regime was getting weaker, that many SS guards were being shipped to the front and replaced by older men from the Wehrmacht and the O.T. To them, this was a sign that we weren't likely to be shot.

Our *Obersturmbannführer* was also sent to the front. His place was taken by a *Hauptmann* from the Wehrmacht. He was an older man, over seventy, very strict and mean. In the last days, I was afraid some provocation would occur that would bring about our liquidation. I remembered how the servant woman across the river Inn had warned me that a terrible end awaited us. I was nervous and distraught.

A rumor reached us that the *Stammlager* in Mühldorf had already been evacuated and that our turn was probably next. Meanwhile the Allies were moving ever closer to us. Berlin had been encircled. The rumor was out that the Führer had committed suicide. The situation was tense. We were caught in a vise and didn't know what tomorrow would bring.

66

The Devil Trips Me Up

The tension in the camp continued to increase. People with wild imaginations who wanted to give the impression that they were important—that they had contacts with the authorities—made up all sorts of fantastic stories, and these stories were swallowed whole by inmates who were anxious for any news. "The Americans have just taken over the *Stammlager* of Mühldorf . . ." "Hitler has hanged himself . . ." "We're all being taken into the forest tonight and murdered—the pits are ready for us . . ."

Our nerves were stretched to the snapping point. None of us could sleep. On April 24 or 25 the *Hauptmann* entered the camp and told us to get ready for a roll call, declaring: "You should know that the war has ended. If you stay calm, nothing will happen to you. We will wait until the Americans arrive and will hand over the camp to them in good order. I have already instructed the guards to lay down their rifles—to carry side arms only, just to keep order."

When we heard this news we hugged and kissed each other. People went crazy with joy. Our understanding at that moment was that the Russians had already captured Berlin. In the bunker of the Reich Chancellery, Hitler had committed suicide, together with his beloved Eva Braun. A group of officers had revolted, establishing a revolutionary council and declaring themselves ready to offer an unconditional surrender, to prevent further bloodshed. The rebels had taken control of the radio station, announced the capitulation, and appealed to the Wehrmacht to surrender to the invading troops.

Having heard the radio appeal, our *Hauptmann* had decided it was pointless to keep fighting. He would wait until Allied troops appeared and then hand over to them the camp and all the slaves. We prisoners decided to remain calm and disciplined. We wanted to avoid any provocation that could endanger our lives. We even appointed our own authorities.

While all this was going on, a guard from the camp's high command approached the *Kapo* of the *Stallkommando* for a horse and wagon. Two doctors had to be taken to the Mühldorf camp. Most of the camp prisoners had been removed from there, but some critical cases had been left behind, and they needed doctors. So our camp was going to lend two. I stood listening to this conversation and trembling for the chance to be assigned to this trip. The *Kapo* noted my eagerness and appointed me the driver. After the guard left, the *Kapo* told me he had assigned me because he could depend on me to bring back news.

I prepared a horse and wagon and seated the two doctors, who were Hungarian Jews. An SS guard sat down with us, but unarmed. The sun beat down on my head. I felt as if I was boiling inside, that I was cracking up with anxiety. I lost my mental balance. I could not stop talking, screaming, laughing, and crying. I became hysterical. I told the guard he had nothing to fear because he had always been decent to us and had never beaten or tortured us. I would therefore defend him. "What need do you have for your SS insignia, those two black snakes?" I asked him. "Tear off that *Dreck*. I began to tear off his insignia. He smiled, and instead of stopping me let me go ahead and do whatever I wanted with him. I hopped off the wagon and then hopped back on. I shouted and screamed, filling the village with my words: "Hitler is dead! He crapped, the dog that he was! We are free! Free!!! The war is over! The bloodshed is finished! No more slave laborers!!!"

The villagers came out of their houses to watch the crazy guy. They even shouted "Bravo!"

I no longer knew what I was doing. I lost my balance completely. I ran around, stumbling like a drunk. The guard tried to calm me down, addressing me very politely, suggesting I control myself and not act so ecstatic. But I couldn't control my hysteria—I was crazed with joy.

Finally we arrived at the *Stammlager*. Here there was also celebrating. The camp inmates were running around in confusion, unsure what was happening. The guards were angry and depressed and afraid of retaliation. When the inmates saw our wagon, they crowded around and started peppering me with questions. As I began telling them what I knew about the situation outside, the crowd began buzzing like a beehive. Some inmates passed my news on, while others told me what had been happening with them. The Mühldorf guards pleaded with the inmates not to gather in groups, not to create disorder, to go to their blocks. But no one could stay calm. Everyone was running around the camp, scratching for any news from outside. When airplanes flew overhead, we all looked up, trying to guess where they were headed.

After three hours at Mühldorf we returned to the *Waldlager*. On the way back we saw people running around looking for anyone with news. We also saw a lot of heavily armed soldiers on transport trucks or on foot. The front was coming closer, and the Germans were digging trenches and throwing up defensive positions.

Halfway home, an O.T. soldier stopped us and asked for a lift. We made room for him in the front. Three of us now sat together, me on the left, the guard in the middle, the O.T. man on the right. I listened to the two of them talking. The O.T. man was telling the guard the latest radio news. There had in fact been an officers' revolt, but it had been put down! The army and the SS security guards had immediately encircled the rebels, taken them prisoner, and executed them for treason.

"The war continues," the radio was now proclaiming. "We have faith in the Führer. We are hopeful that we will soon drive the enemy from our land. The Führer is preparing a great spring offensive that will soon start to roll. We enticed the enemy forces into our territory in order to defeat them here."

When I heard this talk, my stomach began churning and my emotions began somersaulting. My SS guard was afraid to look me in the eye. I drove slowly, not having any reason to rush. My mind began working like a computer, spinning plans for an escape. I considered running immediately but decided it would be too dangerous, since now I had two guards. Besides, German troops were passing by all the time, so I wouldn't get far.

Of one thing I was sure: I must not return to camp that day. After what I had done with the guard's insignia and after the commotion I had caused in the village, I would be shot right away. The guard also sat as if on hot coals. He felt responsible for the scene he had allowed me to make in the village. Hundreds of people had watched it, and it had been his fault because it was his duty to control me. For this negligence he could face a court-martial. Also, he was terrified that I might try to run. He took a revolver out of his inside pocket and placed it in a front one, making sure that I saw.

My mouth was dry and my head was spinning. I could not decide what to do. But I was certain I had to do something now, that I must not return to the camp that day.

67

My Last Chance—Run Away

When I arrived back at the camp I had to unharness the horse. I did this outside the camp between the SS guardroom and the gate. My guard disappeared into the *Schreibstube*. Just as I arrived, so did another wagon, driven by a friend of mine from the *Stallkommando*. His name was Ernst, and he was a German Jew of around twenty. While we were unharnessing our horses I had a talk with him:

"Ernst, we are in a difficult spot. According to what I learned, they're planning to finish us off in the next few days."

Ernst blinked in surprise: "How can that be? The *Hauptmann* promised he would hand us over to the Americans."

"Don't be a fool," I replied, my temper rising. "You still believe what the Germans are telling you? Will you later call them liars? Will you be able to take them to court in the heavenly tribunal, and call me as a witness?"

He stared at me in disbelief and retorted, *"Quwatsch!"* (Nonsense!).

I started to persuade him, telling him the whole story. I even embellished it a little because I wanted to convince him to come with me. It would be better if we were together, I thought. I tried to show him it was our only chance, that we had to run away. If we didn't save ourselves now, our lives would be in danger. I told him I had already prepared a hiding place outside the camp. Ernst couldn't conceive at all the idea of running away. He thought hard and then stared at me as if I was crazy. It is quite possible I *looked* crazy, angry as I was. I thought I was making progress with him, but then he turned to me and said: *"Mach doch keine Dumheiten, das dürfen wir doch nicht"* (Don't make any dumb moves. We don't need that).

I got madder still, and started to talk more sharply: "If you wait for what you need and what you don't need, you can say good-bye to the world.

Maybe you need an invitation?" I was trying to appeal to his heart and mind: "We've come through so much suffering, barely survived until the end of the war. Should we be murdered on the eve of our liberation? Now we have a chance. We should use it because we won't have another chance like it."

I could tell I was starting to convince him, but he still hadn't decided. We returned the horses to the stable and came back out to clear the wagons. I looked around to see how we could run away. We were with the wagons between the camp and the *Schreibstube*. To leave the camp, we would have to pass a perimeter guard. At the edge of the forest, between the *Schreibstube* and the gate in the barbed wire that enclosed our camp, there was a sort of rampart. There was always a guard on this rampart. I noted that the guard that day was carrying a rifle again, and that the tower guards were armed with heavy machine guns. From this I understood that the situation had become serious again and that the O.T. had been right.

I kept glancing at the *Schreibstube* in case they called me again. I was shaking all over and flushed with anger. I felt that my fate was in balance. My mind became as sharp as a sword. I went over to Ernst and said:

"Wait a moment. I'll try to talk with the guard on patrol." I went closer, sat down in the middle of the sector, and started to engage the guard in conversation.

"There has been a change again," I said to him. "This morning the *Hauptmann* told us the war is over, that we only have to wait for the Americans. Now I see there has been a change—the war hasn't ended after all."

"The war is continuing," he replied. "There's no other way but to keep fighting."

I: "You believe, *Herr Wachtmeister,* that the war can still go on for long?"

He: "The whole war is an insanity, a trap from which we can't break loose."

I: "It doesn't make sense to fight any more when the Allies have encircled us on all sides, when the main defense lines have been broken. Why the bloodshed? Wouldn't it be better to sign a peace agreement?"

He: "As far as I'm concerned, the war could end today so that I could return to my family, see my children, and say good-bye to the whole adventure."

I: "That's what you say. Imagine my situation. It's the fifth year that I'm a prisoner, a slave. I've lost my family, my home is destroyed, my belongings are ruined, and I myself am a physical and mental wreck."

He: "It's not much better for us. Many of our homes are destroyed from the bombing raids, and how many millions perished in Russia and Africa?"

I believed I had broken the guard's armor, that I had reached his heart, that he was softening up. I looked around to see if anyone was approaching. Below, Ernst was standing, pretending to repair the wagon and glancing furtively at us. I decided to go all the way:

I: "I would like so much to live to the day of liberation. I'm still young. I've suffered a lot, and borne it all, and I don't want to die now when the war is about to end. In my opinion the war won't last much longer. Perhaps it will last another few days, but certainly not more than that. Who wants to lose his life in the last days?"

He: "You just have to be patient. Just bear the last crisis until it's over."

I: "It's easy to say to bear it, to be patient, when there are so many dangers hanging over us. I'm afraid we're going to be finished off."

He: "Nonsense, that won't happen."

I: "Yes, if everyone was like you, I wouldn't be afraid, but there are others, fanatics, who are still living in their dreams. They can't win on the battlefield so they want to show their heroism over defenseless people. Besides that, there's a chance of more bombardments. Who is to say a few bombs won't fall on the camp? If the war was over, as the *Hauptmann* said today, a few days wouldn't make any difference. We have already suffered so much. We would be able to survive another few days. But this has turned out to be only an illusion. The military have decided to keep fighting, so the war will go on with a terrible ferocity on both sides. Who knows how long it can continue and how many more people will die?"

He: "I don't believe the war will go on much longer. I hope a cease-fire will be reached. To continue the war in these circumstances is crazy."

I: "I wish it were true. Sure, if people like you, sensible and realistic, were in control, things would look different. The trouble is that at the helm stand fanatics who believe the Führer will perform a miracle—people who have no pity for the thousands of victims who die each day."

He: "*Die Vernunft wird noch siegen*" (Common sense will prevail).

I: "Thank you for your words of encouragement and for your humanity. We won't forget those of you who behaved decently and humanely toward us. I always used to comment about this to my comrades, telling them that you and a certain other guard, even though you belonged to the SS and SA, never lost your humanity and always treated us with kindness. We know how to value that, and we won't forget it. If we need to, we will bear witness for this at every opportunity."

I felt that I had broken him down. I could see on his face that he was pleased with my words. Probably, each of them was thinking about what would happen to them later, after the Americans entered and took them prisoner. I decided to launch a direct attack.

"You've already helped us many times. If you were to lend me a hand now, I would never forget it. I don't want to lose my life in the very last days. If you let me disappear into the forest with my friend, you will find we are your best friends and defenders."

The guard gaped at me. He didn't know what to do—whether to get strict with me, or chase me away, or treat me with understanding. And he surely didn't want to forfeit the chance of a strong testimonial. He shouldered his gun as if to clear his thoughts, and said, "Come on, don't be stupid, you'll soon be freed."

But I didn't give up—I could see I had tipped the scale.

I: "The war can't last much longer. It's ending. Every sensible person can see that. It's just a shame we're still being tortured here. You have feelings. We always knew that, so why shouldn't you help me out at such a decisive moment? You were always decent to us. We'll all be ready to tesify on your behalf at all times. You have a wife and children. I also have a wife and children." (Admittedly, a lie.) "They're waiting for me at home. A mother is also waiting, with a fluttering heart, for her son, so why should you refuse me at such a moment when I only want to save myself from death? Maybe tomorrow I'll be able to save you from danger—one hand washes the other. I beg of you, don't refuse me. You will be earning yourself every good word."

I watched him thaw. He was debating with himself, thinking what to answer me. Finally he said quietly:

"As far as I'm concerned, I don't see anything." He turned around and continued on his rounds.

68

The Leap to Freedom

After the guard left, I ran to tell Ernst the good news: we had been given permission to escape. Ernst was still hesitating to risk his life. He also didn't believe I was capable of carrying out something like this. He began to argue with me, telling me we shouldn't risk it, but I closed my ears to him and grabbed him with so much force that he couldn't move. I don't know where my strength came from; I only know that something inhuman overcame me. I dragged him with me into the forest. We ran for a few hundred meters and then collapsed in utter exhaustion.

"You devil!" he shouted at me. "What's going to happen now?"

"The main thing is we're outside the wire," I told him. "Now we'll find our way across the river Inn and hide until the Americans arrive."

Ernst, already regretting having come with me, started firing questions at me: "But we can't stay here in the forest. We'll starve! We can't leave the forest either, dressed in these striped clothes . . . We'd be caught and shot immediately . . ."

I tried to calm him down by saying we would hide somewhere. Now that the war was ending and the Germans had lost, many soldiers would want to make a good impression. "We'll certainly find someone willing to hide us. All we have to do is leave the forest at night or at dawn to find some food till we arrive in the village. But we have to hurry because they'll find out we escaped from the camp during role call and they'll send guards to hunt us down."

I knew more or less the general direction of the river Inn. After resting a while, we began to run. At one point we heard someone walking and dived into a pit. In the distance we saw an O.T. striding down a forest path into the village. We waited till he was out of sight and then started to run again.

We ran the entire night until the break of dawn. It was April 25, 1945. The day emerged, a bright and clear one. We came to the edge of the forest and saw a village, and watched its streets and houses emerge from the darkness.

I started to look around, trying to discern where we were. Finally I recognized the village as Pirten. A blacksmith lived there who used to forge shoes for my horses. At this blacksmith's place there was a Polish slave laborer with whom I used to talk while my horses were being shod. I knew that the blacksmith was a *Partei Genosse* (Nazi Comrade) and proud of it—his membership insignia was hanging on his wall. But at that moment there was no time to speculate: we had to get out of the forest before daybreak while the village was still asleep. If we could hide at the blacksmith's, we would be able to make contact with the Polish gentile, who would probably help us.

We slipped through the streets and houses. A dog began barking, so we moved quickly, praying for it to stop. Finally we reached the blacksmith's. Straight ahead across the yard was a stable and barn. To one side of the yard was his forge, above which were lofts, and to the other his house. We stared at these buildings like lost souls, not knowing what to do or where to hide. Then I saw a ladder leading to the loft.

"Wait here," I said. "I'll see if the loft is open."

I ascended the ladder, shoved the door open and winked to my friend: "Come!" We climbed up to the loft, which was full of hay. I made a hole in the wall from which we could look down on the shop. We covered ourselves with hay and let ourselves relax a little. Only then did we notice that we were aching all over; especially, our feet were swollen.

Ernst fell asleep right away and began to snore. I was unable to fall asleep; my mind was overloaded with plans and impressions. I was assuming that this was only a stopping place and that the next night we would have to run farther to reach the estate where the servant woman had offered me a hiding place. That estate, unfortunately, was across the river Inn, and we would have to see if it was clear.

Ernst woke up and began complaining of hunger. Neither of us had tasted anything for almost twenty-four hours. While we were on the run, we hadn't thought at all about eating; now, while we were resting in the hay, our hunger became painful. We hadn't yet learned to eat hay. I calmed Ernst, telling him that as soon as I saw the Polish gentile I would signal him to come up and he would probably bring us something to eat.

I sat at the crack in the wall and waited for someone to appear. Finally I saw the Polish gentile carrying buckets of food for the livestock and horses. I envied the cows, who had someone to worry about them. The luck of animals. I whistled. He looked around, and not seeing anyone, continued on his way. I told my friend not to show himself so as not to scare our "saviors." It would scare them enough to see one of us. If I could get something to eat, I would share it with him anyhow.

I waited until the Pole came back from the barn. When I saw him I whistled again. He again looked in all directions and did not see anyone, so I whistled again and again until he oriented himself that someone was whistling for him from above. When he came up, I rose from the hay and approached him. When he saw me he crossed himself and looked terrified.

I started to speak to him in Polish: "Do you remember when I used to pass by here with provisions for the camp and when I had the horses shod? You know we are in a camp not far from here near Ampfing. I ran away from the camp because I was afraid they were going to finish us off in the last few days before liberation. Now I'm in your hands, brother. We're both Poles, both slaves of the Germans. We have to help each other."

Almost choking on his words, the Pole replied:

"But what do you want from me? I myself am a slave, a foreigner."

"I know that very well," I said. "I know your situation. You too were dragged from your home, from your family, and forced to work for pennies. But our enslavement is about to end. Soon we'll be free and they'll be the slaves. Now we have to stick together. After all, we're brothers, both Poles. We grew up on the same soil, under the same sky, under the same culture of Slowacki and Mickiewicz. I am a Jew, but I'm still a Polish citizen. We grew up together like brothers. I just want one thing from you: don't let me die of hunger."

He stared at me, thought for a minute, and then said:

"But I can't help you at all. I won't risk my life on your behalf. If it's discovered that I helped someone from the camp, gave him something to eat, they'll send me away like a dog."

I started to plead with him not to let me sink, that at night I would be off again across the river Inn, where I had arranged a hiding place. I pleaded only for something to eat in the meantime, because I didn't have the strength to run any farther.

Avoiding my eye, he shrugged and said: "You have nowhere to run because you won't get across the bridge. It's heavily guarded. The SS are afraid of saboteurs and parachute troops. You'll have to find another place. I'm not going to risk my life for you. If you don't leave here, I'll denounce you to my boss, who is a Party man."

I kept talking, appealing to his conscience, to his patriotism, pleading with him to help me now that the war was ending. I promised I would make it up to him later and repay him more than double for his good heart. Nothing helped. He refused to relent. His cold gray eyes glowed with murder. It was going to be impossible to stir any compassion in him. Seeing that, I told him:

"Good, call your boss. I want to talk to him. But don't tell him beforehand what it's about."

I saw that I had freed him from a heavy burden. He agreed to call the blacksmith to come up, but he did not neglect to remind me: "Remember that he's a Party man and that he can turn you in to the Gestapo."

It was now all the same to me—I was dying of hunger anyway, and obviously it was going to be impossible to cross the bridge. I made ready to play my last card.

The Pole was gone for some time. Meanwhile I went to my friend and told him of my conversation with the Pole. When he heard that my intervention had failed, he was frightened and started to accuse me of bringing misfortune on him, of bringing down the Gestapo on us. According to him, it would be less dangerous to leave immediately.

I tried to calm him, telling him the situation wasn't so dangerous, that it was impossible for us to leave during daylight, that we would leave at night if the blacksmith would not allow us to stay. He was upset with me for asking to see the boss, since he was a Party man who would certainly turn us over to the Gestapo.

My heart was heavy. My mind began working in all directions. Soon enough the blacksmith came up with the Pole. He recognized me at once.

"You're from the *Waldlager*. How did you get here?"

I started to present my arguments: "You know the war is ending. Yesterday the *Hauptmann* notified us that we were free, that we had only to wait until the Allied troops entered and he would then turn the camp over to them."

The blacksmith immediately caught on. "Yes, but that was yesterday, when rebels took over the radio and gave false information about the war's end. But the traitors were captured and immediately charged. The war continues."

When I heard that he knew the whole story, I tried another approach: "You're a sensible man, so you know the war won't continue much longer. If not today, the end will come tomorrow. I ran away from the camp because I was afraid of losing my life at the last moment. It could happen because the Allies bomb us, or because one of the SS guards loses his head, or because the order comes down to finish us all."

"That's impossible," the blacksmith said. "They wouldn't be such fools."

I started to work on him, telling him that not everyone was as clear-headed as him and understood the situation so well. If everyone was like him the war would have ended long ago, because it did not make sense to fight any longer.

He smiled and told me I was right. I continued my argument:

"When I left the camp, I told my close friends I was going to hide at your place because I knew your character and your good heart. I was never afraid of your PG status because you were not a fanatical Party member but a sensible person. You belonged to the Party outwardly, but in your heart you were always a democrat, a liberal. It was probably worth your while, for business reasons, to be a Party member. When the war ends my friends will look for me here. If they don't find me, you will be suspected of killing me. I want very much to prevent this so that you don't have to suffer. On the contrary, I will be the first one to rehabilitate you."

These words made the impression I wanted. He softened, but he was still undecided. Struggling with himself, he replied:

"True, I was never a fanatical Party man. You can ask Anton." He pointed to the Polish gentile. "I always treated the foreign workers decently. I won't turn you over to the Gestapo because I don't want to cause anyone misfortune. You did wrong to leave the camp because nothing would have happened to you there. But I can't keep you here because it's too dangerous. The hounds are sniffing every hole. If you're found on my premises they'll kill my family and burn my house. I'll give you food and provide you with clothes, but you must clear out tonight. You understand, because you're not a fool, that you're asking me to play with fire."

He had not spurted out Nazi talk; if anything, he was trying to show some humanity. Possibly this was to secure himself for the future. Two years earlier or even one, this wouldn't have happened. Without hesitation he himself would have murdered me or would have turned me over to the Gestapo. Now that the Germans knew the war was ending, they were thinking about tomorrow. He understood now that my friends in the camp knew where I was. The Polish worker would also be able to testify that he had murdered me to get rid of me. But I decided not to give up until I had completely convinced him. I pleaded:

"I'm still a young man. I want to live, so why should you send me away from your place to my death? Today you will save me. Perhaps tomorrow I'll be able to save you." I told him that a fine German woman had offered to hide me because she wanted to save me from death, but her house was on the other side of the river and I couldn't cross because the bridge was too heavily guarded. I knelt before him and begged him not so send me away, not to let me die during the last days of the war. "You have children, and because of your merit they will also be saved from death. Later I will defend you. I'll tell the commanders of the Allies how decent you were toward us, how you helped us and protected us. Otherwise, you will be accused of spilling my blood!"

I had placed the blacksmith in a difficult position. Forces for and against us were battling within him. He was afraid of being discovered hiding an escapee from the camp, and he was still a German patriot. At the same time, he was bombarded with feelings of humanity that I had awakened in him, and he wanted to provide himself with an alibi now that the war was ending. He began to plead with me to leave his place. His wife was ill and would not be able to survive something like this. When he mentioned his wife, I said to him:

"Go and ask your wife. Tell her what has happened here. Let her convince you to let me stay."

He agreed to discuss it with her and went away.

69

My Fate Hangs in the Balance

When the blacksmith went down, I went back to Ernst and collapsed in the hay. At that moment I was a pack of nerves and had no thought of food. I knew our lives hung in the balance. If we let ourselves be shoved out, we were lost: we would be captured immediately. At that time there was a manhunt going on for spies and saboteurs, whom the Allies were parachuting in, so we would immediately be grabbed and put up against the wall. If we could cross the river Inn, we would be able to make our way to the estate where the woman had offered to hide me, but according to the Pole, this was impossible: the roads and bridges were too closely guarded, and all suspicious people were being detained for questioning.

Ernst was torturing himself for letting me persuade him to come along. As for me, I was sure I could persuade the blacksmith to help us. As long as he did not act arrogantly toward us, I could get him to bend further. I was certain that once his wife heard our story she would sympathize with us. Also, the two of them would want to have witnesses that they weren't fanatical supporters of the Nazi Party.

I waited with a pounding heart for the blacksmith to return, in the meantime thinking up new arguments to make with him. My mouth was parched and tasted foul: I had had nothing to eat or drink for more than twenty-four hours. Nightmarish thoughts began tormenting me: "Maybe he is gone to denounce us. Maybe he is waiting for the Gestapo."

I was afraid to express my fears to Ernst. He was probably thinking the same ones but afraid to tell me. When he saw how worried I was, I told him: "No matter what happens to me, you remain hidden here. Don't let them know there's someone else." In the worst case he would be able to look for another hiding place the following night.

221

The minutes dragged by, pressing themselves against my lungs, my heart, and my mind. Finally I heard footsteps. The blacksmith opened the door and entered. I breathed lighter when I saw that he had returned alone. I left my hiding place and ran to him with a smile. My smile quickly vanished when I saw that he was white as chalk and biting his lips.

"What happened?" I asked him.

The blacksmith turned away so as to avoid my eye. "When I went down," he said, "and told my wife what happened here, she fainted. We barely managed to revive her. She keeps fainting and has a high fever. I had to bring the doctor, who gave her an injection, and now she has to stay in bed. Now I no longer have anyone to discuss the matter with."

My knees buckled. I asked him to give me a sip of water because my tongue could barely move in my mouth. There was a white foam on my lips that was burning my tongue. He climbed down and brought me up some water, which at that moment smelled better than the best Tokay. I would have drunk it all because I was so dry and thirsty, but I remembered that I had to save some for Ernst. I refreshed myself a little and continued pleading with him.

First, I regretted that my presence had pained his gentle wife so much. Hopefully, she would soon recover. Regarding my leaving here, I would do so, though this might well result in my death. I regretted that I had told my friends in the camp that I was running to hide here. "When they are freed, they will come here to look for me," I told him. "Then they might conclude that you drove me out, that you refused to lend me a hand at this critical moment, and that you caused my death."

The blacksmith wrung his hands and began to plead: "I'm not chasing you out! I would gladly hide you, save you from the dangers you're facing, but you see what has happened here. My wife won't survive this. I had to promise her I would drive you out right away. I'll give you food, and some clothes, too, but at night you have to leave and find another place, in the forest or back to the camp."

When I heard the words "back to the camp," I shook all over. I couldn't tell him why I could not return to the camp—he would have got even angrier and more upset. Just then a new argument came to me:

"Listen, my friend. Pardon me for calling you 'my friend,' but up till now I haven't lost my belief that you *are* my friend, otherwise I wouldn't have run to you. I hope your common sense will rule your head and that we will re-main friends for many long years. I need you to lend me a hand at this diffi-cult moment, when my fate is in the balance. Tomorrow it may be you who needs me to save you from great trouble. So I have another plan for you. Listen well—

"You don't know I'm here. You really don't know. If I hadn't said to call you, knowing of your honesty and humanitarian feelings, you wouldn't know I'm here—after all, I arrived in the night. I came up the ladder and hid here without anyone—not even the Polish worker—knowing about it. So you won't know anything either. I promise you, if even by a slight chance I'm found here I won't under any circumstances—even if I'm severely beaten—reveal that either you or any of yours knew anything about me. Now it's just a matter of something to eat. This won't be a great problem. To start with, I've lost the habit of eating. It will be enough if I have water to drink and a hunk of bread. I don't want you to 'send food up to me' either, because you don't know I'm here. But you have a few hens and ducks up here, so soak a few old pieces of bread and put down a pail of water, and I'll share it with them. They certainly won't give me away."

The blacksmith squirmed. I had pushed him to the wall and offered him two arguments that he would find difficult to reject, but I saw he was still undecided, so I gave him one last push:

"Listen, I have another suggestion for you. I'll stay hidden here for two more days without you knowing anything about it. Rest assured about what I told you—I won't give you away. If in those two days the war still hasn't ended, I'll leave without putting you to any more bother. The way I see it, the war can't last more than a few days more."

I started to sweeten him up. "You're an intelligent man. You understand the situation well because you're a realist. If the Russians have already reached Berlin and the Allies have already crossed the Rhine and reached Bavaria, who can keep the front here? A few old folks and children? I don't know if Hitler is still alive. If he is he'll be captured at any moment because there is no one left to protect him, and his personal guards won't be enough. Once Hitler falls, that will be the end of the war. There are still a few fanat-ics who don't want to betray the Führer, who don't want to surrender, who prefer to die fighting, but their resistance will soon be broken. I believe that very soon you'll need my help and you'll be happy you gave me the chance to save myself—something I'll never forget. I'm also lucky I met such a fine man who has so much empathy for other human beings."

Now I had broken the ice completely. The blacksmith started to smile and conceded that I was right. I offered him my hand and said:

"Relax. If after two days you don't see the correctness of my arguments, you won't have to call me. I'll leave here by myself. Anyway, you know about nothing."

He shook hands with me and left.

70

I Win a Battle

When the blacksmith left, I went over to Ernst and we hugged and kissed each other. Ernst was carried away with joy.

"You're a magician! An artist! What you just did deserves the highest marks for diplomacy."

Personally, I felt deflated. As soon as the tension escaped me, I collapsed in total exhaustion, unable to speak or move. I had only one wish: to sleep! Ernst was still talking, but I didn't hear him: I was in no condition to absorb anything or to think.

A little later we heard someone opening the door. Soon after that we heard the cackling of hens. When it grew quiet again, Ernst got up because I could no longer move. He crossed to the other side and returned soon after with a few chunks of bread and a pot of water. We feasted and then buried ourselves in the hay. Intoxicated by the smell of the hay, I slept until evening.

When I awoke, it was night. Through the cracks in the wall, we could see electric lights flickering. This was our second night outside the camp, but our first night of rest, of freedom from the fear of death. I felt as if we had lived through a ferocious battle, which we had won, but other battles still faced us. I prayed that the two days for which we had permission to stay here would last forever. The thought that the war might not end in two days— that we would have to seek another hiding place—caused me much worry.

In the meantime I tried not to think about anything, so as not to poison my spirit or dampen my joy. We lay in the hay and speculated about how much longer the war would last. In my view, it couldn't continue much longer. If Berlin fell to the Russians and the Allies captured the Ruhr, the

225

Germans would be paralyzed. At that point the people of the countries they occupied would rise up and finish them off.

Late in the following day the Pole came up, bringing me two hunks of bread and margarine, and told me that the Germans were running around in shock because the news on the radio was so frightening. They had lost all hope of victory. The Russians and the Poles were in downtown Berlin and were conducting pogroms on the Germans. A colleague of his who listened to the underground radio had heard all this on the Polish broadcast of Voice of America. He and his friends were just waiting for something to happen in this district and then they would rise up themselves. The blacksmith hadn't betrayed me. He had just told him to make sure that no strangers came near and that the loft was kept locked.

The blacksmith did not show himself to us at all, but from the food that was left—supposedly for the hens—we saw that our situation was improving. We had already seen a piece of fresh white bread, a piece of cheese, a hard-boiled egg from our neighbors the hens.

The following day the Pole returned again and told me that in Italy, Mussolini had been captured and hanged. He added that Hitler was believed to be dead. The Russians were looking for him in the hope of capturing him alive. In the meantime there was still fighting in Bavaria, not far from Munich. His boss was afraid he might be shipped to the front. Anyone who could hold a gun was being sent there.

At this point I told him I wasn't alone and introduced him to Ernst. Without betraying any surprise, he joked: "A boy already has been born?" I told him that though he wasn't a Pole, he was a regular guy. If with God's help we were freed, we should all go together to make ourselves known to the American soldiers. In the meantime, I told him not to say a word—not even to his best friends—because it was too dangerous.

The two days went by. I was afraid the blacksmith would come up and order us to leave, according to the agreement we had made. I had already prepared fresh arguments for persuading him to extend his permission. But he didn't appear at all. It seems that he didn't want to evict us and wasn't going to insist that we keep our word.

Judging from the food the blacksmith was leaving for the hens, it was obvious he had forgiven my debt. Even if I had decided to leave, he probably would have refused to let me go. I was his guarantee that nothing would happen to him later. I had already found a piece of cake and some apples among the "chicken feed." I had even found a pot of milk. My joy was indescribable.

Ernst kept hugging and kissing me. He asked me to forgive him for causing me so much aggravation. He could see now that I had been right, and since the blacksmith had forgiven our agreement, he no longer brought up the subject of our leaving.

71

The Downfall of the Third Reich

On April 29, 1945, we were still hiding in the loft, feverishly awaiting our liberation. Hitler's "Thousand-Year Reich" was collapsing. The last remnants of the Wehrmacht were trying to surrender to the Americans and the British rather than to the Russians. Behind the Führer's back, but separately, Himmler and Goering were trying to negotiate a capitulation with the British and the Americans.

Himmler was negotiating with the Swede, Count Bernadotte, who had lines of communication between the German military and the Allies. He wanted to sign a separate surrender with the British and the Americans so that they could march eastward quickly without interference. But the British and Americans were refusing to deal with Himmler, who was the hangman of Europe, the leader of the SS and the bloody Gestapo. So these negotiations came to nothing.

Goering, who at the time was in southern Germany, was trying to contact the American general Dwight Eisenhower to negotiate a capitulation in the west. The Germans and the Allies could then fight the Russians together. According to a decree of 1941, Goering was supposed to be Hitler's successor. Once he saw that Berlin was about to fall to the Russians, he felt justified in taking over command of the Wehrmacht. However, as wise men say, "The sinners don't repent, even at the gates of hell."

When Hitler heard that Himmler and Goering were trying to negotiate with the British and the Americans, he became enraged because neither had consulted him. He expelled them both from the National Socialist Party and stripped them of their powers. He also appointed as his successor Admiral Doenitz. Hitler was bitter and disappointed and saw himself as betrayed by all his best commanders. In his last order, issued from his bunker on April 29, he announced: "To all Germans, all National Socialists, men, and women, and all soldiers of the Wehrmacht, I command you to be loyal and attentive to the new government and its president, Admiral Doenitz, until death. For all purposes, I charge the government, the nation, and the *Gefolgschaft* with the strict enforcement of the racial laws and with the unceasing opposition to the world poisoners of all nations, international Judaism" [signed April 29, 1945, 4 A.M.].

He then married Eva Braun. The following day, April 30, the newly-weds would commit suicide together. In twelve years Hitler had destroyed half the world; now he would destroy himself and let himself be buried in the rubble of the Reichstag.

When the world learned about Hitler's death, it was understood that the war had ended. The Wehrmacht had no more coal, ammunition, or fuel for its bombers and tanks. Yet some isolated German troops continued to fight hard against the Allies because they hadn't received orders to stop. In the last days, soldiers fell by the thousands on both sides, though mainly on the German side. The Allied air force was very active, destroying the last remnants of the German forces. British and American troops took Hamburg, Magdeburg, and Leipzig and linked up with the Russian armies on the Elbe.

On April 30 the Russians stormed the Reichstag and penetrated its deepest reaches. They did not find Hitler alive, however. Earlier that day he had made an end to his dog's life. His last followers had dragged his body out to the garden of the Reich Chancellery, together with that of Eva Braun, poured gasoline over them, and incinerated them.

Yet still the war continued. The Wehrmacht leaders still hoped to sign a separate surrender with the Allies, in the hope of keeping the Russians off German soil. However, Hitler himself had ended this possibility by punishing Himmler and Goering.

The Russians entered Germany like a herd of wild beasts, destroying and burning everything in their path. They were seeking revenge for the destruction the Germans had done to their own cities and towns. Also, there were many Poles, Romanians, Hungarians, Yugoslavs, and Jews among the Soviet forces, all of whom had reason to seek their own revenge. Berlin was flattened, its houses destroyed, its women raped. Ashes and dust were all that was left.

72

The Last Act of German Resistance

I learned later that two days after we ran away, the *Waldlager* was evacuated. The Germans still had not surrendered. Their new plan was to continue the war from the Alps. For this they would need workers to dig trenches. So it was that the Wehrmacht high command decided to march the slave laborers out of the camps to build trenches, under a hail of bullets and bombs. Besides, they were still committed to Hitler's goal of liquidating Europe's Jews. The slaves would dig the trenches and build new fortifications and would then be exterminated.

Only the sick who could not be moved were left in the *Waldlager*, along with a few functionaries, among them some of the *Stallkommando,* who were needed to look after the animals. According to the plan, all of these people were to be gathered in two blocks afterward and burnt. Those who tried to save themselves were to be shot. But it seems that the *Hauptmann*—a Wehrmacht man, not with the SS—was against this plan and would not let SS troops carry it out.

Those who left on the transport had their train attacked, and many of the camp slaves were killed by bombs. After a day or two, the doors of the transport wagons were opened and the slaves were told they were free. The joy was tremendous. However, before they could get away, a new order was issued: the war was continuing, and everyone was to climb back into the wagons. Many inmates tried to escape right then and were shot to death. All of this was just hours before liberation. The train continued rolling aimlessly until American tanks blocked its way and freed the hungry and suffering slaves.

◆　◆　◆

In the loft we knew nothing about all this. It was precisely such a death that I had feared all along. At times of confusion and chaos, it is very easy to lose one's life—to be in the line of a random bullet, a bomb, or a bully in uniform who is looking for a chance to take out his anger.

On April 30 the Pole came up to us and told us that Hitler had committed suicide, though the war still wasn't "officially" over. Although we had expected it, the news still took us by surprise. Tears flooded my eyes. At last, the devil had breathed his last. How many innocents had he killed, how many families had he destroyed, before killing himself?

At dawn we were awakened by a tremendous commotion in the village. We heard crying, shrieking, shots, and orders being shouted. The last reservists were being rounded up to be taken to the front. Children and old people were being pulled from their beds and taken to assembly points. The children cried, the old people coughed, the women wrung their hands as they watched their children and parents being led away. The entire village had assembled. Our blacksmith was also taken. He became an army commander. For the first time I saw the woman of the house, a thin, pale, sick woman. She glanced up at the loft as if all her hope lay there.

Around eight o'clock the entire "army" was led off, and it once more became quiet in the village. Before long, however, we heard artillery. The shells were being aimed directly over the loft so that the roof was nearly blown away. "Hold up the roof!" I shouted to Ernst. "We may be discovered!"

The shooting continued the whole night of May 1 and 2. Apparently the entire operation was taking place along the banks of the river Inn. The Germans were on one side, the Americans on the other with the Third Army of General George Patton. Soon enough, the Allied air force stilled the German guns. In the silence that ensued, we heard the distant roar of American tanks, which were already on their way from Mühldorf to Ampfing. Soon the Pole came up to us together with the woman of the house, who got acquainted with us and asked us to come down to her house. We were led like grooms to the wedding canopy.

She had prepared a table for us that did indeed resemble a wedding banquet. Everyone wanted to please us. The woman told us she had risked her life for us by not allowing us to be sent away. We began to eat, but the food would not go down, first of all because we were very emotional, psychologically shaken from the experience, and second because we weren't used to such food, which we had not seen in years. The woman begged us to eat and drink. The Pole packed away a meal, had a few drinks, and began to sing Polish songs. He wanted to hug me as if we were brothers.

Ernst drank a little too much and became flushed, but he did not talk, merely stumbled. The woman watched us with both joy and distrust. I drank very little. I was afraid to get drunk because I had to evaluate the situation and plan what to do next. Ernst wanted to go out, but I refused to let him; at night it was safer to stay indoors.

We were led to the bedroom and given the owners' beds. Before going to sleep, I wanted to get washed. I hadn't washed in many days and was terribly itchy. They heated a kettle of water and gave me a basin and some clean clothes, which the blacksmith's wife took from her armoire. I felt as if I had washed away a bucket of dirt. My friend did the same and then we went to bed—the first time in so many years in a clean bed with sheets and comforters.

When I lay down I let out a yell: the mattress was so soft I thought I was sinking. I grabbed the comforter to save myself and fell down. The same thing happened to Ernst. We were no longer used to such beds. Frightened, the woman rushed in. When we told her what had happened, she began to laugh and called in the housemaids to tell them about this most unusual wonder.

73

My First Night as a Free Man

I could not fall asleep. I was full of impressions of the past few days and my heart was so overloaded with joy that I could not calm down. What should I do now? Should I go back to the camp to see what happened to our friends? Should I go out and meet the American troops? I wanted to ask Ernst for advice, but he was sleeping so soundly that I couldn't bring myself to wake him. His face was so calm, so satisfied, his smile so pure. No doubt he was having beautiful dreams.

As soon as daylight started to seep through the shutters, I got out of bed and woke him. It took a long time. When he opened his eyes I started to shout: *"Auf, auf!* Roll call!!! *Komm, Mensch.* We have to go meet General Patton. He's waiting for us."

We washed quickly and got into our striped clothes because those were our insignia, but the woman would not let us go before we ate breakfast.

"You see, Ernst," I said, "lodging has been arranged for us. We no longer have to compete for our food with the hens. Let's go up there and return some food to them so they won't be angry with us."

We went out in the street. People gazed at us as if we had won the war single-handedly.

The Pole immediately called together all the slave laborers in the village: Poles, Czechs, Yugoslavs, Italians, and Ukrainians. I made a speech to them—

"Now we are free and will be able to return home to our families. Unfortunately, many of us will not find our families, who were murdered by the Nazis, or our homes, which were destroyed by them. We shall seek out our murderers and torturers and their henchmen and will pay them back for their brutality. Hitler did not torture and destroy only us foreigners, our

233

houses and cities. He also brought about the destruction of his own land. Millions of victims, millions of widows and orphans—that's the final result of this insane war that one individual wrought upon the world. But let us behave responsibly. Let us not rob and plunder. Before we do anything else we have to meet with the commanders of the American army that has come to free us."

All the non-Jewish slave laborers in the village laughed at my naïveté. Each of them was already dressed in the best clothing of his bosses or neighbors. All of them already had pockets full of "borrowed" goods. Even so, everyone agreed that we ought to go out and meet the American authorities. Someone scrounged a tall pole, and someone else "organized" a sheet from a house. This white banner of truce was given to me to carry. I knew the way to the nearest railway station, through the surrounding forests, so I led the procession.

We came to a crossroads where there was parked a Sherman tank in which there sat a white officer, and behind him a giant black soldier, who was chewing on something. When he saw us his jaw dropped and his eyes moved back and forth in their white sockets.

"Who are you?" the soldier shouted, clenching his machine gun in his hands.

I explained in bad English that we were foreign slave laborers and concentration camp inmates, that we came from various European countries, and that we wanted to present ourselves to the commander.

The soldier sized us up from head to toe and smiled, showing us gleaming white teeth. He opened his rucksack and took out cookies, chocolate, and chewing gum, which he distributed among us. He also told us to go to Ampfing.

In Ampfing's market square a bonfire was burning. Around the fire, soldiers from various divisions and ranks were warming themselves, for a cool wind was sweeping the air. Jeeps and trucks sped past in all directions, directed by orderlies with guide books. The side streets were blocked off by tanks and armored cars. I felt lost, as if at a wedding where I didn't know any of the celebrants. I stood among the soldiers, watching what was happening. Across the square from me stood an American officer, who did not take his eyes off me. It was as if his eyes were punching holes in me. Suddenly he vanished. Not long after that I felt a hand on my shoulder. I turned around and saw him, and heard him ask me: "Are you Jewish? I'm a Jewish boy."

It was as if he had sent an electric charge through me. A Jew! A brother, who is extending a warm hand to me! It was too much for me. I broke down. I lost my speech and my eyes flooded with tears. It was as if a dam had burst inside me and flooded my heart with tears. I sobbed as if in a convulsion. I could not calm down. I fell to the ground and threw myself around. I exploded. Many times during my years in the camps I had felt a need to cry my heart out, to unburden myself of my loneliness and desperation, but at no time could I cry. It was as if my well of tears had gone dry. Now, suddenly, I was flooding myself with tears.

I had imagined that there were no Jews left in Europe, that we were the last remnants of our murdered people. There had been among us Jews from all the European countries, from all the countries that had been emptied of Jews. The greater part of them had been gassed in the chambers and incinerated in the crematoria. Only a handful had been scattered around Europe as slave laborers. Now, here, suddenly, I saw an American Jew, a true flesh-and-blood brother in the uniform of an officer of the armies that had helped behead the Nazi snake. He was extending his hand to me like a brother. My head spun and I fainted.

I do not know what happened to me after that. I only know that I woke up in a bed. I saw at my bedside a military doctor and a nurse, who was wiping the sweat from my forehead. It took two days for me to recover from my shock. During that time I met many high-ranking officers. Some of them spoke broken Yiddish, and some spoke fluent German. They asked me where I came from and whether I had any family. Of my family in Poland I had little hope of finding anyone. I knew my mother had been taken away in a transport to Treblinka. I knew nothing about my brother and his family in Krakow.

Only later did I learn that my brother's entire family had been hiding in a cellar in Krakow-Plaszów. Some traitor snitched on them and their hiding place was discovered. When the Gestapo came, my brother ran, but as soon as he saw that the Gestapo was taking away his wife and their daughter, he joined them because he did not want to be separated from them. The beastly chief of the Krakow Gestapo, Haman, probably had them executed.

My brother and his wife had placed their youngest child, a boy of three, in the safekeeping of a Polish maid who had worked for them for more than five years and was very attached to their children. Of this woman, more later.

I knew I had a brother in Brazil, in Rio de Janeiro, and also relatives in the United States and Canada, but I could not remember their addresses. They promised to search for my relatives and tell them I had survived.

74

I Become a Confidant of the U.S. Army

As soon as I got up from bed, I asked the army commander to drive out to the *Waldlager* to see what had happened to the sick. A caravan of around thirty jeeps was organized, at the head of which were the highest commanders of the U.S. Seventh Army. If I am not mistaken, General Hodges rode along. I rode in the leading jeep with the officers to show them the way.

It was springtime, and the sun warmed our faces. The forest was fragrant with stirring nature. This was one of the most fortunate mornings of my life. Here I was, a free man who had just shed the chains of slavery, leading four of the highest commanders of the U.S. liberation forces to the camp where I had so recently struggled for my existence. I took them to the infirmary, where the beds were full of dying slaves who were too weak to rise. When the commanders saw these skeletal bodies, with their yellow skin covered with sores and boils, several of them started to cry. These were battle-hardened war leaders who had repeatedly seen and faced death, yet when they saw these living dead, they burst into tears.

One of the sick fainted when he saw the American commanders. When we revived him, he whispered through parched lips: "Enough. I was waiting for this. Now I can die." And he did.

The commanders ordered that the O.T. headquarters, one of the largest buildings in Ampfing, be emptied completely and turned into a hospital for camp inmates. Furthermore, the entire German population of the district was to be mobilized to transfer the sick and bring them beds, bedding, and clothing. I was given the responsibility to oversee all of this and was assigned twenty soldiers and officers to assist me.

From all directions, people started bringing beds and bedding. Meanwhile, we drove out with a caravan of twenty wagons and ambulances to the

Waldlager, carried the living skeletons from the barrack, and placed them in the clean beds. All the doctors in the surrounding district were mobilized to examine the sick under the supervision of the American military doctors, and treatments were started. All the necessary medical supplies were requisitioned from pharmacists in the area. The medicines that weren't available were shipped by air from France and even from the United States.

It was impossible to save many of the sick. Many died not of diseases but rather because it was simply too late—they no longer resembled human beings. They were wrecks, skin and bones. In their eyes one could see death looking out.

A large group of German nurses were mobilized to attend to them. These German girls worked very willingly because here they got good food and the opportunity to meet and flirt with the American soldiers.

As soon as I had finished doing what I could for the sick, I was assigned another "job": searching for war criminals. I knew them all and knew where to find them. The Germans themselves also denounced them and showed where they were hiding. I was assigned an officer and two soldiers, and we drove around looking for the SS and Gestapo hangmen. I found them and handed them over to the Americans. To my regret, most of them got off with light punishment.

My name became known among the German civilians. The blacksmith and his wife came to see me. He came, he said, simply to see how I was, but he did not go home empty-handed. I gave them provisions for a whole month, as well as clothing and American nylons for his wife. "This I am giving you, with interest, for feeding me for a week," I told them. "This is for you and for the hens I wronged. I also will not let anyone harm you. If anything happens, let me know right away and I will protect you. And you, lady," I said to the blacksmith's wife, "don't ever faint when you have the opportunity to save someone."

75

Jewish Revenge

Those who were freed from the camps wandered around aimlessly. For the time being they gathered in refugee camps, where the U.S. Army looked after them. Most of them didn't know where to go or what to do with themselves. The Polish Jews knew very well that their homes had been destroyed and their families murdered. Most of them stayed in Mühldorf and Ampfing for the time being, waiting for new documents and making initial contacts. During the day they wandered the streets; in the evening, initially, they had nothing to do. The O.T. building that had been converted into a hospital happened to have a large recreation room, and this was turned into a club for Jewish refugees, who would gather in the evenings to watch films, put on plays, and hold dances. The American soldiers, especially the Jewish soldiers and officers, also came here to enjoy themselves together with us. A similar recreation center for former inmates was established in a destroyed museum in Munich.

Now I want to describe an act of "Jewish revenge," which in comparison with what the Germans did to us seems like child's play. One day, while strolling down a main street of Ampfing, I heard someone approaching me from behind. Suddenly a woman called my name. I turned and saw the woman who had once watched me from her office window in the O.T. headquarters every time I pumped sewage from the tank there. Apparently it amused her to watch me; yet it never occurred to her to toss me a piece of bread. Now she was seeking me out to remind me that we were acquainted.

"You remember," she said to me, "how I used to watch you when you worked in the yard of our headquarters? I used to feel for you so deeply and wonder how I could help you."

"Sure you thought," I replied, "but you didn't reach any conclusions. Your looks didn't satisfy my hunger."

"I *wanted* to help you, but it was too dangerous, so I wanted to at least encourage you with my sympathy."

"Yes," I answered sarcastically, "that's the same sympathy one offers a man who is being hanged while the noose is tightening around his neck."

I wanted to leave, but she clung to me and started to cuddle up:

"My dear, I always sympathized with you and want your friendship in the future. I'm celebrating my birthday today and want to invite you."

I understood very well what lay behind all this: she had heard about my influence and prestige among the Americans and was now trying to get something through me. At that moment it occurred to me to punish her for her hypocrisy. I thanked her for the invitation, took down her address, and promised to come if I could. Then I asked whether I could bring some friends with me. She told me I could and let me know that her friends also wanted to meet me.

I returned to the headquarters and sought out three American soldiers who were known for their drunkenness and brutality. I gave them her name and address, told them the situation, and made sure they took plenty of schnapps along.

The following day, when I met with the soldiers, they were still drunk. They told me about the orgies they had engaged in with this woman. Later she came running to me to complain that I hadn't come and had sent drunken soldiers in my place, who had chased everyone else out of the house and forced her to do things against her will. However, from the way she talked, she didn't sound terribly hurt.

76

I Tear Myself Away from Bloody German Soil

I wanted to get away from the bloody German soil. I could not stand the air, the atmosphere, or the faces. I imagined that I had seen all these faces at the gas chambers and crematoria, at the roundups and transports, at the hangings and executions. As far as I was concerned, all German hands were smeared with Jewish blood. Even if they personally had not murdered, they had known and encouraged those who had. I remembered the old Wehrmacht guard in Sosnowiec: I thought he had been a "good" German, yet while we were being herded down into the courtyard one night, with the rain pouring down, I had asked him to allow me to fetch a blanket for a half-naked child, and he had threatened to beat me with the butt of his rifle.

I also wanted to leave Germany in the hope of finding survivors among my family.

Transportation to France was being arranged for a group of camp survivors, and I signed up to join it. I had many friends among the French Jews. They encouraged me to come with them and made certain I was included in the transport. Every few days groups like this left Munich's airport, Karlsfeld, on American planes. On May 23, 1945, I left with the first of these planes. There was a farewell party for me at the Ampfing recreation center, which several American officers attended, and another at the center in Munich.

Our plane to Paris was bedecked with American and French flags. I was very emotional during the flight. It was my first journey as a free man after so many years as a slave. I had stopped believing this would ever happen, yet now I had emerged from hell and was flying in an American plane to the free world. Also, I would be seeing Paris for the first time. I had read and heard much about this wonderful metropolis of love and freedom. My friends in the camp were never able to stop describing the fantastic life in that city. Now one of my fondest dreams was about to be realized: I was to see it with my own eyes. This had a powerful effect on me.

After a flight of ninety minutes, we landed at an airfield near the town of Nancy. This town is known internationally for its university. Friends of mine had studied there before the war. The mayor and a huge crowd came out to greet us, singing the "Marseillaise," and the city was "handed over to us." One of our group thanked the mayor for this friendly reception: not only were we free again from tyranny, but so was France, and so was the entire world. Practically the whole town had gathered at the airport to cheer us. People tossed flowers at us, and many girls broke through the ropes and kissed us.

A banquet was held for us in the town hall. Everything served was the best and finest. Women volunteers competed to serve us and showered us with so much friendliness and love that we were moved to tears.

This was a turning point in my life. This was a reception for French citizens who had returned from the Nazi camps. On this joyous occasion I was a foreigner, a Polish citizen, so what was I doing here? The girls spoke to me in French. I could not understand them, could not answer them, so I pointed to my neck to suggest that I had lost my voice. They saw tears in my eyes and felt compassion for me, thinking I was ill. I felt drunk from all that I saw and felt here. All of this was new to me; I had never seen anything like it in my old home. Would the Poles have offered a homecoming this warm? I remembered how the Poles had hunted in the forests for Jews to murder or to sell to the Nazis for a kilo of sugar.

Every hour that day another transport arrived at Nancy from Munich. As soon as a few hundred refugees had assembled, we were all paraded to the train station, loaded onto a coach, and taken away to Paris. The train was decorated with French flags, and in all the towns through which we passed, people cheered us and waved to us with flags. The girls threw flowers and kisses to us. I was full of joy. I sat with my friends from the camp and let the French songs intoxicate me. *For this moment alone,* I thought, *the struggle to survive was worth it.*

I deeply regretted that my friend Dr. Avraham Suchodolsky was not among us. He had been made to stay behind in Warsaw while the camp there was being evacuated. I had not yet learned that my dear friend had been killed in Warsaw during the Polish uprising. He had told me so many stories about Paris and had promised me that after we were freed he would take me there to show me the legendary city.

77

We Arrive in Paris

We arrived in Paris—if I remember correctly, at the Gare du Nord. It was a cloudy morning. Here we came upon a painful scene. Scores of women and children were standing on the platform holding up photographs of their loved ones for us to study and asking us tearfully if we had seen or met their husbands, fathers, or brothers. They wanted the truth and waited with trembling hearts for it. Sometimes, to cheer them up, to give them a little hope, I lied: "I think I did meet him in a camp. He'll probably come home soon."

There were also emotional scenes when family members recognized one another. There was no limit to their joy. I held out no hope of meeting anyone from my family. I simply went with the flow. We were taken by bus to a well-known luxury hotel, the Lutecia, which had been the Gestapo headquarters during the war. There we were registered, bathed, and given fresh, clean underwear. Doctors came to examine us and sent the sick to hospitals and sanitariums.

The next day we strode out onto the happy, bustling streets of Paris. People stared at us as if we were from another planet. We were still wearing the striped uniforms of the camp, which immediately identified us as returnees from "that world." The buses, subways, and trains were free for us. The restaurants didn't want to accept our money. It pained us when women or old people rose on the buses or subway trains to give us their seats. Once, when I was walking along the Champs Elysées, a young woman ran up to me, opened her purse, which was full of bank notes, and told me: "Here. Take as much as you want."

I was embarrassed, and took only a small bank note—enough to make her happy.

The gathering place for Jewish refugees in Paris was the house at Guy-

Pétain 9. Old friends met here and new acquaintances were made. Here were refugees from all the camps and from all of Europe's destroyed Jewish communities. Refugees could find meals and clothes and arrange a place to sleep. Also, from here we could announce to the world that we had survived the deluge. I knew I had a brother in Rio de Janeiro and relatives in New York and Toronto, but I could not remember their addresses. However, through the "Joint" (Joint Distribution Committee) and "HIAS" (Hebrew Immigrant Aid Society), I could inform them that I had survived and that they could reach me at the Jewish Centre in Paris.

I would need a passport if I was to leave Paris, so I went to the Polish Consulate, where I encountered Karl Grauer, a former neighbor of mine in Sosnowiec. Now he was the secretary of the Polish Embassy. He started my paperwork and then took me to the home of his in-laws, the Polishuks, where I ate my first home-cooked meal and also received a watch as a gift. Now I was a civilian again, with proper clothing, a decent pair of shoes, a passport, and a watch.

Grauer's brother-in-law, Jack Polishuk, gave me a temporary bed in his bachelor apartment in one of the most elegant quarters of Paris. I now had my own quarters, albeit only borrowed. It was then that I started to write, recalling all I had lived through, putting it all down on paper. I wanted to engrave my memories so that they would never disappear. I also started to write poems, stories, and essays. I even started a play (which I never managed to complete).

One of my friends from Guy-Pétain 9, with whom I had become very close, was the writer Mordechai Strigler. He was already working at the Jewish daily *Undzer Vort*. I showed him one of my pieces, which he took home to read. Meanwhile the French government arranged for me and some of my friends a twenty-one-day stay at the spas at Lourdes and later at a town near the Spanish border in the Pyrenees, all at government expense. Lourdes is famous for its healing waters. It is also famous as a center of pilgrimage for Catholics, many of whom arrive unable to walk and leave on their own feet. One can see hundreds of pairs of crutches hanging on the gates of the healing institutions. At Lourdes there are also famous underground caves that nature has sculpted into wonderful formations.

Lourdes was a magical place for us. The landscape was beautiful and the mild air was a soothing balm. Djer was also magnificent. We encountered many health seekers from Paris and other French cities. The staff and guests at these places were very kind to us and tried to help us in any way they could. A Frenchwoman took it on herself to teach me French. Every day we went walking through the picturesque countryside, and she taught me the names of things. We picked juicy figs from the trees and grapes from vines. On Sundays, picnicking families sent us over wine, fruit, and snacks. It was a blessed time for us after the years of suffering.

One day while we were sitting in the garden of our villa the mail came, with a package for me. I was astonished: a package in the mail for me! I glanced at the return address: M. Strigler, *Undzer Vort*, (*Notre Parole*), Paris. Excitedly, I opened the package and took out several Jewish newspapers. In two of them were articles I had written. Enclosed was the following note:

Dear friend Charmatz: I looked through your material and noted that you have great talent and aptitude to write in a way that appeals greatly to the reader. I permitted myself to publish two of your stories, which evoked a very good response. I advise you to occupy yourself more extensively with writing, because this is definitely your calling [. . .]—Motel.

This was a great surprise for me. I was used to writing merely as a hobby—poems, stories, and essays. I had never written for money, possibly because business life absorbed all my time. Now, on seeing my articles in print and hearing praise from such a gifted man as Mordechai Strigler, journalism began to tempt me as a profession.

When I returned to Paris, Strigler introduced me to the editor of *Undzer Vort*: I. Fink, bless his memory, who hired me to contribute more articles. Now I had an income. It was only a small one, but even so it was as sweet as sugar for me: I would no longer have to rely on the generosity of the "Joint" or the local aid societies. I began to travel in France and other countries as a correspondent for the newspaper. I visited the concentration camps in Germany and Italy and sent back reports, which were well received and quickly became popular with readers. This awakened in me the desire to write more, and I started to become ambitious. I quickly found myself in congenial circles and met a lot of people and made a lot of friends.

Dr. Mark Dworzecki also began working for the newspaper. He quickly became a warm and dear friend, after I got used to him talking unceasingly about "his" Vilna. More and more Jews began arriving from Poland, having returned from the camps and from Russia, and among them I quickly made friends and acquaintances. Among them were a number of writers, artists, and intellectuals, and we quickly made ourselves a "family." Perhaps this circle was our substitute for the families we had lost and missed so much.

Postwar Paris was becoming a great center of Jewish culture, of literary talent. Conferences were held, and special evenings were arranged for concerts and plays. At one of these concerts of Jewish folklore, Yehudit Moretzka and Perl Schechter sang, and I had a very pleasant surprise. Moretzka sang one of my poems, "I had a mother," which she had set to music. Since I was in the audience, I had to go up on the stage and take a bow.

I grew to love Paris very much. In time it became my second home, perhaps because it was here that I first experienced the emotions of freedom. Perhaps, also, it was because of the colors, the magic, and the pulsating life of this international metropolis. After so many years in the ghettoes and camps, it was as if paradise had opened its gates to me and I had permission to draw from all wells of life and pleasure. I had no great aspirations: it took very little to satisfy me because everything was a gain for me.

My circle of acquaintances kept broadening and getting more interesting. Eventually I moved out of Jack Polishuk's apartment and rented a garret near Place de la République, in a hotel that was always cozy and full of people. Mordechai Strigler lived in the same hotel, and so did A. M. Lieberman and the singers Moretzka and Schechter. We would often venture out together and walk and walk the streets of Paris without any particular destination, with all the time in the world at our disposal.

One evening Strigler and I set out from our hotel, strolling the great boulevards and squares—Champs Elysées, Place de la Concorde, and through the Rivoli as far as the Bastille. We never grew tired. We savored every inch of the way, the sight of all the people, the panoramas. We could not get enough of all we saw. And all of the sights were free. Where could we have gotten money?

78

The First Contacts with My Family

My relatives learned that I was alive from the lists that were issued of the survivors of the camps, and that I was in Paris. I began receiving letters from my brother in Rio de Janeiro, from an uncle in New York, Rabbi Elimelech Bleiberg, and from relatives in Toronto. When I received the first letter, I started to cry. It was the first contact with my family, from whom I had been torn away so many years ago. Even from such a great distance, I felt their warmth and support. I no longer felt abandoned in God's world: someone was interested in me and cared about me. I read the letters over and over, as if I couldn't believe my eyes, and absorbed their heartfelt words, which I had not heard for years.

Soon parcels of food and clothing arrived, and well as some money. My situation changed completely. I began to buy household items, to dress better, to live more like a human being.

My brother in Rio started to arrange immigration documents for Brazil. At the same time, my uncle in New York began arranging an affidavit to bring me to the United States. It had been far more difficult before the war, when many Jews tried hard to enter the United States, the "Golden Land," but were prevented from doing so by immigration "quotas."

I was drawn to Brazil. My only brother was there and I wanted to be near him and his family. I waited to see which country would accept me first. Destiny made it Brazil. Soon after that, the Americans also approved me, and the U.S. Consulate invited me over to pick up my immigration papers, but it was too late.

I did not want to leave Europe without visiting the city of my birth and learning more about what had happened to my family. I had known for years that my mother had almost certainly perished in Treblinka, and I held out very little hope of finding her alive. It was possible that someone from my other brother's family had survived. Someone had told me that Akiva had been hiding with his family in a cellar in Plaszów, a suburb of Krakow, until they had been betrayed. Also, that my brother had entrusted to the family maid his youngest child, a three-year-old boy. Against her promise to hide the child, he had given her half of everything he owned. This gave me no rest. I would have to travel to Poland to try to find this child. While there I would investigate what happened to my property in Sosnowiec and my parents' property in Ostrowiec. I would never find peace until I made this journey.

79

I Depart for Poland

On my way to Poland I stopped in Germany to visit a few concentration camps. At Frankfurt am Main I encountered the first wave of Polish refugees. They looked dirty, downtrodden, and in disarray from their long journey. At the Jewish centers they wandered the corridors and stairs or stretched out on their bundles, barely able to stay awake. A young woman was lying on the floor staring suspiciously at every passerby. When I felt her piercing eyes on me, I became uncomfortable and asked: "Why do you look at me with so much anger?"

She sat up, as if ready to start an argument, and asked: "Are you some sort of leader here?"

"I am nothing here," I smiled, wanting to ease the tension. "But why are you so angry at the leaders here?"

"Yes, I'm angry," the woman replied, sinking down again. "They should be sent to where we just came from—then they'd know how to treat exhausted people who have nowhere to rest. We've been en route a whole week with nowhere to wash or rest. We're lying and stinking in our own dirt."

Another woman could hardly lift her head from a heap of rags. One of her eyes was stuck closed, the other was blinking. "Yes," she told me, "committees, offices, but nobody gives us a place to rest our heads."

"Where do you Jews come from?" I asked, the way one asks seriously ill people about their health.

"From Poland." The word fell like a stone from a husky male voice.

When I asked what the news was from there, they began telling me about some of the horrors they had faced, which sent a shudder through me. When they heard I was on my way to Poland, several voices at once cried out in wonder: "Where? To Poland?!"

All around the room, people stared at this specter: a Jew who was going to Poland. Now I was the center of attraction. People stared at me from head to toe and studied me from all sides. No one said a word, but all looked at me suspiciously.

I wandered Frankfurt's streets, taking consolation from the destroyed buildings, wrecks just like the ones I had seen in Warsaw. I stopped in front of a heap of rubble that had once been the city's opera house. All that was left was a burnt shell, with two broken chandeliers to remind one of the building's past glories, and the smoke-blackened sign *"Von dem Schönen, dem Guten und dem Wahren"* (To the beautiful, the good and the true). Opposite the building, before the war, had stood a monumental statue of Schiller. The Nazis had melted it down for the war effort.

I was constantly meeting Jewish refugees who had marched here from the banks of the Volga, the Vistula, and the Don. They had crossed seas and rivers and been tossed on high waves looking for someone to let them in and grant them some rest. I met them in the concentration camps of Zalzheim, Landsberg, Feldafing—refugees from Poland and Russia who had gone through flames of hell until they arrived at this transfer point. All of them were exhausted, and were the only survivors of their families, and had survived by a miracle, but they had not yet found a place to rest. The vast majority wanted to go to Israel to resurrect their lives, but the gates of that land had been shut and they were not being allowed in.

I had heard tragic reports from Poland, but this did not put me off: I was determined to carry out my plan. The thought had wormed itself into my mind: I must go to Poland to see what had happened to my family and all that I owned.

80

First Steps on Polish Soil

The first station on Polish soil was Zebrzydowice, a small town on the Czech border. All the passengers in my train car looked out the windows with curiosity. What did Poland look like now? What did it sound like? We had been torn from our homeland many years before, yet on our faces there was no enthusiasm, no excitement. Certainly, each of us longed to see his land once more. It is just that we didn't know what to expect, and this made us both nervous and cautious. We were sounding things out. When we saw soldiers, we were frightened, as if our country was being invaded again.

The Jews on our train had mixed emotions. It was a moving experience to come upon the Polish customs guards, for this was the land of our birth, and the air was the very air we had grown up breathing, and the soil here had absorbed our sweat and hard work. Here lay the bones of our forefathers. We felt connected to this land by thousands of threads. Yet at the same time, the earth was soaked with our tears, with the blood of our families and communities, and the air was dense with the sobs and wails of our martyrs. Even now that the destruction had stopped, we who had escaped the gas chambers and the crematoria could find no rest. We stood there trembling, waiting for a smile or a welcoming gesture, but we found none of this.

After the Polish anthem was played, we changed trains for Dziedzice, where we presented our repatriation documents. At the desks where we filled out immigration forms, comical scenes took place. The repatriates among us who were Silesian gentiles stood there shattered, not knowing what was being asked of them. They became flushed and didn't know how to answer. They were used to answering "Heil Hitler," but Hitler was dead and their new bosses were the Poles, so they would have to learn to speak Polish. Onlookers smiled at the spectacle.

I took my first cautious steps on Polish soil. I wanted to run, to seek, but what would I have been seeking? I didn't know. Here I had lost my youth, my family, and all that I owned. I had once had so many relatives here, so many friends and acquaintances. Where were they now? The earth had swallowed them. So many doors had once been open for me here, so many friendly faces had once greeted me here. Now all doors were closed to me. I did not meet one friendly face. I was a stranger, an intruder.

I arrived at Katowice, where I wandered the streets aimlessly, without meeting a single familiar face. The stores were the same as before, and the windows were displaying the same goods and advertisements, but the Jewish owners were gone. Other people, strangers, had taken over the Jewish properties and possessions. Those Jews who had escaped the gas chambers, when they returned to their homes, were not given back what had been taken from them. This became clear to me when I returned to Sosnowiec.

81

Sosnowiec

Now I returned to Sosnowiec, the city from which I had been herded into the camps, leaving behind everything I owned. First I went to look for my business. The storerooms were again fully stocked. Functionaries sat at desks, as did vice presidents and minor employees. I introduced myself as the former owner, told them I would be able to document it and told them I wanted my property back. The functionaries stared at me as if I had come from another planet. They sent me to the vice president, who introduced me to the president. All the faces of these people were sour, their eyes cold. The president explained to me that the business was presently owned by the government and that I would have to present myself to the city administration and to the head of government businesses. I was directed from one office to the next until eventually it was explained to me that the matter could be investigated only by the Trade Ministry in Warsaw.

I went to Warsaw and found the minister in charge. He received me in a friendly manner and in an even friendlier manner explained that since it was the Germans that had confiscated my business, I must make my claim to them. It hadn't been the Poles that had stolen it from me, so why was I approaching them about getting it back? It had nothing to do with them. True, the business was mine, but since it wasn't the Poles that had taken it from me, I was complaining to the wrong people. Clearly, Jews had no simple right to their property even if by some miracle they had survived the Nazis. This is how the Polish government reasoned.

I also looked up the *Volksdeutsche,* Polachek, who had denounced me to the Gestapo in 1940 after offering to smuggle me out of Sosnowiec. After I was arrested, I had been tortured for four months and my tormentors had stolen a fortune from me. Now I found Polachek walking free. He had been rehabilitated as an honest Pole with all the rights of a Polish citizen. Of course, it wasn't his fault that a witness to his crimes had returned from the dead. He had been certain that all witnesses to his wrongs had perished in the gas chambers—after all, he had sent them there himself. He had washed the blood from his hands, put on an innocent face, and baptized himself in Polish water, and now he was a "kosher" Pole.

I was told that if I wanted justice I would have to find my own proof and supply my own witnesses. I quickly enough saw that if I showed too much tenacity I would be jeopardizing my very life.

I also searched for another *Volksdeutsche* who during the war had bought valuables from me—not, God forbid, for money, but for bread. He had cheated me and eaten the bread himself; after all, the Jew would go to his death anyhow, so why waste the bread? This one also was now rehabilitated—a "kosher" Pole. He had extra good fortune, though. He had provided himself with testimonials and witnesses stating that he himself had suffered under the Nazis. He had been forced to accept valuable ration cards, to enjoy all the rights of a *Volksdeutsche,* to take a share in the property stolen by the "master race." Any crumbs he had left over he had given secretly to some hungry Poles as insurance. After the war those hungry Poles had served as his witnesses, and now he was as clean as can be. Now I was being told to produce witnesses to prove that he had helped the Nazis. The fact that he had robbed hungry Jews of their valuables was no indication. I would have to take him to court and provide witnesses.

That night in Sosnowiec I could not fall asleep. This was my first night on Polish soil, my first night in Sosnowiec as a free man, a survivor of the deportations and selections. At one time I had had so many friends and acquaintances here, there had been so many homes that had welcomed me and entertained me, so many clubs and organizations for Jews, especially young ones. Now I looked up at the windows and waited for a door to open. Perhaps I would meet someone I knew, recognize a familiar face. But none appeared—not one. An entire world had been wiped away.

I walked the streets with a heavy heart. Now I was on Targowa Street, where I had been living just before being sent to Birkenau. The Judenrat headquarters had been on this street in the house of the Radomsker rebbe. On the opposite side had been the headquarters of the Jewish militia. Here terrible tragedies had played themselves out on people who did not want to die, who did not want to be liquidated. The street tonight was almost dead; only a handful of people were scurrying, as if afraid of the night's shadows. I leaned against a wall, shut my eyes, and remembered those harrowing days. Once again I saw people rushing to work, shoving one another, filling the streets and sidewalks. They were making an uproar, crying and arguing in front of the Judenrat house. Right there on the third floor, Manyek Merin and his murderers had sat, all the lights lit, all the typewriters clacking. On the other side, in the offices of the Jewish militia, there was also light. There all the militiamen in their white caps and polished boots were gathering, preparing to go on a "hunt" for Jews for the next transport. Another few minutes and they would start to soar like ravens over the Jewish homes. The living and the dead would be dragged from the garrets and cellars. I heard sobbing. I wanted to escape before they took me as well.

I awoke from my thoughts and saw in front of me an empty street. A woman told me I had dropped my briefcase.

In my hotel room I shut the heavy curtains so as not to see the street. I wanted to close all the cracks so that nightmares couldn't enter, but it didn't help. They penetrated the walls, seeped under the doors and windows to plague me. I tossed and turned all night. Again I endured those days and nights of panic and fear. Hundreds and thousands of people came running, many of them with familiar faces, tearing my eyes open and shouting in my ears. Each of them carried in a sack their unlived years, which they poured out on an altar. The altar swallowed up all their sacrifices, but the fire did not burn out. It continued to burn, waiting for fresh sacrifices.

The following morning I went walking on the streets where thirty thousand Jews had once lived. I met none of them. There had been wealthy Jews in Sosnowiec, the owners of long-established firms that had been handed down through generations. These families had convinced themselves that they were strong as oak trees, that no storm or crisis could topple or uproot them. I looked for these same Jews now and couldn't find them. The signs of their shops were painted over with new names and insignias. Their order forms were being used as toilet paper.

In Sosnowiec there had been a wealthy Jew, a handsome man with a blond beard, a Hassid of Radom, a regular visitor to the rebbe's court. He owned half a street of houses and a large warehouse with hundreds of employees. The entire city paid attention to every word he spoke. It was no small matter when Reb Feivl said something. When he was asked why he didn't go to *Eretz Israel,* why he had not bought any property there, he laughed at the fools, the naïve dreamers: "What do I need *Eretz Israel* for? I have *Eretz Israel* here. I'll wait for the Messiah."

As he spoke, he looked up at the tall houses that he had constructed and that reached skyward at his command. Now as I walked down Mandzever Street, I saw him at the entrance to a tiny store in one of his houses. He had survived. How? By pure chance, a miracle. But he was no longer the same. His fine blond beard was gone, replaced by only a few gray strands. His cheeks were sunken and his eyes were empty of all feeling. The sign over the store no longer bore his name. The name of a Polish gentile woman was now on the sign. When he saw me he turned pale and shuddered. He took me by the hand, led me into the store, and started speaking nervously to me in Polish:

"I'm not called Feivl anymore, but Pavel, and I don't understand Yiddish."

As he spoke, he pointed to a picture on the wall in which there was an eternal light. I understood everything.

"She's the boss," he added, "and I'm her silent partner," he whispered.

82

I Am Once More in Krakow

I left for Krakow. Revisiting this city was my main reason for returning to Poland. I hoped I would be able to find my young nephew, who had been left for safekeeping with Marisha, my brother's Polish maid. I rode to Stroma 6, the house in Podgórze where my brother once lived, and asked about her, but no one could tell me where she now lived. However, they did know where Marilka, the governess of my brother's children, could be found, and they directed me to her home. I had known her well. She had been young and slender, but now a stout woman with the same face answered my knock. I barely recognized her. She had changed husbands during the war and obviously had not suffered from hunger. When she saw me she made the sign of the cross and gave me the address of Marisha, whom she met from time to time. She knew she had taken the child to hide, but she wasn't certain if the child was still with her.

My heart started to hammer. It was clear that the governess was trying to hide something from me. She invited me into her house, but I didn't want to go in. Instead I went straight to the address she had given me, which was far outside the city.

Here I was, on the street, in front of the house, in front of the door. I summoned my self-control, knowing I was in for a very rude shock. When I knocked, the door opened right away. There stood Marisha in my sister-in-law's housecoat. When she saw me she drew back and turned white as a sheet. She grasped the table so that she wouldn't fall. I sat down on a stool to collect myself and started to speak hurriedly:

"Marisha, I know you took young Marek to hide. My brother and sister-in-law trusted you greatly. They thought of you as a member of the family. So what happened to the child?" She broke down in tears and told me:

"Yes, I did take the child. You know how I loved him like my own life. I wanted to hide him but I couldn't keep him confined indoors. I had to let him out on the street. The neighbors' children started bullying him and shouting 'Zhid! Zhid!' I was afraid the Gestapo would find out and would kill me and the child. My family, the neighbors, and Marilka advised me to take the child to the police. Marilka went with me because she had good friends among the Germans. We gave the child to the police."

When I heard these last words, tears began pouring from my eyes. I couldn't stop weeping. She wanted to give me water, tea, but I didn't want to take anything from her. I rose from the stool in shock and headed for the door. Before leaving, I told her:

"You're an observant Catholic. You may one day be the mother of children. You should know that not in God's eyes or in people's eyes will you ever be able to wash away this sin, which will cling to you all your life. People entrusted you with their most precious possession and gave you a fortune in money and material goods, yet you betrayed them and turned their child over to the murderers. The curse of being a partner to the Nazis will follow you till you die."

She began to cry. She wanted to return some things to me, but I wouldn't accept them. I left, dashing like a madman, trying to outrun my rage. When night fell I boarded a tram and rode it aimlessly. Eventually I reached the city center. I hadn't eaten all day, but I felt no hunger. Nothing would have gone down; I felt as if I was choking.

I entered a hotel on Florianska Street and took a room. I collapsed on the bed but could not fall asleep. I kept imagining children bullying my nephew, shouting "Zhid! Zhid!"; and how he looked at the fiendish world and how he got used to it; and how he was led to the police and handed over like a lamb to the slaughter. I shut my eyes to try to stop imagining the terrible scenes, but they tore my eyes open again. I heard the child wailing and the mocking laughter of the murderers.

It was morning before I could sleep. When I woke up I was a shattered and broken man. I showered and went out to look for Jews.

◆　◆　◆

Those who knew Krakow can never forget it. Krakow is a historic city with many monuments from Poland's greatest days, such as the Florian Gate, the Mariatzka Church, and the Wavel, the residence of the Polish kings. Jewish Krakow was just as ancient, the monuments to its culture just as rich. I knew Krakow well. I had lived there for some time. The Krakow I remembered had been one of Jewish congresses, conferences, and meetings, an important city rich with Jewish traditions and legends. That was the city of my memory.

Now I wandered through the old Jewish streets and courtyards, looking into windows from which Jewish faces once looked out. Here on Esthera Street (named after an early Jewish-Polish queen), Meir Street, Boze Cialo, Józefa, Kuzmark-Stradom, Dajwór Platz, there were old archways and houses, each representing a piece of Jewish history and Jewish tradition. Here one could once meet Jewish patriarchs in their Hassidic garb, wearing *shtreimlech* on their heads and white socks; also enlightened Jews, modernly educated, who played important roles not only in Jewish life but also in Polish arts and sciences.

I wandered like a lost soul through the streets and courtyards of the Jewish quarter. I passed addresses where Jewish synagogues and houses of study had once stood. I passed the old site of the REMUH shul on Szeroka Street. Reb Moishe Isereles had been a famous *gaon,* an brilliant interpreter of the Torah, as well as a philosopher. He had written many important books, among them an interpretation of Rebbe Josef Caro's *Shulchan Aruch.* Among religious Jews he was a legend. His shul had been founded in the fifteenth century. Later, in the sixteenth century, he had prayed here. He had been buried near the shul in an ancient cemetery, beside his brother-in-law Aaron and his sister Miriam. The inscription on their gravestones read: "Moishe, Aaron, and Miriam, names that recall for us Moishe Rabbenu, Aaron HaCohen, and Miriam the prophetess." In the same cemetery were the tombs of Rebbe Yom-Tov Lipman (Tosefot Yom-Tov) and Rebbe Yoel Serkes (the *Ba'ach*), both of them Krakow rabbis, greatly learned in the Torah.

I found myself once more on Miodowa Street, where the temple was still standing. This temple's leader had been Rebbe Yehoshua Tohn, a learned historian and Sejm (Polish Parliament) deputy. I imagined I could hear the prayers, the pleas to God that had been derailed, that had never reached the Seat of Glory. They still floated here in the air, looking for righteousness.

Somehow I found myself standing in front of the restaurant that once belonged to Shapiro. I looked inside for the small, blond Jew with the pencil behind his ear, and for the Hassidic guests who used to get a *Glatt* kosher meal here, but none of them were there now. There were only strangers. The buffet, which had once displayed tasty Jewish foods—pickles, chopped liver, gefilte fish, chopped onions—now carried food to suit a different taste—hams, cabbage salads, and other foods. I walked from there to Tcherinin, a restaurant that had been famous for its Jewish specialties. I looked for the waiters with their caps, half-Hassidic and half-German, but I did not meet anyone. I felt like crying.

Ashamed, I sneaked away from the Jewish street. Despite myself, I looked into a Jewish courtyard. The houses with their gloomy old faces looked down at me angrily. People stared at me and pointed at me as if I was a thief here, an intruder.

I ran off to the city botanical garden and wandered through it, the psychic pain unbearable. The plants were fresh, green, and fragrant. The trees were strong, their leaves glistening in the sunlight. Birds were chirping and pecking the tree bark with their tiny beaks. The sky was blue, sunlight streaming down like gold. It was spring, a beautiful Polish late spring, fragrant with pine needles and acacia blossoms. There was no sign that thirty thousand Jews from the neighboring streets had perished, among them thousands of Jewish children whose voices had once resounded in all this plant life, that one of Europe's most precious Jewish communities had been eradicated. The natural world had not lost its order. The trees and flowers with their many colors were continuing to bloom to cover up the disgrace. The innocent eyes of children had been extinguished by the Nazis and their Polish partners. This earth had swallowed up so many young children, and now their eyes were peering out through the colorful flowers, as if to ask passersby: "Why were our lives so brutally extinguished?"

◆　◆　◆

I visited the Jewish center at Dluga Street 38. Two armed Jewish guards were protecting the entrance. Those Jews who had survived the Nazi war machine were now being threatened by their "dear neighbors." In the courtyard I met Jews from all over Poland. Most of them had just returned from

Russia. Here I met old friends and acquaintances whom I thought had died. Now we rose from our graves and laughed, and cried, and exchanged stories from the vale of tears.

I continued on my way to visit a kibbutz in the former student house at Przemyska 3. This one also had a guard outside the door. Apparently the murderers had not yet had their fill of Jewish blood. Young people gathered at this kibbutz. They were determined to do whatever it took to make *aliyah* to Israel. I also visited the refugee house at Stradom Street 10, at the foot of the Wavel, where there stood a few wooden booths. Here returnees from Russia gathered. It did my heart good to come across entire families: fathers, mothers, and children. My heart beat lighter at the sight of children.

Krakow, which had been one of the world's great Jewish communities, had been torn asunder. There were no more religious Jews here, nor any assimilated Jews. All had been washed away by the deluge. There were still a few individual refugees wandering around, having returned from all number of distant places, and a handful of uprooted and weakened families looking for a home where they could rest from all their wanderings. Here at the foot of the Wavel they were looking for protection, a roof over their heads. But they knew that Poland was offering only the faintest protection for them, that no peace was to be found here. This place was only a hut, a *sukkah,* in the wilderness of the twentieth century. They would rest here a while in the shadow of the Wavel, catch their breath, and wander on until they had found a secure place where they would no longer be persecuted as Jews.

I kept wandering through various other cities in Poland, cities I knew well, places where I once had had many friends. Now all these cities were strange to me, cold and repulsive. I had no friends or relatives left here. I only met lonely individuals unable to find what they were searching for. The old Jewish world had vanished in fire and smoke. It was utterly destroyed. I decided to go to Ostrowiec.

83

In the City of My Birth, Ostrowiec

With a pounding heart, I took the train to the city where I had spent my youth, the loveliest years of my life. Here I had started to envision a future life, to weave dreams, to believe in and hope for a better world. Here I had been when the war broke out, to be near my mother. I knew nearly everyone in this shtetl. Here had been my family and my near and distant relatives, numbering a few hundred, and many friends and acquaintances. Here I had known every stone and tree. I was even friendly with our Polish neighbors. I knew that my shtetl had been destroyed and that I wouldn't find any of my relatives or friends, but I still yearned to see my old home, my old street, the house where I had been rocked in my cradle.

The train passed through familiar cities: Kielce, Skarzysko, Wierzbnik, Kunów. I knew these communities well; in each of them I had had relatives and friends. I had known the institutions and the activists. I had also known the traditional firms, the wealthy of the shtetls, those who had inherited large fortunes from their parents and were planning to leave large fortunes for their children. Now all was dust and ashes.

The sound of the locomotive lulled me to sleep, and as I slept pictures churned in my mind of scenes and people from the past. The magical scenes of my youth replayed themselves before me. I saw my first teacher, Reb Mordechai Lifschitz, on the first day that the assistant teacher brought me to class. I did not see his eyes or his face—only his wild beard and side curls. I remembered the voices of the children reciting after him, and I remembered looking at everything around me with so much anticipation. I remembered the shining eyes of my mother and father when the assistant brought me home in the evening. And I remembered the Hebrew Bible stories to which I would listen in *cheder* on winter evenings, legends from the Book of Genesis, which inspired my imagination so much. I remembered my teachers: Pinyele, the best; Erzl, the quiet one; Myer Pentzik and the Gemara teachers, Leibish, son of Yashe, and Reb Gershon Henech. I remembered also the Hebrew teachers of my yeshiva days and the *shtibl* atmosphere; the patriarchal personalities, Torah authorities, all of whom I remembered with great piety and respect. I remembered the famous *gaon* of Ostrowiec, Rebbe Maier Yechiel Halevi Holchok, bless his memory, an ascetic and a great genius, who tortured his body and fasted for forty years. I often spent time in his study house, his sacred books open in front of me. Sometimes by chance I was there during sessions of the religious court when he and Shimeleh the beadle and a third man would discuss religious cases. All of these scenes replayed themselves again during the night.

Sometimes the rebbe in his silk caftan and fur was too restless to sleep. Something must have been troubling him, so immediately he convened a religious court of three Jews to pray so that the bad thoughts in his dreams and all evil influences would be dispelled. On one such occasion I was attending his study house, studying a sacred text. The beadle had gone out. Suddenly the door of the rebbe's room opened and he appeared in the doorway, with his beard and earlocks and his sharp eyes burning in their deep sockets. When he saw me he asked:

"Are you alone, youngster? Come into my room. Stay with me till Shimeleh comes."

I trembled with fear and respect. I entered and sat on the edge of a stool. The rebbe returned to bed in his clothes and dozed off. I don't know how long I sat there. Every minute felt like a year. Every stroke of the Hebrew-handed clock resounded in my mind. It was as if the rebbe was arguing with angels, which tormented him until Shimeleh the beadle returned, and together we three drove out the spirits that were plaguing the rebbe's dreams.

Now, listening to the clatter of the train wheels, all these scenes came alive in my memory. Hundreds of long-forgotten events sprang into my mind, hundreds of people reminding me of events of my youth, drawing them out of my past. Then the train's sharp whistle woke me from my reveries. I opened my eyes and saw that night had spread its dark wings over the countryside. I pressed my face against the cold glass and saw lighted windows of houses in the forests and fields through which the train was passing. This was a very familiar landscape to me. We were approaching Ostrowiec. I recognized the forests where I often spent my summer days. My heart began to pound as if I was about to meet relatives and friends whom I hadn't seen for many years.

We arrived at the station. The conductor called out: "Ostrowiec Comenyi!" The red brick building was the same, but the people were not the same ones I used to meet here. These were all cold, strange faces. I looked around, searching for my old cabman, Yosl Kobaleh, who used to grab my suitcase as soon as I arrived. But Yosl Kobaleh was nowhere to be seen, and neither was Maneleh, another cabman. There was no Chiyel-Azeh. None of them were here.

The wagons were here but the cabmen were unfamiliar and didn't know me. My world was no longer here: it had vanished along with the people, with the learned ones, with the educated youth and the hard-working Jews, with the wealthy and the poor. Who was I looking for here? Whom should I approach? The people sitting with me in the wagon were also complete strangers. They looked at me suspiciously; they could tell from my face that something strange was passing through my mind. I did not want to speak to anyone, nor could I have. My heart was bursting with pain, and I did not want anyone to see.

I asked to be taken to a hotel. There I collapsed on my bed like the dead. I didn't want to open my eyes because I didn't want to face reality, to see what had become of my hopes and dreams. I fell asleep quickly, but soon woke up, plagued by nightmares and covered with sweat. I had been dreaming that Polish neighbors were chasing me, trying to grab me and take me to Auschwitz. I ran away, hoping to hide in the Kinever forest, but I tripped and fell down. Scores of hands reached for me with axes and knives. When I woke up I was shouting.

Outside it had started to rain. I was afraid to sleep any more in case the nightmares started again. I showered, dressed, and went out. I wanted first to visit the grave of my father, bless his memory. It was right beside the grave of the Ostrowiec rebbe, bless his memory.

It did not take me long to find the cemetery, which had "invaded" the city. Entire streets had been swept away. The walls of the cemetery had also been destroyed, turning the entire city into one huge cemetery. There was no longer a border between the living and the dead because all was dead. The cemetery's main building had also been destroyed, as if a heavy battle had taken place there. But there had been no battle: instead, the Poles had torn it down, along with the other Jewish houses, looking for hoards of treasure. After the war began, a rumor had circulated in the city that the Jews had hidden large fortunes inside the walls of their homes.

The mausoleum of the Ostrowiec rebbe, Reb Meir Yechiel Halevi, bless his memory, had also been destroyed. His stone lay broken on the ground. The stone of my father, bless his memory, was still in one piece, though vandals had torn out the marble plaque. Many tombstones lay broken, and cows were grazing among the plots. Seeing this, I sat on the stone of my father's grave and cried bitterly. I cried my heart out. The Nazis had dragged my mother off to Treblinka. Her ashes were probably scattered over untended fields. May her memory be a blessing, but even the dead are not allowed to rest in peace. Our "loving" neighbors had shattered our tombstones and profaned our graves. No doubt this cemetery would soon be plowed under and houses built on it to wipe away all traces of this once great Jewish center. What will happen then to the graves of our loved ones?

I don't know how long I sat by my father's grave. The sound of voices startled me. When I looked around, I saw a few Jews near me. They recognized me and helped me stand. They told me that around eighty Jews had returned to Ostrowiec from various camps and from their hiding places in the forests, but that most of them had left or were preparing to leave. A short while ago, they told me, a house where a few saved Jews were living had been broken into and three had been murdered. A note had been left behind: "If you don't leave here promptly, you will all be murdered." The three Jews were buried in the cemetery and monuments to them erected. The following day the tombstones were found smashed and the graves disgraced.

I was led to a place where the remaining Jews gathered: the Warszawski Hotel, a small Jewish hotel on Teumah Hill in front of the church. Here I met a few lonely people, the sole survivors of their families. These were not human beings in the normal sense of the word. They were wrecks. Their eyes reflected bitterness, disappointment, and despair. When they heard that I had come from Paris, they peppered me with questions about the situation for refugees there and how they could immigrate. As I looked at these people, I thought more than once to myself: what had been the point of struggling so hard to stay alive? It was not only Hitler who had wanted to liquidate us. The entire world had helped him and was still helping him eradicate the Jews.

♦   ♦   ♦

The following day, I looked into my inheritance. I found the two-story brick building that had belonged to my parents, and the enclosed garden that stretched for three streets from my grandfather's property. Surrounding the garden were houses, most of them of wood, some of brick. In the middle of the area was an orchard. My grandfather, Avraham Leibish Waxman, bless his memory, had been a man of property. He had an estate in Chmielów, near Ostrowiec, and a mill, too. When he bought this property in Ostrowiec, the first thing he did was plant a garden and fruit trees. There we used to spend our leisure time. Near the garden my father had built his house. We had many Christian neighbors. We got along well with them, and as children we used to play with their own children.

One of our neighbors was a slaughterhouse owner named Leshkowitz. He spoke very good Yiddish, which he had learned from his Jewish neighbors. While I was going to see what had happened to my inheritance, I ran into him on Shener Street. He immediately recognized me and greeted me this way: "What! What! You're still alive!?"

My heart felt a blow and tears started to stream from my eyes. A neighbor and so-called friend of so many years, whom my grandfather had helped so much, and with whom we had lived as good neighbors, someone who knew how large a family we were, on seeing that one of them had survived, instead of welcoming him in a friendly manner and inviting him into his house to honor him with a drink, was expressing disappointment that I had survived. He could not stand to see me. Nothing had prepared me for this brutality. I merely answered him:

"Yes, you see with your own eyes that I'm still alive and will probably outlive many of my enemies."

I wiped my eyes and went to see my former home. Another old neighbor, also a slaughterhouse owner, was living in my mother's house. He received me in his kitchen and did not allow me into the salon. Through an open door I saw our green sofa and massive sideboard. On the other side of the house, on the balcony near the kitchen, was a glassed-in porch. Here stood barrels of cabbage and sacks of potatoes. I was dying to enter that room, which had been my writing room. There I had written my poems and stories, sitting near the stove on winter evenings. But he would not open the door. Before I could ask any questions, he dismissed me, telling me he had been awarded the premises by a magistrate and that if I had any questions about it I would have to ask the officials. He glared at me and shoved me toward the door. He immediately locked the door behind me as if he was afraid I might return. I felt as if someone had doused me with ice water and walked away embittered and disappointed.

My grandfather's buildings had also been taken over. The garden had been destroyed. The acacia tree, which I loved so much and from which I would remove branches each year for our *sukkah,* had been chopped down. No sign of it remained. I felt physically and mentally crushed. Only then did I understand the extent of the tragedy: it was not only the Germans, the Nazis, that had rooted us out; other nations had helped them—Poles, Lithuanians, Ukrainians, Russians, Hungarians, Romanians, and others had participated actively in the murders, or at best stood by indifferently.

I wandered the city like a ghost, unable to stop crying. I looked into many Jewish homes and stores where at one time it had been so easy to encounter friends and acquaintances, handsome faces and friendly looks. I encountered none of the former owners. As I looked into the courtyards, scenes of Jewish children at play flashed before my eyes, the Shloimelech, and Peselech, the Hershelech, and Dvorelech. All of them had disappeared. I reminded myself of the long caravans and transports, the executions, the gas chambers and crematoria where I watched them being led to their deaths. The Nazis and their partners had thought of thousands of ways of death for their victims. Their houses, their residences, and their stores had been taken over by strangers, who took possession of the sweat and toil of generations. They stole it all, and now they were parading around in the clothing of the Jews, wearing their jewelry, displaying everything the Jews had once owned. Whenever a survivor of the camps reappeared, they treated him as an enemy, an intruder, an evil spirit who had come to shatter their peace. They were ready to kill him, just as had happened to so many victims.

The market square had once been alive with Jewish shops. The only non-Jewish shop had been the pharmacy. Many of the houses were now in ruins, ripped apart by Polish treasure seekers. That market no longer existed. In its place were empty lots and heaps of rubble. Though the market was still held twice a week, Mondays and Thursdays, it had lost its luster. No longer were there Jewish buyers or sellers. Some stalls remained, but they were run by Poles, and the peasants did not like dealing with them because they didn't know how to sell. They were unfriendly and showed no interest in winning over customers. They treated buyers badly, mocking them and threatening them.

I looked into the tavern of Yosl Horak, where peasants used to come to gorge themselves and get drunk and afterward want to kiss Yosl. Gentile bosses had taken over, stout men with ruddy faces who drank even while they were serving their patrons and afterward tried to rob them. They would start fights, creating havoc. The peasants would run off, cursing the proprietor, recalling fondly their *"Zhid,"* Yosek, who was a *"porzadni chlop"* (decent man).

I looked for other stores, those of Chana-Rivka, Miriam Bayleh, Hindele Monesen, and the *chazanteh* (cantor's wife). Women had run these businesses because their men were not capable, or because they dedicated themselves to study. So these women were the main breadwinners. These stores no longer existed. It was as if the earth had swallowed them. The iron handrail where Jews always used to gather on Sundays and in midweek was deserted. The merchants, the brokers, the money lenders, the cantors, and the matchmakers—all were gone. No one stopped at the handrail any more. A melancholy hung over it all.

The business of Moishe-Mendl Neiholz was locked up. The show window had been knocked out and boarded up. Moishe-Mendl no longer told jokes, no longer whispered into the ears of friends. In Dudl Boifeld's dry goods store I now saw Polish salespeople. They had changed the stock of silk and velvet, brocade and other fine goods, for colored kerchiefs, flashy fabrics. No more gentle talk was heard there. There was only noise and clamor.

I walked away sobbing with pain at the tragic loss of a way of life, until I came to the place where the old Jewish synagogue and the study houses had once stood. All I saw was a grassy knoll and underbrush. The grand old synagogue, built in the sixteenth century, had been torn down. Architecturally, it had been one of the most noteworthy synagogues in Poland—built of wood, with a round cupola on top. The ceiling had been covered with paintings and quotations from the Hebrew Bible, and from it had hung heavy brass lamps with inscriptions of the donors. Legend has it that the painter who had done the ceiling had fallen from it to his death. The Holy Ark, in which the Torah scrolls rested, had been carved from wood, its sides showing birds, flowers, and exotic fruits. On the western wall, also decorated with paintings and quotations from the Hebrew Bible, had hung the "Seat of Elijah the Prophet." The godfather would sit on it during traditional circumcisions. Among the many curtains for the Holy Ark there had been one with a Polish coat of arms, inherited from an important Polish royal family, in recognition of the help the Jewish community had offered during the Polish uprising of 1863. On important Polish national holidays, government officials would come to the synagogue, and the curtain with the initials P.R. (Polska Republic) would be hung.

Near the synagogue, on the right side, had been the old study house, its windows facing Stara Kanowska Street. There, prayers went on all day, one *minyan* after another, and boys would sit at the oak tables engrossed in study. Its windows on the left looked onto the river and meadows. There stood the "New House of Study," where Jews in the trades, minor merchants and craftsmen, fine middle-class men, had once prayed. Down a few stairs was the "Little House of Study" where another class used to pray: porters, butchers, bakers, and teamsters, people whose workday began early. Thousands of Jews had once gathered at these places for prayers. Now all was gone. I sat down on a stone and sobbed at the destruction. I said prayers of mourning. I was flooded with my own tears. My sobs quickly became cries. In my imagination my cries turned into the cries of thousands, tens of thousands; they resounded in my mind and in my ears.

I shut my eyes and imagined the scenes before Yom Kippur, when the synagogue and study houses and prayer houses were filled to overflowing. In the courtyard of the synagogue, thousands of women gathered in wigs or shawls, with tear-filled eyes, holding holiday prayer books in their hands. They were waiting for the rebbe, the *tzaddik* (holy man), to leave his house of study for the old synagogue, where he would recite the Kol Nidrei. A commotion would be heard as the rebbe left the house of study, wearing a white linen robe and a prayer shawl. Thousands of Hassidim, similarly dressed, with flowing beards and side locks, with radiant eyes, would carry the rebbe, so weak, in their hands. Zatylna Street would be jammed with strong young men—butchers, teamsters, porters, coachmen, horse dealers. They would form a pathway through which the rebbe would soon pass, not allowing anyone to break through. Here they would come, or better still, flutter, storm, these hundreds of Hassidim in white linen robes and prayer shawls, carrying the rebbe in their hands. His eyes would be flaming, his wispy beard swaying in the wind. The procession would arrive at the synagogue courtyard, where thousands of voices would call out:

"Holy rebbe! Righteous holy man! Bring prosperity . . . Bring salvation . . . Pray for a good year, redemption for the Jewish people!"

The heavens would tremble, the ground shake, and the whole world seem to be moving.

When I looked up I saw beside me a crowd of Poles, who were talking among themselves and pointing at me as if I was crazy. One came closer and asked me:

"You got lonesome for your *bóznica* [synagogue]. The Germans burned it down and cleared the place for us. We'll plant a garden here."

Yes, the Germans had destroyed the Jewish synagogue with fire, and with it the Torah scrolls and the worshippers. They had cleared a place for the Poles to plant a garden. They were going to make a park out of the cemetery. Polish children would play on the ruins of a destroyed Yiddish world.

◆　◆　◆

That same day I left my home city, Ostrowiec, with a broken heart. I sneaked along the walls like a thief, ashamed to look at the houses, the trees, and the streets, which still remembered me from those fortunate times when I used to stroll hopefully and happily, full of fantasies and dreams. I believed in the world in those days. I believed in humanity and hoped for a better tomorrow when people and nations would live in mutual understanding, helping one another build a better, more just, and more beautiful world; when, in the words of the prophet, "swords shall be beaten into plowshares and the lion will lie down with the lamb." All these hopes and dreams were destroyed. I ran away from the city of my dreams disappointed and bitter, downtrodden and in pain, insulted and spat upon, because my eyes had seen so much of blood and tears, so much brutality and murder, so much despoilment and vileness. I left, never to return. I left for a new world, for a new continent, and for new surprises in life.

Glossary

aliyah: literally, "ascent"; immigration to the Land of Israel; "having an aliyah": the honor of being called up to the Torah for the blessings before and after its reading.

"Avinu Malkainu": literally, "Our Father, our King"; prayer of repentance recited during the High Holidays.

cheder: literally, "room"; traditional Jewish religious school.

Eretz Israel: literally, "Land of Israel"; name used by the Jews for Palestine prior to the establishment of the State of Israel.

gaon: great Torah scholar.

Gefolgschaft: followers or adherents.

Gemara: the part of the Talmud that comments on the Mishnah.

Generalgouvernement: the German government over all conquered territory.

Hagada (pl. *Hagadot*): literally, "The Telling"; the book of the Passover home service which, through narrative and song, recounts the story of Jewish slavery in Egypt and the liberation.

Hassidic: describes a movement of Jewish religious revival which began in Eastern Europe in the latter part of the eighteenth century, characterized by pious devotion and joyful worship.

Hauptmann: army captain.

High Holidays: Rosh Hashana and Yom Kippur.

Himmelkommando: the German group who cajoled and deceived the prisoners in preparation for putting them into the gas chambers.

Judenrat: Jewish council of the ghetto established on Nazi orders during World War II in Jewish communities of Europe, first in Poland in September 1939 and then in the other conquered countries.

Kapo: block or barracks leader in concentration camps. This inmate assisted in the administration of the camp in return for more rations and better living conditions. Many were renowned for their sadism and brutality.

shrut: Jewish dietary laws.

l Nidrei: prayer recited on Yom Kippur eve.

rben Minchah: Jewish women's prayer book.

iegeinsatz: war effort.

'benkommando: group that collected corpses.

aginot Line: a line of defensive fortifications built before the Second World War to protect the eastern border of France but easily outflanked by German invaders.

arranos: Christianized Jews in medieval Spain.

nyan: quorum of minimum of ten Jewish males over the age of thirteen needed for Jewish prayer.

Sheberach: literally, "He who blessed"; a supplication to God for blessing recited in a quorum of Jewish men. In the text it is used as an ironic greeting.

selmänn (pl. *Muselmänner*): emaciated people in the camps.

ersturmbannführer: lieutenant-colonel in the SS.

ganization Todt (abbreviation **O.T.**): engineers who supervised forced laborers to carry out the engineering work.

sover: the eight-day festival during Nissan (March-April) that commemorates the Jews' freedom from Egyptian bondage.

ylacteries: square boxes with leather thongs containing scriptural passages, worn on the arm and head during morning prayer every day except Sabbaths and holidays by male Jews over thirteen.

l: young rogues used for sex in exchange for protection by block elders in the camps.

be: a Hassidic rabbi

ndfunk: Radio broadcasting station.

der: the festive home ritual meal of the first and second nights of Passover at which the Hagada is recited.

lom aleichem: Jewish greeting.

avuot: literally, "weeks"; festival of weeks, celebrated seven weeks after Passover (May-June), and commemorating the revelation at Sinai and the presentation of the Torah to the children of Israel. Like the other two festivals, Passover and Sukkot, Shavuot has agricultural as well as historical and spiritual roots.

na Israel: literally, "Hear oh Israel"; opening words of the central affirmation of Jewish faith.

nates: tatters.

nona-Esrei: eighteen benedictions recited in daily prayer service; core of the Divine service; affirmation of faith.

shtetl(s): small town(s).

shtibl: small Hassidic house of prayer.

shtreimlech: fur-edged hat, worn by rabbis and Hassidic Jews on the Sabbath and holy days.

shul: synagogue.

Sonderkommando: the group who dragged bodies from the gas chambers and set them up for more victims.

Stammlager: main concentration camp that had smaller camps attached to it.

sukkah: outdoor booth where Jews have their meals during Sukkot.

Sukkot: Feast of Tabernacles, celebrated by living in booths.

transport: the transfer of Jews in sealed trains to concentration camps.

Treblinka: concentration camp in Poland.

vidui: final prayer before death.

Volksdeutsche: person of German nationality.

Wehrmacht: German army.

yeshiva: academy of higher Jewish education.

Yivo: acronym for *Yidn Viln Azoi;* this acronym was an insider's code word that meant "that's how Jews want it."

Yomtov: Jewish holiday; celebration.